Build Mobile Apps with Ionic 4 and Firebase

Hybrid Mobile App Development

Second Edition

Fu Cheng

Apress®

Build Mobile Apps with Ionic 4 and Firebase: Hybrid Mobile App Development

Fu Cheng
Sandringham, Auckland, New Zealand

ISBN-13 (pbk): 978-1-4842-3774-8   ISBN-13 (electronic): 978-1-4842-3775-5
https://doi.org/10.1007/978-1-4842-3775-5

Library of Congress Control Number: 2018961558

Managing Director, Apress Media LLC: Welmoed Spahr
Acquisitions Editor: Aaron Black
Development Editor: James Markham
Coordinating Editor: Jessica Vakili

Cover image designed by Freepik (www.freepik.com)

Distributed to the book trade worldwide by Springer Science+Business Media New York, 233 Spring Street, 6th Floor, New York, NY 10013. Phone 1-800-SPRINGER, fax (201) 348-4505, e-mail orders-ny@springer-sbm.com, or visit www.springeronline.com. Apress Media, LLC is a California LLC and the sole member (owner) is Springer Science + Business Media Finance Inc (SSBM Finance Inc). SSBM Finance Inc is a **Delaware** corporation.

For information on translations, please e-mail rights@apress.com, or visit http://www.apress.com/rights-permissions.

Apress titles may be purchased in bulk for academic, corporate, or promotional use. eBook versions and licenses are also available for most titles. For more information, reference our Print and eBook Bulk Sales web page at http://www.apress.com/bulk-sales.

Any source code or other supplementary material referenced by the author in this book is available to readers on GitHub via the book's product page, located at www.apress.com/978-1-4842-3774-8. For more detailed information, please visit http://www.apress.com/source-code.

Printed on acid-free paper

To my wife Andrea and my daughters Olivia and Erica

Table of Contents

About the Author

Fu Cheng is a full-stack software developer living in Auckland, New Zealand, with rich experience in applying best practices in real product development and strong problem-solving skills. He is the author of the book *Exploring Java 9: Build Modularized Applications in Java* (Apress, 2018), which covers the new features of Java SE 9 and provides a deep dive of Java platform core features. He is also a regular contributor to IBM developerWorks China and InfoQ China, with more than 50 published technical articles covering various technical topics.

About the Technical Reviewer

Felipe Laso is a Senior Systems Engineer working at Lextech Global Services. He's also an aspiring game designer/programmer. You can follow him on Twitter as @iFeliLM or on his blog.

Acknowledgments

This book would not have been possible without the help and support of many others. Thank you to my editors, Aaron Black, Jessica Vakili, and James Markham; and the rest of the Apress team, for bringing this book into the world. Thank you to my technical reviewer Felipe Laso Marsetti for your time and insightful feedback.

Many thanks to my whole family for the support during the writing of this book.

Preface

Developing mobile apps is an interesting yet challenging task. Different mobile platforms have their own ecosystems. If you want to start building your own mobile apps, you have to learn new programming languages, frameworks, libraries, and tools. Building complicated mobile apps or games requires a lot of experience. These kinds of apps may not be suitable for beginners. But not all mobile apps are complicated. There are still many mobile apps that are content-centric. This kind of apps focuses on content presentations and doesn't use many native features. For these kinds of apps, PhoneGap and its successor Apache Cordova offer a different way to build them.

Mobile platforms usually have a component called WebView to render web pages. Cordova uses this component to create a wrapper for running web pages inside of native apps. Cordova provides different wrappers for different platforms. The web pages become the mobile apps to develop. After using Cordova, developers can use front-end skills to create cross-platform mobile apps. This empowers front-end developers to create good enough content-centric mobile apps. Many other frameworks build on top of Cordova to provide out-of-box components to make building mobile apps much easier.

This book focuses on the latest version 4 of the popular Ionic framework. The best way to learn a new framework is using it in real-world product development. This book is not a manual for Ionic 4, but a field guide of how to use it. We'll build a Hacker News client app using Ionic 4 and use this as the example to demonstrate different aspects of Ionic 4. This book not only covers the implementation of the Hacker News client app, but also the whole development life cycle, including development, unit tests, end-to-end tests, continuous integration, and app publish. After reading this book, you should get a whole picture of building mobile apps using Ionic 4.

Most of the nontrivial mobile apps need back-end services to work with them. Using mobile apps back-end services is a new trend that eliminates the heavy burden to write extra code and maintain the back-end infrastructure. Google Firebase is a popular choice of mobile apps back-end services. The Hacker News client app uses Firebase to handle user authentication and storage of user favorites data. After reading this book, you should be able to integrate Firebase in your own apps.

Included in This Book

This book is organized around building the Hacker News client app. Starting from the local development setup, each chapter focuses on implementing a user story. Here are some important topics:

- Understanding Web Components and Stencil

- Ionic 4 list component with infinite scrolling and pull-to-refresh

- State management with NgRx

- Routing with Angular Router

- User management and third-party service logins with Firebase

- Data persistence with Firebase Cloud Firestore

- Unit testing with Karma and end-to-end testing with Protractor

- App publishing

- Features provided by Ionic Pro, including Ionic Deploy and Monitor

Below are the versions of main frameworks, libraries, and tools used in the app.

- Angular - 6.1.10

- RxJS - 6.3.3

- NgRx - 6.1.0

- Firebase - 5.5.4

- AngularFire2 - 5.0.2

- Jasmine - 3.2.0

- Karma - 3.0.0

- Protractor - 5.4.1

Not Included in This Book

Before you start reading this book, you should be clear about what is not included in this book.

- This book is NOT an Ionic 4 manual. Although this book covers many Ionic components, it doesn't include details about these components. If you want to know more about Ionic components, you should refer to the official documentation.

- This book is NOT a Firebase manual. The official Firebase documentation should be the place to look for more information about Firebase.

- This book is NOT a guide of building Angular web applications. Even though this book uses Angular as the framework binding for Ionic 4, it focuses on building mobile apps, not web applications. However, some practice used in the sample app can be applied to other Angular applications.

Who Should Read This Book?

This book is a field guide of building mobile apps with Ionic 4 and Firebase. Everyone who is interested in mobile apps development with Ionic 4 should read this book. This book is especially suitable for the following readers.

- Individual developers. This book is a perfect match for individual developers. No matter if you want to build mobile apps for a living or as side projects, as an individual developer, you're responsible for the whole development life cycle. This book covers all the necessary phases in the development life cycle.

- Team members in a small team. If you are on a small team, it's likely that you may need to touch different aspects of product development. This book can help you to understand the development life cycle to easily shift between different roles.

- Development team members in a large team. If you are on a large team, you may only be responsible for some pages or components. This book covers some advanced topics related to web development, including routing, state management with NgRx, and advanced usage of RxJS, which can be useful in development.

How This Book Is Organized

This book is organized around building the example Hacker News client app with Ionic 4 and Firebase. Below is a brief description of all the chapters in this book.

- Chapters 1–4: Introduction of necessary background knowledge and local development environment setup.

- Chapters 5–11: Implementation of all user stories of the example app with Ionic 4 and Firebase.

- Chapters 12–15: Additional topics related to Ionic.

Depending on your skill level, you can choose to skip some of these chapters. If you are an experienced Angular developer, you can skip the first four chapters.

Prerequisites

Ionic 4 is framework agnostic, and this book uses Ionic Angular as the framework binding. Basic knowledge of Angular and TypeScript is required to understand the code in this book. This book provides the basic introduction to Angular and TypeScript, but it's still recommended to refer to other materials for more details.

To build Ionic 4 apps running on iOS platform, macOS is required to run the emulator and Xcode. You may also need real physical iOS or Android devices to test the apps.

CHAPTER 1

Getting Started

Mobile apps development is a hot topic for both companies and individual developers. You can use various kinds of frameworks and tools to build mobile apps for different platforms. In this book, we use Ionic 4 to build so-called hybrid mobile apps. As the first chapter, this chapter provides the basic introduction of hybrid mobile apps and helps you to set up the local environment for development, debugging, and testing.

After reading this chapter, you should have a basic understanding of how hybrid mobile apps are built and get a local development environment ready to use.

Mobile Apps Refresher

With the prevalence of mobile devices, more and more mobile apps have been created to meet all kinds of requirements. Each mobile platform has its own ecosystem. Developers use SDKs provided by the mobile platform to create mobile apps and sell them on the app store. Revenue is shared between the developers and the platform. Table 1-1 shows the statistics of major app stores at the time of writing.

© Fu Cheng 2018
F. Cheng, *Build Mobile Apps with Ionic 4 and Firebase*,
https://doi.org/10.1007/978-1-4842-3775-5_1

Table 1-1. *Statistics of Major App Stores*

App Store	Number of available apps	Downloads to date
App Store (iOS)	2.2 million	140 billion
Google Play	2.8 million	82 billion
Windows Store	669,000+	--
BlackBerry World	245,000+	4 billion

The prevalence of mobile apps also creates a great opportunity for application developers and software companies. A lot of individuals and companies make big money on the mobile apps markets. A classic example is the phenomenal mobile game Flappy Bird. Flappy Bird was developed by Vietnam-based developer Dong Nguyen. The developer claimed that Flappy Bird was earning $50,000 a day from in-app advertisements as well as sales. Those successful stories encourage developers to create more high-quality mobile apps.

Let's now take a look at some key components of mobile app development.

Hybrid Mobile Apps

Developing mobile apps is not an easy task. If you only want to target a single mobile platform, then the effort may be relatively smaller. However, most of the time we want to distribute apps on many app stores to maximize the revenue. To build the kind of apps that can be distributed to various app stores, developers need to use different programming languages, SDKs, and tools: for example, Objective-C/Swift for iOS and Java for Android. We also need to manage different code bases with similar functionalities but implemented using different programming languages. It's hard to maximize the code reusability and reduce code duplications across different code bases, even for the biggest players in the market. That's why cross-platform mobile apps solutions, like Xamarin (`https://www.xamarin.com/`), React Native (`https://facebook.github.io/react-native/`), RubyMotion (`http://www.rubymotion.com/`), and Flutter (`https://flutter.io/`) also receive a lot of attention. All these solutions have a high learning curve for their programming languages and SDKs, which creates a burden for ordinary developers.

Compared to Objective-C/Swift, Java, C#, or Ruby, web development skills – for example, HTML, JavaScript, and CSS are much easier to learn. Building mobile apps with web development skills is made possible by HTML5. This new type of mobile apps is called hybrid mobile apps. In hybrid mobile apps, HTML, JavaScript, and CSS code run in an internal browser (WebView) that is wrapped in a native app. JavaScript code can access native APIs through the wrapper. Apache Cordova (`https://cordova.apache.org/`) is the most popular open source library to develop hybrid mobile apps.

Compared to native apps, hybrid apps have both their benefits and drawbacks. The major benefit is that developers can use existing web development skills to create hybrid apps and use only one code base for different platforms. By leveraging responsive web design techniques, hybrid apps can easily adapt to different screen resolutions. The major drawback is the performance issues with hybrid apps. As the hybrid app is running inside of an internal browser, the performance of hybrid apps cannot compete with native apps. Certain types of apps, such as games or apps that rely on complicated native functionalities, cannot be built as hybrid apps. But many other apps can be built as hybrid apps.

Before making the decision of whether to go with native apps or hybrid apps, the development team needs to understand the nature of the apps to build. Hybrid apps are suitable for content-centric apps, such as news readers, online forums, or showcasing products. These content-centric apps act like traditional web apps with limited user interactions. Another important factor to consider is the development team's skill sets. Most apps companies may need to hire both iOS and Android developers to support these two major platforms for native apps. But for hybrid apps, only front-end developers are enough. It's generally easier to hire front-end developers rather than Java or Swift/Objective-C developers.

Apache Cordova

Apache Cordova is a popular open source framework to develop hybrid mobile apps. It originates from PhoneGap (`http://phonegap.com/`) created by Nitobi. Adobe acquired Nitobi in 2011 and started to provide commercial services for it. The PhoneGap source code contributed to the Apache Software Foundation and the new project Apache Cordova was started from its code base.

An Apache Cordova application is implemented as a web page. This web page can reference JavaScript files, CSS files, images, and other resources. The key component of understanding how Cordova works is the `WebView`. `WebView` is the component provided by native platforms to load and run web pages. Cordova applications run inside the `WebViews`. A powerful feature of Cordova is its plugin interface, which allows JavaScript code running in a web page to communicate with native components. With the help of plugins, Cordova apps can access a device's accelerometer, camera, compass, contacts, and more. There are already many plugins available in Cordova's plugin registry (`http://cordova.apache.org/plugins/`). We can easily find plugins used for common scenarios.

Apache Cordova is just a runtime environment for web apps on native platforms. It can support any kinds of web pages. To create mobile apps that look like native apps, we need other UI frameworks to develop hybrid mobile apps. Popular choices of hybrid mobile apps UI frameworks include Ionic framework (`http://ionicframework.com/`), Sencha Touch (`https://www.sencha.com/products/touch/`), Kendo UI (`http://www.telerik.com/kendo-ui`), and Framework7 (`http://framework7.io/`). Ionic framework is the one we are going to cover in this book.

Ionic Framework

Ionic framework is a powerful tool to build hybrid mobile apps. It's open source (`https://github.com/ionic-team/ionic`) and has over 35,000 stars on GitHub, the popular social coding platform. Ionic framework is not the only player in hybrid mobile apps development, but it's the one that draws a lot of attention and is recommended as the first choice by many developers. Ionic is popular for the following reasons:

- Based on Web Components standards and is framework agnostic. Web Components are W3C specifications of components for the web platform. Ionic components are built as custom elements using its own open source tool, Stencil. Being framework agnostic makes Ionic components work with any framework. Developers are free to choose the framework to use, including Angular, React, and Vue.

- Provides beautifully designed out-of-box UI components that work across different platforms. Common components include lists, cards, modals, menus, and pop-ups. These components are designed to have a similar look and feel as native apps. With these built-in components, developers can quickly create prototypes with good enough user interfaces and continue to improve them.

- Leverages Apache Cordova as the runtime to communicate with native platforms. Ionic apps can use all the Cordova plugins to interact with the native platform. Ionic Native further simplifies the use of Cordova plugins in Ionic apps.

- Performs great on mobile devices. The Ionic team devotes great effort to make it perform well on different platforms.

The current release version of Ionic framework is 4.0. Ionic 4 is the first version of Ionic to be framework agnostic. Ionic Core is the set of components based on Web Components. Ionic Angular is the framework binding of Ionic Core with Angular. This book focuses on Ionic Angular with Angular 6.

Apart from the open source Ionic framework, Ionic also provides a complete solution Ionic Pro for mobile app development, which includes the following products:

- **Ionic Creator** – Ionic Creator is a desktop app to create Ionic apps using drag-and-drop. It helps nontechnical users to quickly create simple apps and prototypes.

- **Ionic View** – Ionic View allows viewing Ionic apps shared by others directly on the phones. It's a great tool for app testing and demonstration.

- **Ionic Deploy** – Ionic Deploy performs hot updates to apps after they are published to app stores.

- **Ionic Package** – Ionic Package builds Ionic apps and generates bundles ready for publishing to app stores. With Ionic Package, we don't to manage local build systems and can use the cloud service instead.

- **Ionic Monitor** – Ionic Monitor can monitor apps and report runtime errors.

This book also covers usage of these products in Ionic Pro. Ionic Pro offers a free starter plan to try out features provided by Ionic Deploy and Ionic Monitor. With a $29 per month plan, you can access all features in Ionic Pro. Check out the pricing (`https://ionicframework.com/pro/pricing`) of Ionic Pro if you want to know more about it. Another important project to mention is Ionic Capacitor (`https://capacitor.ionicframework.com/`), which will replace Apache Cordova to build native progressive web apps. Even though Capacitor is out of the scope of this book, it's still worthwhile to check out this project to see the future of developing hybrid mobile apps with Ionic.

Firebase

Mobile apps usually need back-end services to work with the front-end UI. This means that there should be back-end code and servers to work with mobile apps. Firebase (https://firebase.google.com/) is a cloud service to power apps' back ends. Firebase can provide support for data storage and user authentication. After integrating mobile apps with Firebase, we don't need to write back-end code or manage the infrastructure.

Firebase works very well with Ionic to eliminate the pain of maintaining back-end code. This is especially helpful for hybrid mobile apps developers with only front-end development skills. Front-end developers can use JavaScript code to interact with Firebase.

How to Build Mobile Apps

Even with the frameworks and services mentioned above, it's still not an easy task to build mobile apps. There are multiple stages in the whole development life cycle from ideas to published apps. A typical process may include the following major steps:

- Ideas brainstorming. This is when we identify what kind of mobile apps to build. It usually starts from vague ideas and expands to more concrete solutions.

- Wire-framing and prototyping. This is when we draw on the whiteboard to identify main usage scenarios. Prototypes may be created to demonstrate core usage scenarios for better communications with stakeholders.

- User experiences design. This is when all pages and navigation flows are finalized, and we are now clear what exactly needs to be built.

- Implementation. This is when the development team implements the pages to fulfill requirements.

- Testing. Unit testing should be part of implementation of pages and components. End-to-end testing is also required to verify all usage scenarios. All these tests should be executed automatically.

- Continuous integration. Continuous integration is essential for code quality. If every code commit can be tested automatically, then the development team will be more confident about the product's quality.

- Publishing. This is when the app is published to app stores.

- Operations. After the app is published, we still need to continuously monitor its running status. We need to capture errors and crash logs occurred on users' devices.

This book is a guide to build mobile apps that focuses on implementation and testing. Topics including continuous integration, app publishing, and monitoring are also covered.

Prepare Your Local Development Environment

Before we can build Ionic apps, we first need to set up the local development environment. We'll need various tools to develop, test, and debug Ionic apps.

Node.js

Node.js is the runtime platform for Ionic CLI. To use Ionic CLI, we first need to install Node.js (`https://nodejs.org/`) on the local machine. Node.js is a JavaScript runtime built on Chrome's V8 JavaScript engine. It provides a way to run JavaScript on the desktop machines and servers. Ionic CLI itself is written in JavaScript and executed using Node.js. There are two types of release versions of Node.js – the stable LTS versions and current versions with the latest features. It's recommended to use Node.js version 6 or greater, especially the latest LTS version (8.12.0 at the time of writing).

Installing Node.js also installs the package management tool npm. npm is used to manage Node.js packages used in projects. Thousands of open source packages can be found in the npmjs registry (`https://www.npmjs.com/`). If you have background with other programming languages, you may find npm is similar to Apache Maven (`https://maven.apache.org/`) for Java libraries or Bundler (`http://bundler.io/`) for Ruby gems.

Ionic CLI

After Node.js is installed, we can use npm to install the Ionic command-line tool and Apache Cordova.

```
$ npm i -g cordova ionic
```

Note   You may need to have system administrator privileges to install these two packages. For Linux and macOS, you can use `sudo`. For Windows, you can start a command-line window as the administrator. However, it's recommended to avoid using `sudo` when possible, as it may cause permission errors when installing native packages. Treat this as the last resort. The permission errors usually can be resolved by updating the file permissions of the Node.js installation directory.

Install Ionic CLI Using yarn

yarn (`https://yarnpkg.com/`) is a fast, reliable, and secure dependency management tool. After Facebook open sourced it, it quickly became popular in the Node.js community as a better alternative to npm. If you want to use yarn, follow the official instructions (`https://yarnpkg.com/en/docs/install`) to install it. After installing yarn, we can use the following command to install Ionic CLI and Cordova.

```
$ yarn global add cordova ionic
```

This book still uses npm as the package manager. If you didn't know about yarn before, read this guide (`https://yarnpkg.com/en/docs/migrating-from-npm`) about how to migrate from npm to yarn. Common yarn commands are listed as below:

- `yarn add [package]` – Add packages as the project's dependencies. You can provide multiple packages to install. Version requirements can be specified following the Semantic Versioning spec (`http://semver.org/`). For example, we can use `lodash@4.17.5` to install version 4.17.5 of lodash.

- `yarn upgrade [package]` – Upgrade or downgrade versions of packages.

- `yarn remove [package]` – Remove packages.

- `yarn global` – Manage global dependencies.

The file `yarn.lock` contains the exact version of all resolved dependencies. This file is to make sure that builds are consistent across different machines. This file should be managed in the source code repository.

Note   yarn and npm are both good package managers for Node.js. It's hard to choose between these two. Different development teams may have their own preferences. The main reason to use npm for Ionic apps development is that Cordova CLI only supports npm and has no plan to support yarn (`https://github.com/apache/cordova-cli/pull/292#issuecomment-401331607`). Cordova CLI uses npm to install Cordova plugins. If we use yarn to manage dependencies, then after a Cordova plugin is installed, the existing dependencies in the directory `node_modules` will be in an inconsistent status, and we need to run yarn again to fix the issue.

After finishing installation of Ionic CLI and Cordova, we can use the command `ionic` to start developing Ionic apps.

You are free to use Windows, Linux, or macOS to develop Ionic 4 apps. Node.js is supported across different operating systems. One major limitation of Windows or Linux is that you cannot test iOS apps using the emulator or real devices. Some open source Node.js packages may not have the same test coverage on Windows as Linux or macOS. So they are more likely to have compatibility issues when running on Windows. But this should only affect the CLI or other tools, not Ionic 4 itself.

After Ionic CLI is installed, we can run `ionic info` to print out current runtime environment information and check for any warnings in the output; see Listing 1-1. The output also provides detailed information about how to fix those warnings.

Listing 1-1. Output of ionic info

```
Ionic:

   ionic (Ionic CLI)           : 4.1.0 (/Users/fucheng/
                                 node_modules/ionic)
   Ionic Framework             : @ionic/angular 4.0.0-beta.12
   @angular-devkit/core        : 0.8.5
   @angular-devkit/schematics  : 0.8.5
   @angular/cli                : 6.2.5
   @ionic/ng-toolkit           : 1.0.8
   @ionic/schematics-angular   : 1.0.6

Cordova:

   cordova (Cordova CLI) : 8.0.0
   Cordova Platforms     : android 7.0.0, ios 4.5.4
   Cordova Plugins       : cordova-plugin-ionic 4.1.7,
                           cordova-plugin-ionic-keyboard 2.0.5,
                           cordova-plugin-ionic-webview 2.0.3,
                           (and 12 other plugins)

System:

   Android SDK Tools : 26.1.1
   ios-deploy        : 1.9.0
   ios-sim           : 6.1.3
   NodeJS            : v8.12.0 (/usr/local/bin/node)
   npm               : 6.4.1
   OS                : macOS High Sierra
   Xcode             : Xcode 9.3 Build version 9E145

Environment:

   ANDROID_HOME : /Users/fucheng/Library/Android/sdk
```

iOS

Developing iOS apps with Ionic requires macOS and Xcode (https://developer.apple.com/xcode/). You need to install Xcode and Xcode command-line tools on macOS. After installing Xcode, you can open a terminal window and type command shown below.

```
$ xcode-select -p
```

If you see output like that below, then command-line tools have already been installed.

```
/Applications/Xcode.app/Contents/Developer
```

Otherwise, you need to use the following command to install it.

```
$ xcode-select --install
```

After the installation is finished, you can use xcode-select -p to verify.

To run Ionic apps on the iOS simulator using Ionic CLI, package ios-sim is required. Another package ios-deploy is also required for deploying to install and debug apps. You can install both packages using the following command.

```
$ npm i -g ios-sim ios-deploy
```

Android

To develop Ionic apps for Android, Android SDK must be installed. Before installing Android SDK, you should have JDK installed first. Read this guide (https://docs.oracle.com/javase/8/docs/technotes/guides/install/) about how to install JDK 8 on different platforms. It's recommended to install Android Studio (https://developer.android.com/studio/index.html), which provides a nice IDE and bundled Android SDK tools. If you don't want to use Android Studio, you can install stand-alone SDK tools.

Note   Android API level 22 is required to run Ionic apps. Make sure that the required SDK platform is installed.

Stand-alone SDK tools is just a ZIP file; unpack this file into a directory and it's ready to use. The downloaded SDK only contains basic SDK tools without any Android platform or third-party libraries. You need to install the platform tools and at least one version of the Android platform. Run android in `tools` directory to start **Android SDK Manager** to install platform tools and other required libraries.

After installing Android SDK, you need to add SDK's `tools` and `platform-tools` directories into your PATH environment variable, so that SDK's commands can be found by Ionic. Suppose that the SDK tools is unpacked into /Development/android-sdk, then add /Development/android-sdk/tools and /Development/android-sdk/platform-tools to PATH environment variable. For Android Studio, the Android SDK is installed into directory /Users/<username>/Library/Android/sdk.

To modify PATH environment variable on Linux and macOS, you can edit ~/.bash_profile file to update PATH as shown below. The PATH environment below uses the Android SDK from Android Studio. You can replace it with another directory if stand-alone SDK tools is used.

```
export PATH=${PATH}/:/Users/<username>/Library/Android/sdk
/platform-tools \
  : /Users/<username>/Library/Android/sdk/tools
```

To modify the PATH environment variable on Windows, you can follow the steps below.

1. Click **Start** menu, then right-click **Computer** and select **Properties**.

2. Click **Advanced System Settings** to open a dialog.

3. Click **Environment Variables** in the dialog and find **PATH** variable in the list, then click **Edit**.

4. Append the path of `tools` and `platform-tools` directories to the end of **PATH** variable.

It's highly recommended to use Android Studio instead of stand-alone SDK tools. Stand-alone SDK tools is more likely to have configuration issues.

Genymotion

Genymotion (`https://www.genymotion.com/`) is a commercial Android emulator with better performance than the standard emulators. It's recommended to use Genymotion for Android emulation instead of the standard emulators. You can start from the free Genymotion personal edition (`https://www.genymotion.com/fun-zone/`) to emulate apps.

IDEs and Editors

You are free to use your favorite IDEs and editors when developing Ionic apps. IDEs and editors should have good support for editing HTML, TypeScript, and Sass files. For commercial IDEs, WebStorm (`https://www.jetbrains.com/webstorm/`) is recommended for its excellent support of various programming languages and tools. For open source alternatives, Visual Studio Code (`https://code.visualstudio.com/`) and Atom (`https://atom.io/`) are both popular choices.

Create an App Skeleton

After the local development environment is set up successfully, it's time to create new Ionic apps. The easiest way to create Ionic apps is using Ionic CLI. Before we can create Ionic 4 apps using Ionic CLI, we need to enable the feature `project-angular` first by running the following command.

```
$ ionic config set -g features.project-angular true
```

Apps are created using the command `ionic start`. Below is the syntax of using ionic start.

```
$ ionic start <name> <template> [options]
```

The first argument of `ionic start` is the name of the new app, while the second argument is the template name. We can also pass extra options after these two arguments. If not enough arguments are provided, Ionic CLI can help you to finish the setup interactively with prompts. Ionic CLI supports creation of projects of three types. Project types are specified using the option `--type`, for example, `--type=angular`.

- `angular` – Ionic Angular projects for Ionic 4.

- `ionic-angular` – Ionic 2/3 projects.

- `ionic1` – Ionic 1 projects.

For project templates, Ionic provides different types of application templates. All available templates can be listed with the following command. A template may have versions for different project types.

```
$ ionic start --list
```

We can choose a proper template to create the skeleton code of the app. It's also possible to pass URLs of other Git repositories as the templates to use. Ionic also maintains a marketplace (`https://market.ionicframework.com/starters/`) for the community to share project starters. You can find many paid or free project starters in the marketplace.

Below are the available options of `ionic start`.

- `--type` – Allowed values are `angular`, `ionic-angular` and `ionic1`.

- `--cordova` – Enable Cordova integration.

- `--capacitor` - Enable Capacitor integration.

- `--pro-id` – Link this app with Ionic Dashboard.

- `--no-deps` – Do not install npm dependencies. Useful when you only want to explore the content of a project starter.

- `--no-git` – Do not initialize a Git repo.

- `--no-link` – Skip the prompt about connecting the app with Ionic Dashboard.

- `--project-id` – Specify the slug for the app. The slug is used for the directory name and npm package name.

- `--package-id` – Specify the bundle ID/application ID for the app. This is the unique ID of the app when publishing to the Apple store or Google Play. It's highly recommended to set this value when Cordova integration is enabled. The value of this option should be in the reverse domain format, for example, `com.mycompany.myapp`. If not specified, the default value `io.ionic.starter` is used.

Application Templates

We'll take a look at these application templates.

Blank App

This template blank only generates basic code for the app. This template should be used when you want to start from a clean code base; see Figure 1-1.

```
$ ionic start blankApp blank
```

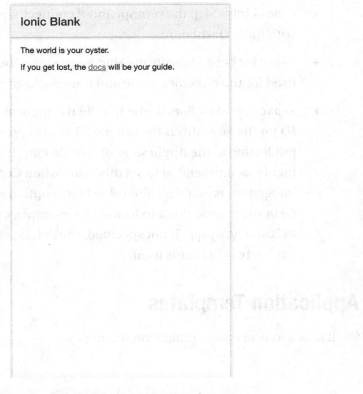

Ionic Blank

The world is your oyster.

If you get lost, the docs will be your guide.

Figure 1-1. *App created using the blank template*

Tabbed App

This template tabs generates apps with a header at the top and tabs at the bottom; see Figure 1-2. This template should be used for apps with multiple views.

```
$ ionic start tabsApp tabs
```

Figure 1-2. *App created using the tabs template*

Sidemenu

This template `sidemenu` generates apps with a side menu that opens itself when sliding to the left or clicking the menu icon; see Figure 1-3. This template can also be used for apps with multiple views, but it uses a menu to switch to different views.

```
$ ionic start sidemenuApp sidemenu
```

Figure 1-3. *App created using the sidemenu template*

Local Development

After a new app is created using `ionic start`, we can navigate to the app directory and run `ionic serve` to start the local development server. The browser should automatically open a new window or tab that points to the address `http://localhost:8100/`. You should see the UI of this Ionic app. Ionic sets up livereload by default, so when any HTML, TypeScript or Sass code is changed, it automatically refreshes the page to load the page with updated code. There is no need for a manual refresh.

The default port for the Ionic local development server is 8100. The port can be configured using the option `--port` or `-p`. For example, we can use `ionic serve -p 9090` to start the server on port 9090.

Use Chrome for Development

Using iOS or Android emulators to test and debug Ionic apps is not quite convenient because emulators usually consume a lot of system resources and take a long time to start or reload apps. A better alternative is to use Chrome browser for basic testing and debugging. To open Chrome DevTools, you can open the Chrome system menu and select **More Tools ➤ Developer Tools**. Once the developer tools window is opened, you need to click the mobile phone icon on the top menu bar to enable device mode. Then you can select different devices as rendering targets: for example, Apple iPhone X or Nexus 6P. Figure 1-4 shows the app created from the template tabs running in Chrome as Nexus 6P.

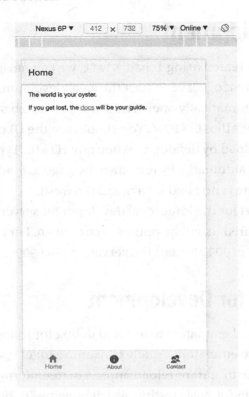

Figure 1-4. *Use Chrome for development*

Use Chrome DevTools for Android Debugging

For Android platform, when an Ionic app is running on the emulator or a real device, we can use Chrome DevTools (`https://developers.google.com/web/tools/chrome-devtools/`) to debug the running app. Navigate to `chrome://inspect/#devices` in Chrome and you should see a list of running apps; see Figure 1-5. Clicking `inspect` launches the DevTools to inspect the running app. If you cannot see the app in the list, make sure that the device is listed in the result of the command `adb devices`.

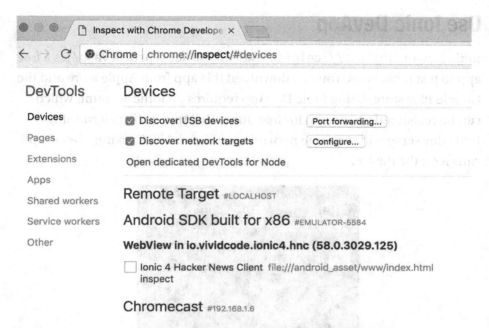

Figure 1-5. *Chrome DevTools for Android remote debugging*

Use Safari Web Inspector for iOS Debugging

For an iOS platform, when an Ionic app is running on the emulator or a real device, we can use Safari Web Inspector (https://developer.apple. com/safari/tools/) to debug the running app. After opening Safari, in the **Develop** menu, you should see a menu item like **Simulator - iPhone X - iOS 11.3 (15E217)**. This menu item has a subitem called **localhost - index. html**. Clicking this menu item opens the Web Inspector for debugging.

Use Ionic DevApp

Ionic DevApp (`https://ionicframework.com/docs/pro/devapp/`) is a free
app to test Ionic apps. You can download this app from Apple store and the
Google Play store. Using Ionic DevApp requires an Ionic account, which
can be registered on the app for free. Ionic DevApp can list all running
Ionic dev servers in the same network; see Figure 1-6. Clicking a listed app
runs it on the device.

Figure 1-6. *Ionic DevApp*

To view the logs generated when testing the app, we need to add the
option `-c` when running the dev server, that is, `ionic serve -c`.

Test on Emulators

After finishing the basic testing using browsers, it's time to test on device emulators. First, we need to configure the platforms' support for the app. Ionic apps created by Ionic CLI have no platforms added by default.

iOS

We can use the following command to add iOS platform support.

```
$ ionic cordova platform add ios --save
```

Then the app can be built for iOS platform using the following command. If you just installed Xcode, you may need to open Xcode to install additional components first.

```
$ ionic cordova build ios
```

Now you can start the emulator and test your app.

```
$ ionic cordova emulate ios
```

Running the code above will launch the default iOS emulator. If you want to use a different emulator, you can use --target flag to specify the emulator name. To get a list of all the targets available in your local environment, use the following command.

```
$ cordova emulate ios --list
```

Then you can copy the target name from the output and use it in the command ionic cordova emulate ios, see the code below to use the iPhone 8 with the iOS 11.3 emulator.

```
$ ionic cordova emulate ios --target=" iPhone-8, 11.3"
```

Android

To add the Android platform, we can use the following command.

```
$ ionic cordova platform add android --save
```

Then we need to finish several tasks before building the app for Android.

- Install Gradle. Gradle is the build tool for Android apps. Follow the official instructions (`https://gradle.org/install/`) to install Gradle on your local machine.

- Accept Android SDK licenses. Use the `sdkmanager` tool in Android SDK to accept all SDK package licenses by running `sdkmanager --licenses`. The tool `sdkmanager` can be found in the directory of `<Android_Home>/sdk/tools/bin`.

- Create an Android Virtual Device (AVD). Follow the official instructions (`https://developer.android.com/studio/run/managing-avds`) to create a new AVD.

Now the app can be built for the Android platform using the following command.

```
$ ionic cordova build android
```

We can start the emulator and test the app; see Figure 1-7 for a screenshot of an Ionic app running on the Android 8.1 emulator. If the emulator is not started, the following command will try to start it.

```
$ ionic cordova emulate android
```

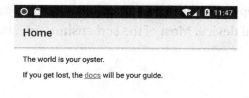

Figure 1-7. *Ionic app running on Android 8.1 emulator*

Note   If you are using Genymotion for testing, you need to use the
`ionic cordova run android` command to run Ionic apps on the
emulator; this is because Genymotion emulators are treated as real
devices instead of emulators.

When running on the emulator, we can also use the option
`--livereload` to enable livereload, so the app refreshes automatically
when the code changes.

The sample app in this book is primarily tested on the Android 8.1 emulator and a real device. Most of the screenshots are also taken on the Android platform.

Summary

As the first chapter of this book, this chapter provides a basic introduction of hybrid mobile apps created with Ionic 4. After finishing this chapter, you should be able to set up your local environment to be ready for developing, debugging, and testing Ionic 4 apps. In the next chapter, we'll introduce programming languages, frameworks, libraries, and tools that are required in the actual development.

CHAPTER 2

Languages, Frameworks, Libraries, and Tools

Building hybrid mobile apps with Ionic requires mostly front-end skills, including HTML, JavaScript, and CSS. You should have basic knowledge of these programming languages before reading this book. This chapter doesn't contain a basic introduction of these languages. You can find a lot of online resources if you do need to learn HTML, JavaScript, and CSS. Modern front-end development requires a lot more than just simple HTML, JavaScript, and CSS code. We need to deal with different languages, frameworks, libraries, and tools.

We'll discuss the following languages, frameworks, libraries, and tools in this chapter first.

- TypeScript

- Angular

- RxJS

- Sass

- Jasmine and Karma

- Jest

© Fu Cheng 2018
F. Cheng, *Build Mobile Apps with Ionic 4 and Firebase*,
https://doi.org/10.1007/978-1-4842-3775-5_2

This book only covers the basics of these languages, frameworks, libraries, and tools. You may need to read more related materials to understand their details. If you are confident that you have a good understanding of these, you can skip the whole chapter or related sections.

After reading this chapter, you should be familiar with all necessary languages, frameworks, libraries, and tools used across this book.

TypeScript

In the first chapter, we mentioned that Ionic 4 has Ionic Core and other framework bindings. Ionic Angular is the framework binding for the Angular framework, and it's also the framework used in this book. Other than standard JavaScript, Ionic Angular uses TypeScript (`https://www.typescriptlang.org/`) by default. This is because Angular uses TypeScript by default. You are still free to use JavaScript if you don't want to learn a new programming language. But TypeScript is strongly recommended for enterprise applications development. As the name suggests, TypeScript adds type information to JavaScript. Developers with knowledge of other static-typing programming languages, for example, Java or C#, may find TypeScript very easy to understand. The official TypeScript documentation (`https://www.typescriptlang.org/docs/index.html`) is a good starting point to learn TypeScript.

Note   It's no longer possible to use Ionic CLI to create Ionic projects using JavaScript. Ionic CLI always uses TypeScript. Although it's still possible to bypass Ionic CLI and use JavaScript to build Ionic apps, the configuration is quite complex and not recommended for most cases.

Why TypeScript?

The reason why TypeScript is recommended for Ionic apps development is because TypeScript offers several benefits compared to standard JavaScript.

Compile-Time Type Checks

TypeScript code needs to be compiled into JavaScript code before it can run inside of the browsers because browsers don't understand TypeScript. This process is called transpiling (https://en.wikipedia.org/wiki/Source-to-source_compiler). During the compiling, the compiler does type checks using type declarations written in the source code. These static type checks can eliminate potential errors in the early stage of development. JavaScript has no static-typing information in the source code. A variable declared with var can reference to any type of data. Even though this provides maximum flexibility when dealing with variables in JavaScript, it tends to cause more latent issues due to incompatible types in the runtime. For most of the variables and function arguments, their types are static and won't change in the runtime. For example, it's most likely an error when assigning a string to a variable that should only contain a number. This kind of error can be reported by the TypeScript compiler in the compile time.

In Listing 2-1, the variable port represents the port that a server listens on. Even though this variable should only contain a number, it's still valid to assign a string 9090 to port in JavaScript. This error may only be detected in the runtime.

Listing 2-1. Valid JavaScript with type errors

```
var port = 8080;
port = '9090';
// -> valid assignment
```

However, the TypeScript code in Listing 2-2 declares the type of port is number. The following assignment causes a compiler error. So developers can find out this error immediately and fix it right away.

Listing 2-2. Type checking in TypeScript

```
let port: number = 8080;
port = '9090';
// -> compiler error!
```

Rich Feature Sets

Apart from the essential compile-time type checks, TypeScript is also a powerful programming language with rich feature sets. Most of these features come from current or future versions of ECMAScript, including ES6, ES7, and ES8. Using these features can dramatically increase the productivity of front-end developers. You'll see the usages of these features in the code of the sample app.

Better IDE Support

With type information in the TypeScript source code, modern IDEs can provide smart code complete suggestions to increase developers' productivity. IDEs can also do refactoring for TypeScript code. Navigation between different files, classes, or functions is easy and intuitive. Front-end developers can enjoy the same coding experiences as Java and C# developers.

Basic Types

The key point of writing TypeScript code is to declare types for variables, properties, and functions. TypeScript has a predefined set of basic types. Some of those types come from JavaScript, while other types are unique in TypeScript.

Boolean

Boolean type represents a simple true or false value. A Boolean value is declared using type boolean in TypeScript.

```
let isActive: boolean = false;
isActive = true;
```

Number

Numbers are all floating-point values in TypeScript. A number is declared using type number in TypeScript. TypeScript supports decimal, hexadecimal, binary, and octal literals for numbers. All these four numbers in the code below have the same decimal value 20.

```
let n1: number = 20;        // decimal
let n2: number = 0x14;      // hexadecimal
let n3: number = 0b10100;   // binary
let n4: number = 0o24;      // octal
```

String

String type represents a textual value. A string is declared using type string in TypeScript. Strings are surrounded by double quotes (") or single quotes ('). It's up to the development team to choose whether to use double quotes or single quotes. The key point is to remain consistent across the whole code base. Single quotes are more popular because they are easier to type than double quotes that require the shift key.

```
let text: string = 'Hello World';
```

TypeScript also supports ES6 template literals, which allow embedded expressions in string literals. Template literals are surrounded by backticks (`). Expressions in the template literals are specified in the form of ${expression}.

```
let a: number = 1;
let b: number = 2;
let result: string = `${a} + ${b} = ${a + b}`;
// -> string "1 + 2 = 3"
```

Null and Undefined

null and undefined are special values in JavaScript. In TypeScript, null and undefined also have a type with name null and undefined, respectively. These two types only have a single value.

```
let v1: null = null;
let v2: undefined = undefined;
```

By default, it's allowed to assign null and undefined to variables declared with other types. For example, the code below assigns null to the variable v with type string.

```
let v: string = null;
```

However, null values generally cause errors in the runtime and should be avoided when possible. TypeScript compiler supports the option --strictNullChecks. When this option is enabled, TypeScript compiler does a strict check on null and undefined values. null and undefined can only be assigned to themselves and variables with type any. The code above will have a compile error when strictNullChecks is enabled.

Array

Array type represents a sequence of values. The type of an array depends on the type of its elements. Appending [ ] to the element type creates the array type. In the code below, number[ ] is the type of arrays with numbers, while string[ ] is the type of arrays with strings. Array type can also be used for custom classes or interfaces. For example, Point[ ] represents an array of Point objects.

```
let numbers: number[] = [1, 2, 3];
let strings: string[] = ['a', 'b', 'c'];
```

Tuple

The elements of an array are generally of the same type, that is, a homogeneous array. If an array contains a fixed number of elements of different types, that is, a heterogeneous array, it's called a tuple. The tuple type is declared as an array of element types. In the code below, the tuple points has three elements with types number, number, and string.

```
let points: [number, number, string] = [10, 10, 'P1'];
```

Tuples are useful when returning multiple values from a function because a function can only have at most one return value. Tuples of two elements, a.k.a. pairs, are commonly used. Be careful when using tuples with more than two elements, because elements of tuples can only be accessed using array indices, so it reduces the code readability. In this case, tuples should be replaced with objects with named properties. So it's better to change the type of points to an actual interface.

Enum

Enum type represents a fixed set of values. Each value in the set has a meaningful name and a numeric value associated with the name. In the code below, the value of status is a number with value 1. By default, the numeric values of enum members start from 0 and increase in sequence. In the enum Status, Status.Started has value 0, Status.Stopped has value 1, and so on.

```
enum Status { Started, Stopped, Error };
let status: Status = Status.Stopped;
```

It's also possible to assign specific numeric values to enum values. In the code below, enum values Read, Write, and Execute have their assigned values. The value of permission is 3.

```
enum Permission { Read = 1, Write = 2, Execute = 4 };
let permission = Permission.Read | Permission.Write;
```

To convert an enum value back to its textual format, we can do the lookup by treating the enum type as an array.

```
let status: string = Status[1];
// -> 'Stopped'
```

Any

Any type is the escape bridge from the TypeScript world to the JavaScript world. When a value is declared with type any, no type checking is done for this value. While type information is valuable, there are some cases when type information is not available, so we need the any type to bypass the compile-time check. Below are two common cases of using the type any.

- Migrate a JavaScript code base to TypeScript. During the migration, we can annotate unfinished values as any to make the TypeScript code compile.

- Integrate with third-party JavaScript libraries. If TypeScript code uses a third-party JavaScript library, we can declare values from this library as any to bypass type checks for this library. However, it's better to add type definitions for this kind of libraries, either by loading type definitions from community-driven repositories or creating your own type definitions files.

In the code below, the variable val is declared as any type. We can assign a string, a number, and a Boolean value to it.

```
let val: any = 'Hello World';
val = 100; // valid
val = true; // valid
```

Void

Void means no type. It's commonly used as the return type of functions that don't return a value. The return type of the sayHello function below is void.

```
function sayHello(): void {
  console.log('Hello');
}
```

void can also be used as a variable type. In this case, the only allowed values for this variable are undefined and null.

Never

Never is a special type related to control flow. It represents the type of values that should never occur. If a function always throws an exception or it contains an infinite loop that makes the function never return, the return type of this function is never. The function neverHappens in the code below always throws an Error object, so its return type is never.

```
function neverHappens(): never {
  throw new Error('Boom!');
}
```

Union

Union type represents a value that can be one of several types. The allowed types are separated with a vertical bar (|). In the code below, the type of the variable stringOrNumber can be either string or number.

```
let stringOrNumber: string | number = 'Hello World';
stringOrNumber = 3;
stringOrNumber = 'Test';
```

Union types can also be used to create enum-like string literals. In the code below, the type TrafficColor only allows three values.

```
type TrafficColor = 'Red' | 'Green' | 'Yellow';
let color: TrafficColor = 'Red';
```

Functions

Functions are important building blocks of JavaScript applications. TypeScript adds type information to functions. The type of a function is defined by the types of its arguments and return values.

As shown in Listing 2-3, we only need to declare function types either on the variable declaration side or on the function declaration side. TypeScript compiler can infer the types from context information.

Listing 2-3. Declaring function types

```
let size: (str: string) => number = function(str) {
  return str.length;
};

let multiply = function(v1: number, v2: number): number {
  return v1 * v2;
}
```

Function types are useful when declaring high-order functions, that is, functions that take other functions as arguments or return other functions as results. When specifying types of functions used as arguments or return values, only type information is required, for example, (string) => number or (number, number) => number. We don't need to provide the formal parameters. In Listing 2-4, forEach is a high-order function that takes functions of type (any) => void as the second argument.

Listing 2-4. Use function types in high-order functions

```
function forEach(array: any[], iterator: (any) => void) {
  for (let item in array) {
    iterator(item);
  }
}

forEach([1, 2, 3], item => console.log(item));
// -> Output 1, 2, 3
```

Arguments

JavaScript uses a very flexible strategy to handle function arguments. A function can declare any number of formal parameters. When the function is invoked, the caller can pass any number of actual arguments. Formal parameters are assigned based on their position in the arguments list. Extra arguments are ignored during the assignment. When not enough arguments are passed, missing formal parameters are assigned to undefined. In the function body, all the arguments can be accessed using the array-like arguments object. For example, using arguments[0] to access the first actual argument. This flexibility of arguments handling is a powerful feature and enables many elegant solutions with arguments manipulation in JavaScript. However, this flexibility causes an unnecessary burden on developers to understand. TypeScript adopts a stricter restriction on arguments. The number of arguments passed to a function must match the number of formal parameters declared by this function. Passing more or fewer arguments when invoking a function is a compile-time error.

If a parameter is optional, we can add ? to the end of the parameter name, then the compiler doesn't complain when this parameter is not provided when invoking this function. Optional parameters must come after all the required parameters in the function's formal parameters list. Otherwise, there is no way to correctly assign arguments to those parameters. For example, given a function func(v1?: any, v2: any, v3?: any), when it's invoked using func(1, 2), we could not determine whether value 1 should be assigned to v1 or v2.

We can also set a default value to a parameter. If the caller doesn't provide a value or the value is undefined, the parameter will use the default value. In Listing 2-5, the parameter timeout of function delay has a default value 1000. The first invocation of delay function uses the default value of timeout, while the second invocation uses the provided value 3000.

Listing 2-5. Default value of a parameter

```
function delay(func: () => void, timeout = 1000) {
  setTimeout(func, timeout);
}

delay(() => console.log('Hello'));
// -> delay 1000ms
delay(() => console.log('Hello'), 3000);
// -> delay 3000ms
```

TypeScript also supports using ellipses (...) to collect all remaining unmatched arguments into an array. This allows developers to deal with a list of arguments. In Listing 2-6, all the arguments of the format function are collected into the array values.

Listing 2-6. Collect unmatched arguments

```
function format(...values: string[]): string {
  return values.join('\n');
}

console.log(format('a', 'b', 'c'));
```

Interfaces and Classes

TypeScript adds common concepts from object-oriented programming languages. This makes it very easy for developers familiar with other object-oriented programming languages to move to TypeScript.

Interfaces

Interfaces in TypeScript have two types of usage scenarios. Interfaces can be used to describe the shape of values or act as classes contracts.

Describe the Shape of Values

In typical JavaScript code, we use plain JavaScript objects as the payload of communication. But the format of these JavaScript objects is opaque. The caller and receiver need to implicitly agree on the data format, which usually involves collaboration between different team members. This type of opacity usually causes maintenance problems.

For example, a receiver function may accept an object that contains the properties name, email, and age. After a later refactoring, the development team found that the date of birth should be passed instead of the age. The caller code was changed to pass an object that contains the properties name, email, and dateOfBirth. Then the receiver code failed to work anymore. These kinds of errors can only be found in the runtime if developers failed to spot all those places that rely on this hidden data format contract during refactoring. Because of this potential

code breaking, developers tend to only add new properties while still
keeping those old properties, even though those properties were not used
anymore. This introduces "bad smells" to the code base and makes future
maintenance much harder.

Interfaces in TypeScript provide a way to describe the shape of an
object. As shown in Listing 2-7, if we update interface User to remove the
property age and add a new property dateOfBirth, TypeScript compiler
will throw errors on all the places where the age property is used in
the whole code base. This is a huge benefit for code refactoring and
maintenance.

Listing 2-7. Use interface to describe the shape of values

```
interface User {
  name: string;
  email: string;
  age: number;
}

function processUser(user: User) {
  console.log(user.name);
}

processUser({
  name: 'Alex',
  email: 'alex@example.org',
  age: 34,
});
```

interface can also be used to describe function types, which can
provide consistent names for function types. Considering the forEach
function in Listing 2-8, interface Iterator describes the function type of
the second parameter.

Listing 2-8. Use interface to describe function types

```
interface Iterator {
  (item: any): void
}

function forEach(array: any[], iterator: Iterator) {
  for (let item in array) {
    iterator(item);
  }
}

forEach([1, 2, 3], item => console.log(item));
// -> Output 1, 2, 3
```

As Classes Contracts

Interfaces in TypeScript can also be used as contracts for classes. This is the typical usage of interfaces in object-oriented programming languages like Java or C#. In Listing 2-9, interface DataLoader has two implementations: DatabaseLoader and NetworkLoader. These two classes have different implementations of the method load().

Listing 2-9. Interfaces as classes contracts

```
interface DataLoader {
  load(): string;
}

class DatabaseLoader implements DataLoader {
  load() {
    return 'DB';
  }
}
```

```
class NetworkLoader implements DataLoader {
  load() {
    return 'Network';
  }
}

let dataLoader: DataLoader = new DatabaseLoader();
console.log(dataLoader.load());
// -> Output 'DB'
```

Classes

Class is the fundamental concept in object-oriented programming languages. ES6 added the classes concept to JavaScript. TypeScript also supports classes.

Listing 2-10 shows important aspects of classes in TypeScript. A class can be abstract. An abstract class cannot be instantiated directly, and it contains abstract methods that must be implemented in derived classes. Classes also support inheritance. The members of a class are public by default. public, protected, and private modifiers are supported with similar meanings as in other object-oriented programming languages.

Classes can have constructor functions to create new instances. In the constructor function of a subclass, the constructor of its parent class must be invoked using super(). The constructor of Rectangle takes two parameters width and height, but the constructor of the subclass Square takes only one parameter, so super(width, width) is used to pass the same value width for both parameters width and height in the Rectangle constructor function.

Listing 2-10. Classes

```
abstract class Shape {
  abstract area(): number;
}
```

44

```
class Rectangle extends Shape {
  private width: number;
  private height: number;
  constructor(width: number, height: number) {
    super();
    this.width = width;
    this.height = height;
  }
  area() {
    return this.width * this.height;
  }
}

class Square extends Rectangle {
  constructor(width: number) {
    super(width, width);
  }
}

class Circle extends Shape {
  private radius: number;
  constructor(radius: number) {
    super();
    this.radius = radius;
  }
  area() {
    return Math.PI * this.radius * this.radius;
  }
}

let rectangle = new Rectangle(5, 4);
let square = new Square(10);
let circle = new Circle(10);
```

```
console.log(rectangle.area());
// -> 20
console.log(square.area());
// -> 100
console.log(circle.area());
// -> 314.1592653589793
```

Decorators

Decorator is an experimental yet powerful feature in JavaScript. It's the JavaScript way of adding annotations and meta-programming support. Java developers may find decorators are easy to understand since Java already has annotations with similar syntax. Since the support of decorators is now experimental, it needs to be enabled explicitly using the `experimentalDecorators` option on TypeScript compiler. Understanding decorators is important as they are fundamental building blocks in Angular.

A decorator can be attached to a class declaration, method, accessor, property, or parameter. Decorators are declared using the form @expression, where `expression` must be evaluated to a function that will be invoked with information about the decorated element. In the decorator's function, it can retrieve, modify, and replace the definition it decorates. You can add multiple decorators to the same class declaration, method, property, or parameter.

In practice, it's common to use another function to create the actual decorator functions. These kinds of functions are called decorator factories. Decorator factories allow further customizations on how decorators are applied in the runtime.

Class Decorators

A class decorator is added to a class declaration and applied to the constructor of the class. The decorator function receives the constructor as the only argument. If the decorator function returns a value, the value is used as the new constructor that replaces the existing constructor. Class decorators allow us to replace the classes constructors when necessary. The decorator function is called when the class is declared. Instantiation of objects of a class doesn't call the class decorators on it.

In Listing 2-11, we create a class decorator refCount to keep track of the number of instances created for a class. refCount is a decorator factory that takes a name argument that is used as the key in the data structure refCountMap. The decorator function creates a new constructor newCtor that records the count and invokes the original constructor. The new constructor replaces the existing constructor of the decorated class.

Listing 2-11. Class decorators

```
@refCount('sample')
class Sample {
  constructor(value: string) {

  }
}

const refCountMap = {};

function refCount(name: string) {
  return (constructor: any) => {
    const originalCtor = constructor;
    const newCtor:any = function (...args) {
      if (!refCountMap[name]) {
        refCountMap[name] = 1;
      } else {
        refCountMap[name]++;
      }
      return originalCtor.apply(this, args);
    }
```

```
    newCtor.proptotype = originalCtor.proptotype;
    return newCtor;
  };
}

const s1 = new Sample('hello');
const s2 = new Sample('world');
console.log(refCountMap['sample']);
// -> 2
```

Method Decorators

A method decorator is added to a method declaration. The decorator
function receives three arguments:

1. `target` - For a static method of a class, it's the
    constructor function; for an instance method, it's
    the prototype of the class.

2. `propertyKey` - The name of the function.

3. `descriptor` - The `PropertyDescriptor` that
    contains information about the function.

In Listing 2-12, we create a method decorator `fixedValue` that
makes a function return a provided fixed value regardless of the actual
argument. In the decorator function, we set the `value` of the method's
`PropertyDescriptor` instance to a function that simply returns the
provided value. Updating the property `value` of the `PropertyDescriptor`
instance replaces the method declaration.

Listing 2-12. Method decorator

```
class Sample {
  @fixedValue('world')
  test() {
```

```
    return 'hello';
  };
}

function fixedValue(value: any) {
  return (target: any, propertyKey: string, descriptor:
PropertyDescriptor) => {
    descriptor.value = () => value;
  };
}

const sample = new Sample();
console.log(sample.test());
// -> 'world'
```

The PropertyDescriptor contains other properties like writable, enumerable, and configurable. These properties can also be updated.

Property Decorators

A property decorator is added to a property declaration. The decorator function receives two arguments: target and propertyKey, which are the same as the first two arguments of method decorators. To replace a property in the decorator function, we need to return a new PropertyDescriptor object.

In Listing 2-13, we create a property decorator fixedValue with the same functionality as the method decorator in Listing 2-12 but applies to properties. This property decorator fixedValue sets the property's value to the provided value. The return value of the decorator function is the property descriptor of the new property. Here we only set the property value of the PropertyDescriptor and use default values for other properties.

Listing 2-13. Property decorator

```
class Sample {
  @fixedValue('world')
  value: string = 'hello';
}

function fixedValue(value: any) {
  return (target: any, propertyKey: string) => {
    return {
      value,
    };
  };
}

const sample = new Sample();
console.log(sample.value);
// -> 'world'
```

Angular

Angular is the next version of the popular JavaScript framework AngularJS 1. Angular is a full–fledged framework for developing web applications. Angular itself is out of the scope of this book. There are plenty of online resources about learning Angular. Angular is the default framework binding of Ionic 4. Developing any nontrivial app requires the use of frameworks. This book uses Angular as the example, so it's important for developers to have a basic understanding of Angular when building Ionic 4 apps. This section covers essential parts of Angular. More detailed documentation can be found on the Angular official site (https:// angular.io/docs). The Angular version used in this book is 6.1.10.

We'll go through following core building blocks of Angular.

- Modules

- Components

- Templates

- Metadata

- Data binding

- Directives

- Services

- Dependency injection

Modules

Angular modules provide the solution to break application logic into separate units. Each app must have at least one module, the root module, for bootstrapping the whole app. For small apps, one module is generally enough. For complex apps, it's common to have different modules grouping by functionalities.

From the implementation point of view, a module is just a class with a `NgModule` decorator factory. When declaring a module, we just need to provide necessary metadata to the `NgModule()` method and Angular will create the module instance. Metadata of the module is provided as properties of the only parameter of `NgModule()`. Here we list important properties of `NgModule` metadata.

- `declarations` - Components, directives, and pipes that belong to this module.

- `exports` - Set of declarations that are usable in other modules.

- `imports` - Set of imported modules. Declarations exported from imported modules are usable in the current module.

- `providers` - Set of services that are available for dependency injection in this module.

- `entryComponents` - Set of components that should be compiled when the module is defined.

- `bootstrap` - Set of components that should be bootstrapped when the module is bootstrapped. This property should only be set for the root module.

Listing 2-14 declares a module `MyModule`. It declares a component `MyComponent`, a service `MyService`, and imports `CommonModule`.

Listing 2-14. Angular module

```
@NgModule({
  declarations: [
    MyComponent,
  ],
  providers: [
    MyService,
  ],
  imports: [
    CommonModule,
  ]
})
export class MyModule {

}
```

Components

A component is responsible for managing a portion of an app's user interface. An Angular app consists of a hierarchical structure of components. A component has a template associated with it. The template defines the HTML markup to display when the component is rendered.

The rendered HTML of a component usually depends on the data passed to the component. Some parts of a template may use a special syntax to define the binding to the data passed to it. During the rendering, those placeholders in the template will be replaced with data values that come from runtime, for example, from server-side or local storage. Data binding makes writing dynamic HTML elegant and easy to maintain.

Directives are used to attach extra behaviors to standard DOM elements. Structural directives can add, remove, or replace DOM elements. For example, ngFor creates repeated elements based on an array of items. ngIf only adds elements when the predicate matches. Attribute directives change the appearance or behavior of an element. For example, ngClass adds extra CSS classes to the element.

A component is created by annotating a class with a Component decorator factory. Component decorator supports a list of different properties to configure the component, including the following:

- template - Inline HTML template for the view.

- templateUrl - URL to an external template file for the view.

- selector - CSS selector for this component when referenced in other templates.

- style - Inline CSS styles for the view.

- styleUrls - List of URLs to external stylesheets.

- providers - List of providers available for the component and its children.

53

Listing 2-15 creates a component MyComponent with the selector my-component. It can be created using `<my-component></my-component>` in other components.

Listing 2-15. Angular component

```
@Component({
  template: '<p>Hello {{name}}!</p>',
  selector: 'my-component',
})
export class MyComponent {
  name: string = 'Alex';
}
```

Template Syntax

In Angular, we can embed different types of expressions in the template for data binding.

- {{expr}} - String interpolation to be used in HTML text or attribute assignments.

- [name] - Property binding, for example, `<img [src]="profileImageUrl">`.

- (event) - Event binding, e.g. `<button (click)="save()">Save</button>`.

- [(ngModel)] - Two-way property and event binding, for example, `<input [(ngModel)]="username">`.

- [attr.attr-name] - Attribute binding, for example, `<td [attr.colspan]="colspan"></td>`.

- [class.class-name] - class property binding, for example, `<div [class.header]="isHeader"></div>`.

- [style.style-property] - style property binding, for example, <span [style.color]="textColor"> </span>.

Services

Unlike modules or components, Angular doesn't have a definition for services. There is no limitation on what could be a service. It can be a class or a value. Services are designed to encapsulate the logic that is unrelated to the view. Components should only handle view presentation and user interactions. All other logic, like communication with the back-end server, logging, and input validation should be organized into services.

Listing 2-16 shows a Logger service that logs different types of messages. The Injectable decorator factory makes the Logger service available in dependency injection.

Listing 2-16. Angular service

```
@Injectable()
export class Logger {
  debug(message: string) {}
  info(message: string) {}
  warn(message: string) {}
  error(message: string) {}
}
```

Dependency Injection

Services can be used everywhere in a module. Components can declare their dependencies to services using constructor parameters. Injector in Angular is responsible for providing the actual instances of services when components are instantiated.

The injector creates instances of services when necessary. It needs to know how to create new instances. This is done by modules or components to declare providers. Providers are recipes of creating service instances. There are three types of providers: class, value, and factory.

Class Providers

This is the default type of provider. Class providers are specified using the classes. New instances are created by invoking the constructors. For example, `providers: [Logger]` in the module declaration means using the constructor of `Logger` class to create new instances. This is actually a shorthand expression of `[{ provide: Logger, useClass: Logger }]`. The property `provide` specifies the token to get the created instance. We can change to a different class using the property `useClass`, for example, `[{ provide: Logger, useClass: AnotherLogger }]`.

Value Providers

Value providers use existing objects as the values for the injector. For example, `[provide: Logger, useValue: myLogger]` uses the object `myLogger` as the value of `Logger` instances.

Factory Providers

Sometimes, we need to use complex logic to create new instances, or external dependencies are required for the creation. In this case, we can use the factory providers, which are custom functions. The parameters of provider functions can be dependencies resolved by the injector.

In Listing 2-17, `loggerFactory` is the function to create new instances of `Logger` service. It accepts two arguments of types `StorageService` and `UserService`. In the implementation of this function, we can use these two arguments to decide the actual service instances to create.

Listing 2-17. Function to create new service instances

```
const loggerFactory = (storageService: StorageService,
userService: UserService) => {
  return new Logger();
}
```

Listing 2-18 shows how to use a factory provider.
loggerServiceProvider is the provider for Logger service. The property
useFactory specifies the provider function loggerFactory. The property
deps specifies the dependent services as the arguments of loggerFactory.

Listing 2-18. Use factory provider

```
const loggerServiceProvider =
  { provide: Logger,
    useFactory: loggerFactory,
    deps: [StorageService, UserService],
  };
```

Tokens

In the previous examples of using providers, we always use the class type
as the value of the property provide. The value is called a dependency
injection token, which is the key to getting the associated provider.
If we don't have a class for the provider, we can use an OpaqueToken. In
Listing 2-19, we create an OpaqueToken TITLE with the value app.title.

Listing 2-19. Dependency injection tokens

```
import { OpaqueToken } from '@angular/core';

export let TITLE = new OpaqueToken('app.title');
```

Then we can use this OpaqueToken in the property provide.

```
providers: [{ provide: TITLE, useValue: 'My app' }]
```

Because the OpaqueToken has no class type, we need to use the Inject decorator to inject it into constructors.

```
constructor(@Inject(TITLE) title: string) {
}
```

Use Services in Components

To use the services in a component, we need to add the service to the array of providers in the NgModule decorator, as shown in Listing 2-20.

Listing 2-20. Add services to module

```
@NgModule({
  providers: [
    Logger,
  ]
})
export class MyModule {

}
```

We only need to add the service dependency in the constructor. The Angular injector injects the instance when the component is created, as shown in Listing 2-21.

Listing 2-21. Add service dependency in the constructor

```
export class MyComponent {
  constructor(public logger: Logger) {
  }
}
```

Metadata

Metadata is related to how Angular works internally. Angular uses decorators to declaratively add behaviors to normal classes. Metadata is provided when using decorators. We already see the usage of metadata in NgModule and Component decorators. Those properties passed to the decorator factories are metadata.

Bootstrapping

An Angular app is started by bootstrapping the root module. Angular apps can run on different platforms, for example, browsers or server-side. In Listing 2-22, we use the browser dynamic platform to bootstrap the AppModule.

Listing 2-22. Bootstrap Angular app

```
import { platformBrowserDynamic } from '@angular/platform-
                                         browser-dynamic';
import { AppModule }              from './app.module';

platformBrowserDynamic().bootstrapModule(AppModule);
```

RxJS

RxJS is another complicated yet important library used in Angular apps. RxJS is very powerful for apps using asynchronous and event-based data processing. The core of RxJS is observable sequences that allow pushing multiple values into consumers synchronously or asynchronously. A RxJS observable can produce multiple values at its own pace. An observer that is interested in the observable can subscribe to the observable by providing callback functions for different scenarios. These callback functions will be invoked when the observable produces different types of values.

This section only provides a basic introduction of RxJS; see this link (`http://blog.angular-university.io/functional-reactive-programming-for-angular-2-developers-rxjs-and-observables/`) for in-depth discussion.

The sample in this book uses the latest RxJS 6.x. If you are still using RxJS 5.x, check out the migration guide (`https://github.com/ReactiveX/rxjs/blob/master/docs_app/content/guide/v6/migration.md`) to see how to use the backward-compatibility package `rxjs-compat` or migrate the code.

Observable

RxJS provides two different approaches to create observables. The first approach is using the method `Observable.create()`. The argument of the method `create()` is a function that defines how values are produced. The function receives an observer instance and uses methods `next()`, `complete()`, and `error()` to produce different notifications.

- `next` - Produces a normal value.

- `complete` - Produces a notification that the observable completes its value production.

- `error` - Produces a notification that an error occurred during its value production.

Both `complete` and `error` notifications are terminal, which means there won't be any values for the observable after these two types of notifications.

In Listing 2-23, we create an observable that produces two values `hello` and `world`, then produces the `complete` notification.

Listing 2-23. Create Observables with observers

```
Observable.create(observer => {
  observer.next('hello');
  observer.next('world');
  observer.complete();
});
```

The second approach is using built-in RxJS operators to create observables. In Listing 2-24, of() method creates an observable with two values. from() method creates an observable from an iterable object.

Listing 2-24. Create Observables with operators

```
of('hello', 'world');
// -> Observable with values "hello" and "world"

from([1, 2, 3]);
// -> Observable with values 1, 2 and 3
```

Observers

To receive notifications from an observable, we need to subscribe to it using the method subscribe(). When subscribing to an observable, we can provide any number of callback handlers for those three different types of notifications. In the code below, we only add a callback handler for the next notification and ignore the error and complete notifications. In the handler of next notification, we simply log out the value to the console.

```
from([1, 2, 3]).subscribe(v => console.log(v));
```

The return value of the method subscribe() is an instance of RxJS Subscription class that can be used to manage the subscription. It's important to call the method unsubscribe() to release resources or cancel executions when the subscription is no longer used.

```
const subscription = from([1, 2, 3]).subscribe(v => console.log(v));
subscription.unsubscribe();
```

Subjects

A subject is a special type of Observable that can be both an Observable and an Observer. As an Observable, we can subscribe to it to receive notifications. As an Observer, we can use next(v), error(e), and complete()methods to send different notifications. These notifications will be multicasted to other observers that subscribed to the subject, as shown in Listing 2-25.

Listing 2-25. Subjects

```
const subject = new Subject();
subject.subscribe(v => console.log(v));

subject.next(1);
subject.next(2);
subject.next(3);
```

Operators

The power of RxJS comes from all the provided operators. When an operator is invoked on an Observable, it returns a new Observable. The previous Observable stays unmodified.

In Listing 2-26, for the given `Observable`, we use a `map` operator to change the values to be multiplied by 100, then we use a `filter` operator to filter the values using given predicate function. The final result `Observable` contains only value 300.

Listing 2-26. Operators

```
Observable.from([1, 2, 3])
  .map(v => v * 100)
  .filter(v => v % 3 == 0)
  .subscribe(v => console.log(v));
```

Sass

Sass is a powerful CSS extension language. It belongs to the group of CSS preprocessors with other alternatives like LESS and Stylus. These CSS preprocessors take code written in their own format and turn it into CSS style sheets. Preprocessors allow developers to use the latest features in CSS, which is the same motivation of using TypeScript over JavaScript.

Variables

We can define variables in Sass files, just like other programming languages. Variables are defined using $ as the prefix. See Listing 2-27.

Listing 2-27. Sass variables

```
$primary-color: red;

h1 {
  color: $primary-color;
}
```

Nesting

We can nest CSS selectors in Sass to match the visual hierarchy of HTML elements. See Listing 2-28.

Listing 2-28. Sass nesting

```
article {
  padding: 10px;

  header {
    font-weight: bold;
  }

  section {
    font-size: 12px;
  }
}
article {
  padding: 10px;
}
article header {
  font-weight: bold;
}
article section {
  font-size: 12px;
}
```

Mixins

Mixins, as shown in Listing 2-29, are reusable functions that can be shared in different modules.

Listing 2-29. Sass mixins

```
@mixin important-text($font-size) {
  font-weight: bold;
  font-size: $font-size;
}

header {
  @include important-text(12px);
}
header {
  font-weight: bold;
  font-size: 12px;
}
```

Jasmine and Karma

Jasmine (`https://jasmine.github.io/`) is a behavior-driven development framework for testing JavaScript code. Testing code with Jasmine is organized as suites. Each suite can include multiple specs. A spec contains one or more expectations that represent the actual testing logic to run.

A suite is created by calling the method `describe()` with a string as the name and a function as the body to execute. A spec is created by calling the method `it()` with the same parameters as the method `describe()`. An expectation is created by calling the method `expect()` with the value to check, then chained with different matcher functions for verifications.

Listing 2-30 is a simple suite with one spec.

Listing 2-30. Jasmine test suite

```
describe('A sample suite', () => {
  it('true is true', () => {
    expect(true).toBe(true);
  });
});
```

In the suite, we can also use methods `beforeEach()`, `afterEach()`, `beforeAll()`, and `afterAll()` to add custom setup and teardown code.

Karma (`http://karma-runner.github.io/2.0/index.html`) is the tool to run tests on different platforms. We use Karma to run tests written with Jasmine. Karma can launch different browsers to run the tests.

Jest

Jest (`https://facebook.github.io/jest/`) is another JavaScript testing framework. Jest is used by Facebook to test all JavaScript code including React applications. We can use a similar syntax as Jasmine to write test suites and specs. The test suite in Listing 2-30 can also be run using Jest. In this book, Jest is used to test components created by Stencil.

Summary

Building Ionic 4 apps requires knowledge of different programming languages, frameworks, libraries, and tools. This chapter provides basic introduction of TypeScript, Angular, RxJS, Sass, Jasmine, Karma, and Jest. You may still need to refer to other online resources to gain further understanding. In the next chapter, we'll discuss Web Components and Stencil.

CHAPTER 3

Web Components and Stencil

Ionic 4 has two layers of implementations. The bottom layer is Ionic Core that consists of common components built as custom elements in Web Components. These components can be used in any web page with vanilla JavaScript or any JavaScript framework. The top layer consists of bindings for different frameworks. The Ionic team provides the framework bindings of Angular, React and Vue. This chapter covers basic concepts related to Web Components, Stencil and Ionic Core.

Compared to previous versions of Ionic framework, building Ionic components as Web Components in Ionic 4 is a great step to embrace web standards. This change removes the tight coupling between Ionic and Angular and opens up the opportunity for using Ionic with other frameworks. You are free to skip this chapter if you are not interested in understanding how Ionic components themselves are built. After reading this chapter, you should be familiar with W3C specifications related to Web Components and know how to build components using Stencil.

© Fu Cheng 2018
F. Cheng, *Build Mobile Apps with Ionic 4 and Firebase*,
https://doi.org/10.1007/978-1-4842-3775-5_3

Web Components

Componentization is a common software development practice. A large project can be divided into small components. The development team can work on different components in parallel. Components can be easily reused across different projects. Components contributed by the open source community can also be used in product development to reduce the efforts. Other popular programming platforms, like Java, Ruby, and Python all have their own component ecosystems. For the web platform, the standardization process of component modeling is still very slow.

Web Components is a set of platform APIs for creating reusable components for web pages and web apps. Specifications related to Web Components (`https://github.com/w3c/webcomponents/`) have changed several times. There are four major concepts related to Web Components, including custom elements, shadow DOM, HTML imports, and HTML template. Each of these concepts used to have its own W3C specification. Now they are being merged to DOM and HTML standards.

- **Custom Elements** – Custom Elements (`https://html.
  spec.whatwg.org/multipage/custom-elements.
  html#custom-elements`) enables the creation of custom
  HTML elements. These custom HTML elements are
  the embodiment of components for the web platform.
  Custom elements can be used in HTML pages like
  standard built-in elements.

- **Shadow DOM** – A proper implementation of
  componentization cannot live without encapsulation.
  Encapsulation protects components from unexpected
  conflicts with other components that run on the
  same platform. Shadow DOM makes it possible
  to encapsulate HTML markups and styles in web
  components. Most of the parts of Shadow DOM are

merged into the DOM standard (`https://dom.spec.whatwg.org/#shadow-trees`) with the new name "shadow tree."

- **HTML Imports** – Custom elements need to be imported into the current HTML page first before they can be used. The HTML imports specification (`https://www.w3.org/TR/2016/WD-html-imports-20160225/`) defines the inclusion and reuse of HTML documents in other HTML documents.

- **HTML Template** – Dynamically importing HTML documents may have a runtime performance penalty. HTML templates are fragments of markup that are included in the page, but they are not used at page load time. Templates can be instantiated at runtime when necessary. The HTML template is merged into the HTML standard (`https://html.spec.whatwg.org/multipage/scripting.html#the-template-element`).

The effort related to Web Components specifications started quite a long time ago, but only in recent days has it gained more attention. There are mainly three reasons why Web Components has become popular.

The first reason is the pressing demand of high-performance web pages and web apps. Nowadays, the componentization of web apps highly depends on the selected frameworks and libraries. Angular, React, and Vue all have their own component models. These frameworks all include the basic code to satisfy the requirements of componentization. This inevitably increases the bundle size of web apps, which means longer delays for downloading and more runtime memory consumption. With Web Components, the componentization mechanism is provided by the underlying platforms, so the bundle size can be dramatically reduced. Using the platform APIs also means future-proof solutions that can benefit from platform improvements for free.

The second reason is the growing browsers support for Web Components. Browser compatibility is always an important consideration when introducing new techniques into web development. Although the browser support of Web Components is still not satisfying, the future is promising as major browser vendors have plans to enhance support. So far Chrome has the best support for Web Components.

The last reason is the increasing support of development libraries and tools for Web Components. The platform APIs of Web Components are low-level APIs, so it's not very convenient to use them directly. There are many open source libraries available for development with Web Components. Stencil (`https://stenciljs.com/`) is a tool developed and maintained by the Ionic team, and other popular choices include Polymer (`https://www.polymer-project.org/`) supported by Google and X-Tag (`https://x-tag.github.io/`). Ionic Core is built on top of Stencil.

In the following section, I'll go through these four concepts related to Web Components. The introduction will focus on the basic platform APIs with concrete examples.

Why Do We Need Web Components?

Web apps are created with HTML markups, CSS styles, and JavaScript code. Markups are the backbone of web apps that lay out the structure with content. HTML specification provides a set of standard built-in elements, including `div`, `span`, `p`, `h1` to `h6`, `section`, etc. The set of built-in elements may expand in different specifications. For example, HTML5 introduces more semantic elements like `main`, `article`, `section`, `header`, `footer`, etc. These built-in elements are for general purposes only and provide limited semantics. However, modern web development requires much more than those simple elements.

When developing with existing web frameworks, a typical component usually consists of the following three parts.

- A fragment of HTML markup for the component to operate on. The markup can contain standard HTML elements and other components developed using the same framework.

- A JavaScript object that manages the component's internal states and interactions with end users and other components. This usually involves event handling and data bindings. Event handlers receive the user's actions to trigger changes of internal states and communications with the back-end server. Data bindings render the HTML markup with dynamic content retrieved from the back-end server. Some frameworks also support bindings of HTML form elements with the component's internal states.

- Some CSS styles for the component's look and feel. It's recommended for these CSS styles to be scoped in the current component to avoid unexpected conflicts and overrides with styles from other components. A typical practice is to use a unique CSS class name for the root element of the component's markup, and all the component's styles are nested under this class name; see CSS Modules (https://github.com/css-modules/css-modules).

Since each framework has its own opinionated way to implement the component model, switching between different frameworks requires developers to learn a lot of new stuff. It's also very hard to share components between different frameworks. For example, it's not practical to use a React component in an Angular app and vice versa. That's why the community has duplicate components to work with different frameworks. It defeats the purpose of componentization when components cannot be freely reused. If browsers provide the basic support for componentization, then it's much easier to reuse components.

Custom Elements

Custom elements are created by web app authors, not the user agents. There are two types of custom elements: autonomous custom elements and customized built-in elements.

Autonomous Custom Elements

Autonomous custom elements are fully customized by authors. Let's use an example to explore the platform API for custom elements. We are going to create a custom element to show numbers as badges. It's a common component seen in modern web apps.

To create a custom element, we need to define the class of the new element. In Listing 3-1, the class SimpleBadge extends from the built-in HTMLElement. In the constructor, it's required to call super() in the first statement. _number is the internal state for the number to display in the badge. The function observedAttributes returns the names of observed attributes. Any change of the values of the observed attributes will trigger the callback function attributeChangedCallback. SimpleBadge only has one observed attribute number, so the name passed to the callback is always number. In the callback, the internal state _number is updated and the function _render is invoked to update the UI. After the custom element is inserted into the document tree, the function connectedCallback is invoked. connectedCallback should be the place to add initialization logic. In the setter function of number, the function setAttribute from HTMLElement is invoked to update the attribute value, thus triggering the attributeChangedCallback. In the function _render, a span element is created to show the number.

Listing 3-1. JavaScript class of the custom element

```
class SimpleBadge extends HTMLElement {
  constructor() {
    super();
    this._number = null;
  }

  static get observedAttributes() {
    return ['number'];
  }

  attributeChangedCallback(name, oldValue, newValue) {
    this._number = newValue;
    this._render();
  }

  connectedCallback() {
    this._render();
  }

  get number() {
    return this._number;
  }

  set number(v) {
    this.setAttribute('number', v);
  }

  _render() {
    if (this._number == null) {
      return;
    }
```

```
    let span = this.querySelector('span');
    if (span == null) {
      span = document.createElement('span');
      this.appendChild(span);
    }
    span.innerText = this._number;
  }
}
```

Now we can use this custom element in the page. To use the custom element, it needs to be registered first. The registration is done by calling the function define of the global object customElements. The first parameter is the name of the custom element, and the second parameter is the constructor of the new element. The name of the custom element must contain a hyphen in the middle and start with a lowercase ASCII letter. After the custom element is defined, it can be created just like built-in elements using the DOM API document.createElement. It can also be used in the markup directly. CSS styles can also be applied using the element selector. In Listing 3-2, we register the custom element with name simple-badge. Two simple-badge elements will be created.

Listing 3-2. Use custom element

```
<!DOCTYPE html>
<html lang="en">
<head>
  <meta charset="UTF-8">
  <meta name="viewport" content="width=device-width,
  initial-scale=1.0">
  <meta http-equiv="X-UA-Compatible" content="ie=edge">
  <title>Simple badge</title>
  <style>
    simple-badge {
```

```
    border: 1px solid black;
    border-radius: 5px;
    padding: 2px 8px;
    margin: 2px 5px;
  }
</style>
<script src="badge.js"></script>
<script>
  customElements.define('simple-badge', SimpleBadge);
  document.addEventListener('DOMContentLoaded', () => {
    const badge = document.createElement('simple-badge');
    badge.number = 10;
    document.body.appendChild(badge);
  });
</script>
</head>
<body>
  <simple-badge number="100"/>
</body>
</html>
```

Customized Built-In Elements

Creating a brand-new custom element may not be that easy as shown in
Listings 3-1 and 3-2. Especially when it comes to accessibility, the effort
to make a new custom element compliant with regulations in different
countries is quite large. In this case, a better alternative is to customize
built-in elements to inherit the semantics and behavior.

Creating customized built-in elements also needs a constructor. But
this constructor extends from the class of the built-in element, not the
generic HTMLElement. The API to define customized built-in elements is
also slightly different from autonomous custom elements.

As an example, we'll create a counter button based on a built-in button element. This kind of button maintains an internal counter. The value of the counter is displayed as the button's text. Clicking the button will increase the value of the counter. Listing 3-3 shows the constructor CounterButton of this element. CounterButton extends from HTMLButtonElement, so it inherits the semantics and behavior of the button element.

Listing 3-3. Customized button element

```
class CounterButton extends HTMLButtonElement {
  constructor() {
    super();
    this._value = 0;
    this.addEventListener('click', () => {
      this._value++;
      this._render();
    });
  }

  connectedCallback() {
    this._render();
  }

  _render() {
    this.innerHTML = this._value;
  }
}
```

Customized built-in elements are defined using the same function customElements.define, but they need to provide the third parameter to specify the element type to extend. In Listing 3-4, when creating the element, the base name button is used, and the actual element type counter-button is specified as the value of the attribute is.

Listing 3-4. Create customized button

```
customElements.define('counter-button', CounterButton, {
extends: 'button' });
document.addEventListener('DOMContentLoaded', () => {
  const button = document.createElement('button', { is:
'counter-button' });
  document.body.appendChild(button);
});
```

Custom Elements v0 and v1

The code examples of autonomous custom elements and customize built-in elements are using the platform APIs in the Custom Elements v1 specification. Unfortunately, at the time of writing, the latest version of Chrome (Chrome 68) only supports the API to create autonomous custom elements using the v1 specification. The code examples of customized built-in elements cannot run on any browser. To create customized built-in elements, the API in the Custom Elements v0 specification should be used.

Listing 3-5 shows the usage of v0 API to create customized built-in elements. ES6 classes are not supported in v0 API, so the prototype chain needs to be set up manually for inheritance to work. The function `createdCallback` is invoked when the custom element is created, so it's the right place to initiate internal states and add event listeners. In v0, the function `document.registerElement` is used to register custom elements.

Listing 3-5. Use v0 specification to create customized element

```
<!DOCTYPE html>
<html lang="en">
<head>
  <meta charset="UTF-8">
```

```
<meta name="viewport" content="width=device-width,
initial-scale=1.0">
<meta http-equiv="X-UA-Compatible" content="ie=edge">
<title>Counter Button</title>
<script>
  const prototype = Object.create(HTMLButtonElement.prototype);
  prototype.createdCallback = function() {
    this._value = 0;
    this.addEventListener('click', () => {
      this._value++;
      this.innerHTML = this._value;
    });
  };
  document.registerElement('counter-button', {
    prototype,
    extends: 'button'
  });
</script>
</head>
<body>
  <button is="counter-button">0</button>
</body>
</html>
```

Shadow DOM

The implementation of the custom element simple-badge uses DOM API
to create new span elements for display. These elements are still in the
same document tree as other elements. Styling of custom elements is also
done in the main document. Custom elements provide the mechanism
to create components, but shadow DOM is required to support necessary
encapsulation for components.

Shadow DOM or shadow tree is a scoped subtree inside of an element. This element is the host element of the shadow root that attached to it. The shadow root itself is a document fragment and can have its own children. For a custom element, a shadow root should be created as the root node of its content. A shadow root is created using the function `attachShadow` of `Element`. Not all elements are allowed to have shadow DOM attached to it. Allowed element types are `article`, `aside`, `blockquote`, `body`, `div`, `footer`, `h1`, `h2`, `h3`, `h4`, `h5`, `h6`, `header`, `main`, `nav`, `p`, `section`, and `span`. The function `attachShadow` accepts only one parameter, which is a JavaScript object with only one possible property `mode`. This property has two valid values, `open` and `close`.

- `open` – Specifies the open encapsulation mode, which means elements of the shadow root are accessible from JavaScript code outside the root using the property `shadowRoot`.

- `closed` – Specifies the closed encapsulation mode, which denies any access to the elements of the shadow root from JavaScript code outside the root, that is, the getter of the property `shadowRoot` returns `null`.

The `closed` encapsulation mode should not be used.

We can add styles to the shadow DOM. These styles are scoped to the shadow DOM only. Styles from the outer page don't apply inside the shadow DOM. Styles defined inside of the shadow DOM don't leak to the outer page. Styles inside of shadow DOM only need to deal with the simple DOM tree of the shadow root, so the styles can be very simple and perform well. DOM nodes inside of the shadow DOM cannot be queried directly using DOM APIs. For example, `document.querySelectorAll` doesn't return nodes inside the shadow DOM. To access those nodes, we need to query the shadow hosts first, then get the shadow root using the property `shadowRoot`, and finally query the nodes.

Listing 3-6 shows the basic example to create and query a shadow DOM. After creating the shadow DOM, we can use DOM API or innerHTML to manipulate its content. The first query `document.querySelectorAll('span')` can only find the span element in the main page. The second query `document.querySelector('#root').shadowRoot.querySelectorAll('span')` finds the span element inside of the shadow DOM.

Listing 3-6. Create and query shadow DOM

```
<!DOCTYPE html>
<html lang="en">
<head>
  <meta charset="UTF-8">
  <meta name="viewport" content="width=device-width,
  initial-scale=1.0">
  <meta http-equiv="X-UA-Compatible" content="ie=edge">
  <title>Shadow DOM query</title>
</head>
<body>
  <div id="root"></div>
  <span>In the outer page</span>
  <script>
    const shadowRoot = document.querySelector('#root').attach
    Shadow({mode: 'open'});
    shadowRoot.innerHTML = '<span>Inside of the shadow DOM
    </span>';
    console.log(document.querySelectorAll('span').length);
    // The output is 1.
    const spans = document.querySelector('#root').shadowRoot.
    querySelectorAll('span');
```

```
      console.log(spans.length); // The output is 1.
    </script>
  </body>
</html>
```

Although it's not required for custom elements to use shadow DOM, with the help of shadow DOM, we can create better components. Listing 3-7 shows the updated implementation of SimpleBadge with shadow DOM. _root is the shadow root of the component.

Listing 3-7. Use shadow DOM in custom elements

```
class SimpleBadge extends HTMLElement {
  constructor() {
    super();
    this._number = null;
    this._root = this.attachShadow({ mode: 'open' });
  }

  static get observedAttributes() {
    return ['number'];
  }

  attributeChangedCallback(name, oldValue, newValue) {
    this._number = newValue;
    this._render();
  }

  connectedCallback() {
    this._render();
  }

  get number() {
    return this._number;
  }
```

81

```
set number(v) {
  this.setAttribute('number', v);
}

_render() {
  if (this._number == null) {
    return;
  }
  let span = this._root.querySelector('span');
  if (span == null) {
    span = document.createElement('span');
    const style = document.createElement('style');
    style.textContent = 'span {'
      + 'border: 1px solid black;'
      + 'border-radius: 5px;'
      + 'padding: 2px 8px;'
      + 'margin: 2px 5px;'
      + '}';
    this._root.appendChild(span);
    this._root.appendChild(style);
  }
  span.innerText = this._number;
}
}
```

The custom element in Listing 3-7 has no child nodes when added to the page. Some components may allow developers to provide child nodes as the content. A typical example is the dialog component. A dialog component provides the basic layout and styles for its title, content, and footer. The actual content of these three parts is provided when using the component in the page. To support this kind of usage scenarios, we can use slot elements inside of the shadow DOM to define extension points.

A slot can specify its name using the attribute name. It can also provide default content. When the custom element is used on the page, its children can be distributed into the shadow DOM based on the slot names. The default content will be rendered when there is no distributed content for a slot.

Listing 3-8 is the custom element of a dialog. It defines three slot elements for dialog title, body, and footer, respectively. Each slot has its name.

Listing 3-8. Dialog element with slots

```
class SimpleDialog extends HTMLElement {
  constructor() {
    super();
    this._root = this.attachShadow({ mode: 'open' });
    this._root.innerHTML = '<div><h1><slot name="title"/></h1>'
      + '<div><slot name="body"/></div>'
      + '<div style="border-top: 1px solid black;"><slot
        name="footer"/></div>'
      + '</div>';
  }
}
```

Listing 3-9 shows how to use this custom element. The attribute slot specifies the slot to assign the element.

Listing 3-9. Use simple dialog

```
<simple-dialog>
  <span slot="title">My title</span>
  <div slot="body">body</div>
  <div slot="footer">footer</div>
</simple-dialog>
```

HTML Templates

The custom element `simple-badge` is very simple, so it uses DOM API `createElement` and `appendChild` to build the DOM structure. If the custom element is complicated, using DOM API results in a lot of hard-to-maintain code. It's better to use the new element `template`. `template` elements are containers of the actual content. They are added to the page directly but not used on the page load time.

In Listing 3-10, the `template` element contains the markup for the items in the list. The property `content` of the `template` element is the document fragment for its content. To use the template, the document fragment can be cloned and added to the document tree.

Listing 3-10. Use template element

```
<!DOCTYPE html>
<html lang="en">
<head>
  <meta charset="UTF-8">
  <meta name="viewport" content="width=device-width,
  initial-scale=1.0">
  <meta http-equiv="X-UA-Compatible" content="ie=edge">
  <title>Use template</title>
  <script>
    document.addEventListener('DOMContentLoaded', () => {
      const data = [
        { name: 'Alex', email: 'alex@example.com' },
        { name: 'Bob', email: 'bob@example.com' },
        { name: 'David', email: 'david@example.com' },
      ];
      const usersContainer = document.getElementById('users');
      const template = document.getElementById('user-template');
```

```
    data.forEach(user => {
      const node = template.content.cloneNode(true);
      node.querySelector('strong').textContent = user.name;
      node.querySelector('span').textContent = user.email;
      usersContainer.appendChild(node);
    });
  });
</script>
</head>
<body>
  <template id="user-template">
    <li>
      <strong></strong>
      <span></span>
    </li>
  </template>
  <ul id="users"></ul>
</body>
</html>
```

HTML Imports

To enable reuse of web components, we need to be able to publish and consume web components. With HTML imports, HTML pages can also be included in a HTML page. The element link can be used to include another HTML page with the attribute rel set to import. Imported HTML pages are treated like they are added directly in the current document.

When working with custom elements, we can put all related code into a single HTML page and import this page to use the custom element. In Listing 3-11, the definition of simple-badge is contained in the page badge-template.html. After importing this page, the custom element can be used directly.

Listing 3-11. Import custom elements in a HTML page

```
<!DOCTYPE html>
<html lang="en">
<head>
  <meta charset="UTF-8">
  <meta name="viewport" content="width=device-width,
  initial-scale=1.0">
  <meta http-equiv="X-UA-Compatible" content="ie=edge">
  <title>Badge using template</title>
  <link rel="import" href="badge-template.html">
</head>
<body>
  <simple-badge number="100"/>
</body>
</html>
```

The browser support of Web Components is improving. The best place to check for browser compatibility is caniuse.com.

- Custom elements – v0 (https://caniuse.com/#feat=custom-elements) and v1 (https://caniuse.com/#feat=custom-elementsv1)

- Shadow DOM – v0 (https://caniuse.com/#feat=shadowdom) and v1 (https://caniuse.com/#feat=shadowdomv1)

- HTML template (https://caniuse.com/#feat=template)

- HTML imports (https://caniuse.com/#feat=imports)

Stencil

It's possible to build web components based on the platform APIs defined in Web Components specifications. However, the development experiences with these low-level APIs may not be that pleasant. Code written with low-level APIs are more verbose and harder to read, just like comparing DOM APIs with jQuery APIs for DOM manipulations. Since not all browsers support Web Components yet, using platform APIs needs to deal with browser compatibility issues. It's better to leave these hard-lifting tasks to frameworks and libraries. Stencil is the framework created by Ionic team for Ionic Core. Stencil is also a general framework for building web components. In this section, we'll go through Stencil with examples.

Stencil is a Web Components compiler. The inputs of the compiler are source code written with modern programming languages and techniques, including TypeScript and JSX. The outputs of the compiler are standards-based web components that can be used directly in web pages or as parts of other frameworks.

Let's start from rebuilding the simple badge component with Stencil. The easiest way to start a new Stencil project is to clone its sample project from GitHub (`https://github.com/ionic-team/stencil-component-starter`). This sample project already includes the implementation of a sample component called `my-component`. We simply remove the directory `my-component` in `src/components` and add a new directory `badge` for the new component.

Listing 3-12 shows the file `badge.tsx` for the component. The syntax of TSX is similar with JSX that is used extensively in React, except that TSX uses TypeScript instead of JavaScript. The way to declare Stencil components is also similar to Angular. The decorator `@Component` from `@stencil/core` annotates components. For `@Component`, the property `tag` is the name of the generated custom element. `styleUrl` is the URL of the CSS file that contains the styles. The Boolean property `shadow` controls whether shadow DOM should be used for this custom element.

SimpleBadge is the class of the component. The decorator @Prop annotates the property number. The method render returns the markup of the component. {this.number} is the expression to render the property number. Any property decorated with @Prop is automatically watched for changes. If the property's value is changed, the function render is called again to update the content. There is no need to write your own attributeChangedCallback for the component.

Listing 3-12. Stencil component of simple badge

```
import { Component, Prop } from '@stencil/core';
@Component({
  tag: 'simple-badge',
  styleUrl: 'badge.css',
  shadow: true,
})
export class SimpleBadge {
  @Prop() number: number = 0;

  render() {
    return (
      <span>{this.number}</span>
    );
  }
}
```

The file badge.css contains the styles shown in Listing 3-2 of the original simple-badge implementation. To build the component, simply run npm run build. A JavaScript file badge.js will be generated in the directory dist. This is the file to distribute. To use this component, we can include the built JavaScript and use the custom element simple-badge.

The function render in Listing 3-12 only returns a single node as the result. The return node is the root of the component's DOM tree. It's also possible to return an array of nodes as the result. These nodes will be rendered as siblings.

Using Slots

Stencil components also support slots. Listing 3-13 declares two slots with names body and footer.

Listing 3-13. Add slots to Stencil component

```
import { Component, Prop } from '@stencil/core';

@Component({
  tag: 'simple-card',
  styleUrl: 'card.css',
  shadow: true,
})
export class SimpleCard {
  @Prop() title: string;

  render() {
    return (
      <div>
        <h1>{this.title}</h1>
        <div class="separator" />
        <slot name="body" />
        <div class="separator" />
        <slot name="footer" />
      </div>
    );
  }
}
```

Listing 3-14 shows how to use the component simple-card.

Listing 3-14. Use simple-card

```
<simple-card title="Hello World">
  <div slot="body">This is the body.</div>
  <div slot="footer">This is the footer.</div>
</simple-card>
```

@Prop

Stencil components can export public properties using the decorator @Prop. These kinds of properties are designed to be set by users of the components. By default, they cannot be changed by components themselves. Once they are set, they are immutable inside of the components. When they are changed by the users, the components will re-render by calling the function render. These types of properties can be number, boolean, string, Object, and Array. When using properties of types Object and Array, the re-render is only triggered when the reference is changed. That means updating the actual object or array won't trigger the re-render. A new object reference is required when updating the properties.

Even though properties annotated with @Prop are designed to be immutable, it's still possible to make them mutable. This is done by setting the property mutable of @Prop to true, for example, @Prop({ mutable: true }) name: string.

There are three different ways that properties can be set. The first way is to set them as attribute values in HTML. The attribute names should be in dash-case, for example, label-color or is-selected. The second way is to set them as attribute values in JSX. The attribute names should be in camel case, for example, labelColor or isSelected. The last way is to set directly on the DOM elements as properties.

Sometimes we may need to get notified when the value of a property is changed. We can use @Watch to decorate a function to be the handler of change notifications. In Listing 3-15, the function watchHandler will be invoked with the new value and old value when the value of the property label is changed.

Listing 3-15. Change listeners using @Watch

```
export class SimpleTag {
  @Prop() label: string;

  @Watch('label')
  watchHandler(newValue: string, oldValue: string) {
    console.log('The new value of label is: ', newValue);
  }
}
```

@State

Properties in components can also be decorated with @State. @State is the opposite of @Prop. @State is used for properties designed to be a component's internal state. These kinds of properties are invisible to users. Similar to @Prop, updating properties annotated with @State also triggers the re-render.

@Prop and @State are both used to control when components should re-render. Properties annotated with @Prop are part of a component's public contract, while those with @State are part of a component's implementation details. Apart from public properties, a component can also export public methods using @Method. Some components may need to access the host element. @Element can be used to get the reference to the HTMLElement instance of the host element.

Events

Events are an import mechanism for communications between components, especially for publisher-subscriber scenarios. Stencil provides two decorators for event publishers and subscribers, respectively. @Event decorator is used on properties of type EventEmitter. The name of the decorated property is also the name of the custom event. @Listen decorator is used on the handler of events published by @Event. @Event can also be used to handle DOM events like keyup, keydown, etc. Native DOM events can be handled using attributes on the DOM elements. For example, a function can be assigned to the attribute onClick as the handler of click event.

Component Life Cycle

During a component's life cycle, Stencil fires different events at particular stages. To provide custom logic to handle these events, certain methods can be added as the handler.

- componentWillLoad – The component will load but has not rendered yet.

- componentDidLoad – The component finished loading and has rendered.

- componentWillUpdate – The component will update and re-render.

- componentDidUpdate – The component finished updating.

- componentDidUnload – The component finished unloading and the element will be destroyed.

Tag Selector Example

We'll use a more complicated example to demonstrate different aspects of Stencil. This example is a tag selector to select tags to apply. The user can select from a drop-down of available tags. Applied tags can also be removed. Two components, `simple-tag` and `simple-tag-selector`, are created.

Listing 3-16 shows the code of the component `simple-tag`. It has a public property `label` to set the label of the tag. It also publishes the custom event `tagRemoved` when the tag is removed by clicking the close icon. There are two approaches to add native DOM event listeners. The first approach is what is used in Listing 3-16, which is creating a new anonymous function using the arrow syntax. This is to make sure that `this` binds to the current component object. Another approach is to use the method `bind` to bind `this` value, for example, `onClick={this.handleTagRemoved.bind(this)}`. In the method `handleTagRemoved`, the label of the removed tag is published using function `emit` of `EventEmitter`.

Listing 3-16. Simple tag component

```
import { Component, Event, EventEmitter, Prop } from
'@stencil/core';

@Component({
  tag: 'simple-tag',
  styleUrl: 'tag.css',
  shadow: true,
})
export class SimpleTag {
  @Prop() label: string;
  @Event() tagRemoved: EventEmitter;
```

```
handleTagRemoved(label: string) {
  this.tagRemoved.emit(label);
}

render() {
  return (
      <span class="container">
        <strong>{this.label}</strong>
        <span class="close" onClick={() => this.
        handleTagRemoved(this.label)}>X</span>
      </span>
  );
}
}
```

Listing 3-17 shows the code of the component simple-tag-selector. This component uses Set from ImmutableJS (https://facebook.github. io/immutable-js/) to manage selected tags. Each update to immutable Set results in a new reference, thus making it perfect to work with the Stencil change detection mechanism. The public property tags represents the list of available tags. The internal state property selectedTags manages selected tags. Available tags are rendered as options of the HTML select element. Selected tags are rendered using the component simple-tag. Since Stencil components are standard custom elements, there is no need to import them explicitly beforehand. The handler of the custom event tagRemoved receives the event object of type CustomEvent. The actual event payload can be retrieved from its property detail. The object reference selectedTags is assigned directly when updating, which essentially triggers the re-render of the component.

Listing 3-17. Simple tag selector

```
import { Component, Listen, Prop, State } from '@stencil/core';
import { Set } from 'immutable';

@Component({
  tag: 'simple-tag-selector',
  styleUrl: 'tag-selector.css',
  shadow: true,
})
export class SimpleTagSelector {
  @Prop() tags: string[] = ['Stencil', 'React', 'Angular', 'Vue'];
  @State() selectedTags: Set<string> = Set.of('Stencil');

  selectTag(tag) {
    this.selectedTags = this.selectedTags.add(tag)
  }

  @Listen('tagRemoved')
  tagRemoved(event: CustomEvent) {
    this.selectedTags = this.selectedTags.remove(event.detail);
  }

  render() {
    return (
      <div>
        <div class="selected">
          {this.selectedTags.map((tag) =>
            <simple-tag label={tag}/>
          ).toArray()}
        </div>
        <div class="to-select">
          <select onInput={(event: any) => this.select
          Tag(event.target.value)}>
```

```
        {this.tags.map((tag) =>
          <option value={tag}>{tag}</option>
        )}
      </select>
    </div>
  </div>
);
  }
}
```

Context

Context in Stencil is a global object to store global variables and singleton objects. These objects can be bound in components as properties annotated with @Prop. Context is the Stencil way of dependency injection.

The context object is defined in a TypeScript file that exports the global object Context. All the global variables and singleton objects are added as properties of this object. By convention, this TypeScript file is called src/global/index.ts. Files to define global variables and singleton objects are put into the directory src/global.

Listing 3-18 shows the content of the file src/global/index.ts. The Context object has a global variable appTitle and a global function formatLabel.

Listing 3-18. Declare the Context object

```
declare var Context: any;

Context.appTitle = 'My app';
Context.formatLabel = (str: string) => {
  return `_${str}_`;
};
```

Then we need to update the file stencil.config.js to set this global script file; see Listing 3-19.

Listing 3-19. Update Stencil config to include global file

```
export.config = {
  globalScript: 'src/global/index.ts'
};
```

To use the objects declared in the Context, we need to change the usage of @Prop as shown in Listing 3-20. The property context specifies the name of the object to bind. Then we can use formatLabel in the component code.

Listing 3-20. Use objects in the Context

```
@Prop({context: 'formatLabel'}) formatLabel: any;
```

Use Sass

Stencil uses CSS for components styling by default. It also has a plugin to enable Sass support. To use this plugin, the dependency @stencil/sass should be installed first. Then stencil.config.js is updated with the configuration in Listing 3-21. This plugin uses node-sass (https://www.npmjs.com/package/node-sass) to compile Sass files, and options supported by node-sass can be passed directly when invoking the function sass.

Listing 3-21. Enable Sass plugin

```
const sass = require('@stencil/sass');

exports.config = {
  plugins: [
    sass()
  ]
};
```

Sass is not the only supported CSS preprocessor. Stencil also has plugins @stencil/less and @stencil/stylus for LESS (http://lesscss.org/) and Stylus (http://stylus-lang.com/), respectively. We can also use the plugin @stencil/postcss for PostCSS (https://github.com/postcss/postcss).

Unit Testing

Stencil provides unit testing support for components using Jest. The component starter project already has configured Jest support. Unit testing in Stencil is very easy with TestWindow. TestWindow simulates the standardized browser environment built on top of window and document. Each test should have its own TestWindow instance to avoid global objects getting reused and affecting the testing results.

Listing 3-22 is the unit test for the component simple-badge. The function load of TestWindow creates the element to test. The only parameter is a JavaScript with two properties. The property components is the array of component classes used in the rendering. The property html is the markup to render. The returned value of load is a Promise resolved with the rendered element. The function load is usually used in beforeEach to prepare the element for testing. The function flush re-renders the element after property changes. The return value is also a Promise.

Listing 3-22. Unit testing

```
import { TestWindow } from '@stencil/core/testing';
import { SimpleBadge } from './badge';

describe('badge', () => {
  let window;
  let element;
```

```
beforeEach(async () => {
  window = new TestWindow();
  element = await window.load({
    components: [SimpleBadge],
    html: '<simple-badge/>',
  });
});

it('should display default value', () => {
  expect(element.textContent.trim()).toEqual('0');
});

it('should display assigned value', async () => {
  element.number = 10;
  await window.flush(element);
  expect(element.textContent.trim()).toEqual('10');
});
});
```

Distribution

Stencil provides two types of distributions for components. The first type is for components designed to be shared and reused. The second type is for components used in web apps. Distribution types are configured in the file stencil.config.js.

The file stencil.config.js in Listing 3-23 enables both types of distributions. In the property outputTargets, the type dist means the distribution for reusable components. Once this distribution is enabled, the directory dist contains all the files required to distribute these components. The name of the entry point file matches the property namespace in the config file. To use the distributed files, we can simply include the JavaScript file using the script tags.

Listing 3-23. Distribution configuration

```
exports.config = {
  namespace: 'myapp',
  outputTargets: [
    {type: 'dist'},
    {type: 'www'}
  ]
};
```

To enable distribution type `dist`, configurations in Listing 3-24 also need to be added in `package.json`. The property `types` specifies the output file of the TypeScript definition file. The property `collection` specifies the output file of the manifest of the collection of distributed components.

Listing 3-24. Configurations in package.json

```
{
  "main": "dist/myapp.js",
  "types": "dist/types/index.d.ts",
  "collection": "dist/collection/collection-manifest.json",
  "files": [
    "dist/"
  ],
  "browser": "dist/myapp.js"
}
```

The second type `www` means the distribution for web apps. Once this distribution is enabled, the HTML page `index.html` is processed to include necessary files. The output directory is `www`. We can simply serve static files in this directory.

Use Ionic Core

Ionic Core contains a rich set of reusable components, so it's a good example to demonstrate how to use public Stencil components. Ionic Core is published to NPM. We can include the published JavaScript file directly from unpkg.com. For example, `https://unpkg.com/@ionic/core@4.0.0/dist/ionic.js` is the URL of Ionic Core version `4.0.0`. We can also install the package `@ionic/core` locally and copy its files to the directory www.

In Listing 3-25, the script `/ionic/ionic.js` is the copied file of Ionic Core. In the page, Ionic Core components like `ion-app`, `ion-header`, and `ion-content` can be used directly.

Listing 3-25. Use Ionic Core

```
<!DOCTYPE html>
<html lang="en"><head>
  <meta charset="UTF-8">
  <meta name="viewport" content="width=device-width,
  initial-scale=1.0">
  <meta http-equiv="X-UA-Compatible" content="ie=edge">
  <title>Ionic App</title>
  <script src="/ionic/ionic.js"></script>
  <script src="/build/myapp.js"></script>
</head>
<body>
  <ion-app>
    <ion-header>
      <ion-title>Stencil App</ion-title>
    </ion-header>
    <ion-content>
      <simple-tag-selector></simple-tag-selector>
    </ion-content>
  </ion-app>
</body></html>
```

101

Summary

In this chapter, we discussed Web Components and Stencil. Ionic Core of Ionic 4 consists of components following Web Components standards. This chapter covers four W3C concepts related to Web Components. Ionic Core components are built using Stencil. This chapter also covers important aspects of Stencil. In the next chapter, we'll go through the skeleton code generated by Ionic CLI to see how Ionic 4 apps are organized.

CHAPTER 4

Basic App Structure

After we have prepared the local Ionic development environment and learned the basics of developing Ionic apps, it's time to dive into the details of Ionic framework. To better explain Ionic framework, we need to build a good sample app. In this book, we are going to create a mobile app for the popular Hacker News using Ionic 4.

If you search for Hacker News apps in major app stores, you can find a lot of existing apps. But this book still uses Hacker News app as the sample for the following reasons:

- Hacker News is very popular in the community, so it's easy for developers to understand what this app is for. We don't need to explain the background for the app.

- This app represents many content-centric mobile apps that are suitable for building with Ionic. What we discussed in this book can be applied in real-world product development.

- Hacker News has a Firebase-based API to retrieve its data, so it's a good example of both Ionic and Firebase.

To describe the app's requirements, we list the main user stories as below.

- View top stories – Users can view a list of top stories on Hacker News and view the page of each story.

© Fu Cheng 2018
F. Cheng, *Build Mobile Apps with Ionic 4 and Firebase*,
https://doi.org/10.1007/978-1-4842-3775-5_4

- View comments – For each story, users can view its comments. For each comment, users can also view replies to that comment.

- Add stories to favorites – Users can add a story to favorites and see a list of all favorite stories.

- Share stories – Users can share stories to the social network.

In the following chapters, we are going to implement these user stories. In this chapter, we'll create the basic skeleton code for the app and explore the app structure. This is important to understand code structure and conventions for Ionic 4 apps. After reading this chapter, you should be familiar with the code structure and know where to add new code.

Understanding the Basic App Structure

Once we are clear about the user stories that need to be implemented in the app, we can start building the app.

An Ionic 4 app typically starts from a starter template. For this app, we choose blank as the starter template. We use the following command to create the basic code structure of this app. The app name is hacker-news-app-v4. We also enabled Cordova integration for this app. The command also prompts whether the Ionic Pro SDK should be installed. We can simply answer "no" and deal with Ionic Pro later.

```
$ ionic start hacker-news-app-v4 blank --package-id=
io.vividcode.ionic4.hnc  --type angular --cordova
```

Then we add the support for both iOS and Android platforms by running the following command in the newly created project's directory.

```
$ ionic cordova platform add ios --save
$ ionic cordova platform add android --save
```

After the basic code is generated, we'll go through the code base first to get a rough idea about how source code is organized in Ionic 4 apps. This is a very important step for us to know where to add new code.

Since Ionic is built on top of Apache Cordova, an Ionic app is also a Cordova app, so some of the app's code is related to Cordova.

Config Files

At the root directory of the project, we can find several config files. These config files are used by different libraries or tools.

package.json

package.json is a JSON file that describes this Node.js project. This file contains various metadata of this project, including name, description, version, license, and other information. This file is also used by npm or yarn to manage a project's dependencies.

package.json also contains metadata used by Cordova. All Cordova-related configurations are specified in the property cordova. The value of this property is a JavaScript object with other configuration values. For example, plugins specifies the installed plugins for this app, while platforms specifies supported platforms.

The content of package.json file can be managed by tools like npm, yarn, or Ionic CLI, or edited manually using text editors.

config.xml

config.xml is the configuration file for Apache Cordova. More information about this file can be found at the Apache Cordova website (http://cordova. apache.org/docs/en/dev/config_ref/index.html#The%20config.xml%20 File). The content of this file is usually managed by Cordova CLI.

tsconfig.json

tsconfig.json in Listing 4-1 is the JSON file to configure how TypeScript compiler compiles the TypeScript code into JavaScript. For example, compilerOptions specifies the compiler options. In these compiler options, emitDecoratorMetadata and experimentalDecorators must be enabled to use Angular decorators. More details about tsconfig.json can be found in the official website (http://www.typescriptlang.org/docs/handbook/tsconfig-json.html).

Listing 4-1. tsconfig.json file

```
{
  "compileOnSave": false,
  "compilerOptions": {
    "outDir": "./dist/out-tsc",
    "sourceMap": true,
    "declaration": false,
    "moduleResolution": "node",
    "emitDecoratorMetadata": true,
    "experimentalDecorators": true,
    "target": "es5",
    "lib": [
      "es2017",
      "dom"
    ]
  }
}
```

ionic.config.json

ionic.config.json in Listing 4-2 is the config file for Ionic itself. From this file, we can see the app is an Ionic 4 project with Cordova integration. Because the project is created from an Ionic starter template, it also has the file ionic.starter.json to describe the template used to create it. The file ionic.starter.json can be removed after the code skeleton is generated.

Listing 4-2. ionic.config.json file

```
{
  "name": "hacker-news-app-v4",
  "type": "angular",
  "integrations": {
    "cordova": {}
  }
}
```

tslint.json

tslint.json is the config file for TSLint. Ionic 4 provides a default configuration. More rules (https://palantir.github.io/tslint/rules/) can be added to match the development team's style guide.

angular.json

angular.json is the configuration file of Angular CLI.

Cordova Files

Besides the config.xml in the root directory, the directories hooks, platforms, plugins, and www are all managed by Cordova.

platforms

For each supported platform, there is a subdirectory in the directory `platforms` to contain built files for this platform. This app has subdirectories `ios` and `android` for iOS and Android platforms, respectively. These files are generated by Cordova and should not be edited manually.

plugins

This directory contains various Cordova plugins used in this app.

www

The directory `www` contains static files of this app. This is also the directory of the whole app's static files, including built JavaScript and CSS files and other assets.

App Files

All the app's main source code is in the directory `src`. The directory `resources` contains the image files for the app icons and the splash screen.

index.html

As we know, an Ionic app is just a web app running inside the browser-like `WebView` component. The `index.html` is the entry point of the whole Ionic app. The markup in index.html is very simple with only one element `app-root`.

assets

The directory `assets` contains various assets used in the app, including favicon and fonts.

theme

The directory theme contains Sass files to customize the look and feel of the app. The file `variables.scss` contains colors for different themes. If you don't need to customize the look and feel of Ionic 4, just leave this file unchanged.

Environment Files

The directory `environments` contains configuration files for different environments. Development and production environments are defined by default. Listing 4-3 shows the content of the file `environment.ts` for the development environment.

Listing 4-3. environment.ts

```
// The file contents for the current environment will overwrite
   these during build.
// The build system defaults to the dev environment which uses
   `environment.ts`, but if you do
// `ng build --env=prod` then `environment.prod.ts` will be
   used instead.
// The list of which env maps to which file can be found in
   `.angular-cli.json`.
export const environment = {
  production: false
};

/*
 * In development mode, to ignore zone related error stack
   frames such as `zone.run`, `zoneDelegate.invokeTask` for
   easier debugging, you can import the following file, but
   please comment it out in production mode because it will
   have performance impact when throw error
 */
```

```
// import 'zone.js/dist/zone-error';  // Included with Angular
CLI.
```

Listing 4-4 shows the content of the file environment.prod.ts for the production enviroment.

Listing 4-4. environment.prod.ts

```
export const environment = {
  production: true
};
```

The difference between these two environments is the value of the property production. We can add extra environment-specific configurations into these two files. To use the production environment, we can add the option --env, for example, ng build --env=prod.

app

The directory app contains modules and components of the app.

components

The directory components contains components declared in the app.

pages

The directory pages contains code for different pages. Each page has its own subdirectory.

Skeleton Code

The template blank already includes some basic code. It has only one page.

app.module.ts

The file app.module.ts in Listing 4-5 declares the root module of the app. This file contains only a single empty class AppModule. Most of the code is using @NgModule decorator to annotate the class AppModule. The imported module IonicModule.forRoot() in the array of property imports is the difference between normal Angular modules and Ionic modules. The method IonicModule.forRoot() makes sure that the service providers, components, and directives from Ionic Angular are provided when the module is loaded. These components and directives can be used anywhere in the module. AppComponent is the root component of the app, so it's in the array of the property bootstrap to bootstrap the Ionic app. The property declarations contains only the AppComponent, while entryComponents is an empty array. StatusBar and SplashScreen in the property providers are used by Cordova. RouteReuseStrategy is related to Angular Router and will be discussed in Chapter 8.

Listing 4-5. app.module.ts

```
import { NgModule } from '@angular/core';
import { BrowserModule } from '@angular/platform-browser';
import { RouterModule, RouteReuseStrategy, Routes } from
'@angular/router';

import { IonicModule, IonicRouteStrategy } from '@ionic/angular';
import { SplashScreen } from '@ionic-native/splash-screen/ngx';
import { StatusBar } from '@ionic-native/status-bar/ngx';

import { AppComponent } from './app.component';
import { AppRoutingModule } from './app-routing.module';
```

111

```
@NgModule({
  declarations: [AppComponent],
  entryComponents: [],
  imports: [BrowserModule, IonicModule.forRoot(),
  AppRoutingModule],
  providers: [
    StatusBar,
    SplashScreen,
    { provide: RouteReuseStrategy, useClass: IonicRouteStrategy }
  ],
  bootstrap: [AppComponent]
})
export class AppModule {}
```

app-routing.module.ts

The file app-routing.module.ts in Listing 4-6 defines the routes used by Angular Router in the app. Here the path home points to the HomePageModule. We'll see more details of routing in Chapter 8.

Listing 4-6. app-routing.module.ts

```
import { NgModule } from '@angular/core';
import { Routes, RouterModule } from '@angular/router';

const routes: Routes = [
  { path: ", redirectTo: 'home', pathMatch: 'full' },
  { path: 'home', loadChildren: './home/home.
  module#HomePageModule' },
];
```

```
@NgModule({
  imports: [RouterModule.forRoot(routes)],
  exports: [RouterModule]
})
export class AppRoutingModule { }
```

app.component.ts

The file app.component.ts in Listing 4-7 declares the main component of the app. In the decorator @Component, the property templateUrl is set to the file app.component.html. The constructor function declares a public parameter platform of type Platform. Angular injector creates the instance of Platform and provides it when this component is instantiated. The method ready() of Platform returns a promise that is resolved when the Cordova platform is ready to use. Here it set the styles of the status bar and hide the splash screen.

Listing 4-7. app.component.ts

```
import { Component } from '@angular/core';

import { Platform } from '@ionic/angular';
import { SplashScreen } from '@ionic-native/splash-screen/ngx';
import { StatusBar } from '@ionic-native/status-bar/ngx';

@Component({
  selector: 'app-root',
  templateUrl: 'app.component.html'
})
export class AppComponent {
  constructor(
    private platform: Platform,
```

```
    private splashScreen: SplashScreen,
    private statusBar: StatusBar
  ) {
    this.initializeApp();
  }

  initializeApp() {
    this.platform.ready().then(() => {
      this.statusBar.styleDefault();
      this.splashScreen.hide();
    });
  }
}
```

app.component.html

The template file `app.component.html` in Listing 4-8 uses `ion-app` as the root element of the app. The component `ion-router-outlet` is the Ionic Angular integration of Angular Router.

Listing 4-8. app.component.html

```
<ion-app>
  <ion-router-outlet></ion-router-outlet>
</ion-app>
```

main.ts

The `main.ts` file in Listing 4-9 contains the logic to bootstrap the Ionic app. In the production environment, the method `enableProdMode` is invoked to enable Angular's production mode for better performance.

Listing 4-9. main.ts

```
import { enableProdMode } from '@angular/core';
import { platformBrowserDynamic } from '@angular/platform-
browser-dynamic';

import { AppModule } from './app/app.module';
import { environment } from './environments/environment';

if (environment.production) {
  enableProdMode();
}

platformBrowserDynamic().bootstrapModule(AppModule)
  .catch(err => console.log(err));
```

global.scss

The file global.scss contains additional global CSS styles. This file can also be used as the entry point to import other Sass files. If you don't need to customize the styles of the app, just leave this file empty.

Home Page Files

The home page has its own subdirectory home under the directory app. Each component has five files with similar names.

- home.page.ts – TypeScript file for the component class.

- home.module.ts – TypeScript file for the module.

- home.page.spec.ts – TypeScript file for the Jasmine test spec.

- `home.page.html` – HTML file as the view template.

- `home.page.scss` – Scss file for styles.

This is the common code convention when developing components in Ionic 4.

Unit Test Files

There are three files related to Jasmine unit tests.

- `test.ts` – The entry point file for Karma to load unit tests.

- `karma.conf.js` – The configuration file of Karma.

- `tsconfig.spec.json` – The configuration file for TypeScript to compile Jasmine test specs. It extends from the app's default TypeScript configuration file `tsconfig.json`.

Extra Files

There are two files not included in the previous sections.

- `polyfills.ts` – This file contains different polyfills required by Angular and is loaded before the app. Some of these polyfills are commented out. You can selectively enable them based on the browser compatibility requirements for your apps.

- `tsconfig.app.json` – The configuration file for TypeScript to compile app files. It extends from the app's default TypeScript configuration file `tsconfig.json`. This file is referenced in `angular.json`.

Run the App

We can use the command `ionic serve` to start the Ionic dev server and see the running app using the browser. Since we haven't made any change to the skeleton code, the app looks exactly the same as Figure 1-1 of the `blank` template in Chapter 1.

Summary

In this chapter, we discussed the user stories of the example Hacker News app and use Ionic CLI to generate the skeleton code of the app. We went through the skeleton code to understand how the code of an Ionic 4 app is organized. This skeleton code is the starting point of the example app. In the next chapter, we'll see how to implement the first user story of listing top stories on Hacker News.

CHAPTER 5

List Stories

Based on the existing `blank` template code, we start implementing the first user story that lists Hacker News's top stories. Because this is the first chapter about implementing user stories, some common concepts are introduced in this chapter. We are going to cover the following topics in this long chapter.

- Use the component `ion-list` to show top stories and test with Jasmine and Karma.

- Angular services to load top stories.

- Firebase basics and Hacker News API.

- Infinite scrolling and pull-to-refresh in list view.

- Loading indicators and error handling.

This chapter also shows how to gradually improve the implementation of a user story to make it more user friendly and reliable, which is a recommended practice in actual product development. We start from a simple list with dummy data and improve it to a full–fledged component with real data from Hacker News API. After reading this chapter, you should know how to use the component `ion-list` to render a list of items and use JavaScript to interact with Firebase database.

© Fu Cheng 2018
F. Cheng, *Build Mobile Apps with Ionic 4 and Firebase*,
https://doi.org/10.1007/978-1-4842-3775-5_5

Define the Model

As we mentioned before, Hacker News has a public API to list top stories. The API is actually a public Firebase database. It's a bad idea to jump directly into the implementation details. We should start from the user experience that we want to provide.

After the app starts, the user is presented with a list of top stories on Hacker News. The user can see basic information of each story in the list, including title, URL, author, published time, and score. The information for each story should be declared in the model. Each story has these properties: id, title, url, by, time, and score. We declare the model as a TypeScript interface in Listing 5-1. Here we use a more general model name Item instead of Story because comments and replies to comments are also items and can share the same model.

Listing 5-1. Item model

```
export interface Item {
  id: number;
  title: string;
  url: string;
  by: string;
  time: number;
  score: number;
}
```

The list of top stories can be represented as an array of items, that is, Item[ ]. However, we define a type Items in Listing 5-2 to represent a list of items. Even though Items is currently just an alias of Item[ ], declaring a dedicated type Items enables potential future improvements without changing existing code. For example, the list of items may only represent a paginated subset of all items, so properties related to pagination like limit, offset, or total may need to be added to the model Items in the future. All the existing code can still use the same type Items.

Listing 5-2. Items model

```
import { Item } from './Item';

export type Items =  Item[];
```

List Component

After we have a list of items, we need to find a UI component to display them. We can use the Ionic component ion-list. The component ion-list is a generic container of an array of items. Items in the list can be text only or text with icons, avatars, or thumbnails. Items can be a single line or multiple lines. We can use the component ion-list to display top stories. Let's start with the introduction of the component ion-list.

Simple List

Listing 5-3 shows a simple list with three text-only items. The component ion-list is the container of items, while the component ion-item represents a single item in the list. The component ion-item has three slots. The default slot is for content displayed in the item. The slots with name start and end appear at the start or end position of the item, respectively.

Listing 5-3. Simple list

```
<ion-list>
  <ion-item>
    Item 1
  </ion-item>
  <ion-item>
    Item 2
  </ion-item>
```

```
<ion-item>
  Item 3
</ion-item>
</ion-list>
```

Header and Separators

A list can contain a header to display a title at the top of the list. The header is created by adding the component ion-list-header as the child of the ion-list. Items in the list can be separated using the component ion-item-divider.

In Listing 5-4, a title is added to the list and a divider separates two items. The component ion-list-divider has three slots. The default slot is for content displayed in the divider. The slots with name start and end appear at the start or end position of the divider, respectively.

Listing 5-4. List with header and dividers

```
<ion-list>
  <ion-list-header>
    Items
  </ion-list-header>
  <ion-item>
    Item 1
  </ion-item>
  <ion-item-divider>
    <ion-button slot="start">Start</ion-button>
    <ion-label>Divider</ion-label>
    <ion-icon slot="end" name="book"></ion-icon>
  </ion-item-divider>
  <ion-item>
    Item 2
  </ion-item>
</ion-list>
```

Grouping of Items

If a list contains a lot of items, it's better to group those items for users to view and find them easily. A typical example is the contact list, which is usually grouped by the first character of each contact's first name. Grouping of items can be done using the component ion-item-group.

Listing 5-5 is an example of the simple contacts list. We use the component ion-item-divider to show the name of each group. We don't need to use the component ion-list when grouping items.

Listing 5-5. Grouping of items

```
<ion-item-group>
  <ion-item-divider>A</ion-item-divider>
  <ion-item>Alex</ion-item>
  <ion-item>Amber</ion-item>
</ion-item-group>
<ion-item-group>
  <ion-item-divider>B</ion-item-divider>
  <ion-item>Bob</ion-item>
  <ion-item>Brenda</ion-item>
</ion-item-group>
```

Icons

Ionic provides over 700 ready-to-use icons (http://ionicons.com/). These icons can be displayed using the component ion-icon with the name of the icon. For each icon, there may be three variations for different platforms, that is, iOS, iOS-Outline, and Material Design. For example, the icon book has three variations with names ios-book, ios-book-outline, and md-book. If the name book is used, the displayed icon is auto-selected based on the current platform. We can also use the property ios and md to explicitly set the icon for different platforms.

In Listing 5-6, the first `ion-item` has the icon book to the left of the text. The second `ion-item` has the icon build at both sides of the text, but the icon on the left side is inactive. The last `ion-item` shows the icon `ios-happy` on iOS, but shows the icon `md-sad` on Android.

Listing 5-6. List with icons

```
<ion-list>
  <ion-item>
    <ion-icon name="book" slot="start"></ion-icon>
    Book
  </ion-item>
  <ion-item>
    <ion-icon name="build" is-active="false" slot="start">
    </ion-icon>
    Build
    <ion-icon name="build" slot="end"></ion-icon>
  </ion-item>
  <ion-item>
    <ion-icon ios="ios-happy" md="md-sad" slot="end">
    </ion-icon>
    Happy or Sad
  </ion-item>
</ion-list>
```

Avatars

Avatars create circular images. They are typically used to display users' profile images. In Ionic Core, avatars are created by using the component `ion-avatar` to wrap img elements.

Listing 5-7 shows a list of three items that have avatars.

Listing 5-7. List with avatars

```
<ion-list>
  <ion-item>
    <ion-avatar slot="start">
      <img src="http://placehold.it/60?text=A">
    </ion-avatar>
    Alex
  </ion-item>
  <ion-item>
    <ion-avatar slot="start">
      <img src="http://placehold.it/60?text=B">
    </ion-avatar>
    Bob
  </ion-item>
  <ion-item>
    <ion-avatar slot="start">
      <img src="http://placehold.it/60?text=D">
    </ion-avatar>
    David
  </ion-item>
</ion-list>
```

Thumbnails

Thumbnails are rectangular images larger than avatars. In Ionic Core, thumbnails are created by using the component ion-thumnail to wrap img elements.

Listing 5-8 shows a list of three items that have thumbnails.

Listing 5-8. List with thumbnails

```
<ion-list>
  <ion-item>
    <ion-thumbnail slot="start">
      <img src="http://placehold.it/100x60?text=F1">
    </ion-thumbnail>
    Apple
  </ion-item>
  <ion-item>
    <ion-thumbnail slot="start">
      <img src="http://placehold.it/100x60?text=F2">
    </ion-thumbnail>
    Banana
  </ion-item>
  <ion-item>
    <ion-thumbnail slot="start">
      <img src="http://placehold.it/100x60?text=F3">
    </ion-thumbnail>
    Orange
  </ion-item>
</ion-list>
```

In Listings 5-6, 5-7, and 5-8, the attribute slot="start" or slot="end" is used in the components ion-icon, ion-avatar, or ion-thumbnail to place the icon, avatar, or thumbnail to the left or right side of the item. There is a difference between slot="start" and slot="end" regarding the element's position. The element with slot="start" is placed outside of the main item wrapper, but the element with slot="end" is placed inside of the main item wrapper. This is made clear by checking the position of the bottom line that separates each item.

Display a List of Items

After defining the model Item and learning the component ion-list, we are now ready to display a list of items in the app. We need to create a component for the list of items and another component for each item in the list. These two components are added to the module components that are created using the following command. The option --flat false means generating a separate directory for the module.

```
$ ng g module components --flat false
```

To use Ionic Core components, we need to add CUSTOM_ELEMENTS_ SCHEMA in the array schemas of the module declaration to make Angular recognize custom elements; see Listing 5-9.

Listing 5-9. Use CUSTOM_ELEMENTS_SCHEMA in the module

```
import { CUSTOM_ELEMENTS_SCHEMA, NgModule } from '@angular/core';
@NgModule({
  schemas: [CUSTOM_ELEMENTS_SCHEMA],
})
export class ComponentsModule { }
```

Item Component

The easiest way to create a new component is by using Ionic CLI or Angular CLI. Ionic CLI has the sub-command generate or g to generate different objects. Ionic CLI simply delegates to Angular CLI to finish the tasks after applying the naming convention for Ionic projects. It's recommended to use Angular CLI directly for its flexibility. We can use the following command to generate the component to display items. The name components/item means the component files will be generated in the directory components. The option --flat false means the components files will be put into its own directory.

```
$ ng g component components/item --flat false
```

For each component, four files will be generated, including the TypeScript file for the component and test spec, HTML template file, and Scss file. Let's start from the TypeScript file item.component.ts of the component ItemComponent. In Listing 5-10, class ItemComponent is decorated with @Component. The value of the property selector is app-item, which means that this component can be created using the element app-item in the template, for example, <app-item></app-item>. The property item is the Item object to display. The type of the property item is the model interface Item we defined in Listing 5-1. The @Input decorator factory of the class instance property item means the value of this property is bound to the value of the property item in its parent component. The @Input decorator factory can take an optional argument that specifies a different name of the bound property in the parent component: for example, @Input('myItem') binds to the property myItem in the parent component.

Listing 5-10. Item component

```
import { Component, Input } from '@angular/core';
import { Item } from '../../model/Item';

@Component({
  selector: 'item',
  templateUrl: 'item.html',
})
export class ItemComponent {
  @Input() item: Item;
}
```

Listing 5-11 shows the template file `item.component.html` of the component Item. In the template, we can use `item.title`, `item.score`, `item.by`, `item.time`, and `item.url` to access properties of the current bound item. The layout of the item is simple. The title is displayed in an HTML h2 element. The score, author, and published time are displayed in the same row after the title. The URL is displayed at the bottom.

Listing 5-11. Template of the item component

```
<div>
  <h2 class="title">{{ item.title }}</h2>
  <div>
    <span>
      <ion-icon name="bulb"></ion-icon>
      {{ item.score }}
    </span>
    <span>
      <ion-icon name="person"></ion-icon>
      {{ item.by }}
    </span>
    <span>
      <ion-icon name="time"></ion-icon>
      {{ item.time | timeAgo }} ago
    </span>
  </div>
  <div>
    <span>
      <ion-icon name="link"></ion-icon>
      {{ item.url }}
    </span>
  </div>
</div>
```

The `timeAgo` used in `{{ item.time | timeAgo }}` is an Angular pipe to transform the timestamp `item.time` into a human-readable text, like `1 minute` or `5 hours`. The implementation of `timeAgo` uses the moment.js (`https://momentjs.com/`) library to generate a human-readable text; see Listing 5-12.

Listing 5-12. timeAgo pipe

```
import { Pipe, PipeTransform } from '@angular/core';
import * as moment from 'moment';

@Pipe({
  name: 'timeAgo'
})
export class TimeAgoPipe implements PipeTransform {

  transform(time: number): string {
    return moment.duration(moment().diff(moment(time * 1000))).
    humanize();
  }

}
```

The file `item.component.scss` in Listing 5-13 contains the basic style of the component `Item`. All the CSS style rules are scoped in the component to make sure that styles defined for this component won't conflict with styles from other components. The styles in Listing 5-13 only apply to `ItemComponent`. When we inspect the DOM structure for `ItemComponent`, we can see unique CSS classes like `_ngcontent-c1` assigned to the DOM elements. The scoped CSS is supported by Angular by default. The pseudo-class selector `:host` targets styles in the element that hosts the component.

Listing 5-13. Styles of the item component

```
:host {
  width: 100%;
}

.title {
  color: #488aff;
  font-size: 18px;
  font-weight: 500;
  margin-bottom: 5px;
}

.link {
  font-size: 14px;
}

div {
  margin: 1px;
}

ion-icon {
  margin-right: 2px;
}

div > span:not(:last-child) {
  padding-right: 10px;
}
```

Items Component

The ItemsComponent is used to render a list of items. In Listing 5-14 of its main TypeScript file items.component.ts, the selector for this component is app-items. It also has the property items of type Items.

Listing 5-14. Items component

```
import { Component, Input } from '@angular/core';
import { Items } from '../../models/items';
import { Item } from '../../models/item';

@Component({
  selector: 'app-items',
  templateUrl: './items.component.html',
  styleUrls: ['./items.component.scss']
})
export class ItemsComponent {
  @Input() items: Items;
}
```

In the template file `items.component.html` shown in Listing 5-15, we use the component `ion-list` as the container. The Angular directive `ngFor` is used to loop through the array of items. For each item in the list `items`, a component `ion-item` is created to wrap a component `app-item`.

Listing 5-15. Template of items component

```
<ion-list>
  <ion-item *ngFor="let item of items">
    <app-item [item]="item"></app-item>
  </ion-item>
</ion-list>
```

Empty List

If a list contains no items, it should display a message to inform the user. We can use the directive `ngIf` to display different views based on the length of the list; see Listing 5-16.

Listing 5-16. Show empty list

```
<ion-list *ngIf="items && items.length > 0">
  <ion-item *ngFor="let item of items">
    <app-item [item]="item"></app-item>
  </ion-item>
</ion-list>
<p *ngIf="items && items.length === 0">
  No items.
</p>
<p *ngIf="!items">
  Loading...
</p>
```

Unit Tests of Components

Even though the component ItemsComponent is very simple so far, it's still a good practice to add tests for this component. The project created using Ionic starter template already has support for unit test, so we'll go through the process of configuring the basic tools for testing. We usually need two kinds of tests:

- Unit tests - Test a single code unit, for example, a component, a service, or a pipe.

- End-to-end tests - Test a user story, usually for testing integration between different components.

So far, we only need to add unit tests for the component ItemsComponent. We'll use Jasmine and Karma for unit testing, which are both used in standard Angular projects. Jasmine is used to write test specs, while Karma is used to run tests on different browsers. The sample Ionic project is also an Ionic CLI project with Jasmine and Karma configured. We'll go through the testing configuration first.

Testing Configuration

The file angular.json in the project's root directory is the configuration file of Angular CLI. The configuration in angular.json is very complicated with many options. Listing 5-17 shows the partial configuration related to testing. From the configuration, we can see that the entry point file for Karma is src/test.ts. The Karma configuration file is src/karma.conf.js.

Listing 5-17. angular.json configuration for testing

```json
{
  "$schema": "./node_modules/@angular-devkit/core/src/
  workspace/workspace-schema.json",
  "version": 1,
  "projects": {
    "app": {
      "root": "",
      "projectType": "application",
      "architect": {
        "test": {
          "builder": "@angular-devkit/build-angular:karma",
          "options": {
            "main": "src/test.ts",
            "polyfills": "src/polyfills.ts",
            "tsConfig": "src/tsconfig.spec.json",
            "karmaConfig": "src/karma.conf.js",
            "styles": [
              { "input": "styles.css" }
            ],
            "scripts": [],
            "assets": [
              {
```

```
                        "glob": "favicon.ico",
                        "input": "src/",
                        "output": "/"
                    },
                    {
                        "glob": "**/*",
                        "input": "src/assets",
                        "output": "/assets"
                    }
                ]
            }
          }
        }
      }
    }
}
```

Listing 5-18 shows the Karma configuration file karma.conf.js.

Listing 5-18. karma.conf.js

```
module.exports = function (config) {
  config.set({
    basePath: ",
    frameworks: ['jasmine', '@angular-devkit/build-angular'],
    plugins: [
      require('karma-jasmine'),
      require('karma-chrome-launcher'),
      require('karma-jasmine-html-reporter'),
      require('karma-coverage-istanbul-reporter'),
      require('@angular-devkit/build-angular/plugins/karma')
    ],
    client: {
```

```
    clearContext: false
  },
  coverageIstanbulReporter: {
    dir: require('path').join(__dirname, 'coverage'),
    reports: ['html', 'lcovonly'],
    fixWebpackSourcePaths: true
  },
  angularCli: {
    environment: 'dev'
  },
  reporters: ['progress', 'kjhtml'],
  port: 9876,
  colors: true,
  logLevel: config.LOG_INFO,
  autoWatch: true,
  browsers: ['Chrome'],
  singleRun: false,
});
};
```

The file karma.conf.js has different configurations.

- basePath – The base path to resolve other relative paths.

- frameworks – Frameworks to use. Here we use Jasmine and Angular devkit.

- plugins – Plugins for Karma. Here we use plugins for Jasmine, Chrome launcher, Angular devkit, and different reporters.

- client.clearContext – Whether Karma should clear the context window upon the completion of running the tests.

- angularCli – Configurations for the Angular CLI.

- reporters – Names of all reporters.

- coverageIstanbulReporter – Configuration of the istanbul coverage reporter.

- port – Server port.

- colors – Show colors in the console.

- logLevel – Set the log level to INFO.

- autoWatch – Watch for file changes and rerun tests.

- browsers – Browsers to launch. Here we only use Chrome.

- singleRun – Whether Karma should shut down after the first run. Here it's set to false, so Karma keeps running tests after file changes.

The file test.ts in Listing 5-19 is the entry point to bootstrap the testing. After Angular core testing modules are imported, we initialize the test bed for component testing, then start the testing. All test spec files with suffix .spec.ts are loaded and executed.

Listing 5-19. test.ts

```
import 'zone.js/dist/zone-testing';
import { getTestBed } from '@angular/core/testing';
import {
  BrowserDynamicTestingModule,
  platformBrowserDynamicTesting
} from '@angular/platform-browser-dynamic/testing';

declare const require: any;
```

```
getTestBed().initTestEnvironment(
  BrowserDynamicTestingModule,
  platformBrowserDynamicTesting()
);
const context = require.context('./', true, /\.spec\.ts$/);
context.keys().map(context);
```

Testing Items Component

Now we can add a test suite for the items component. A test suite file uses the same name as the component it describes but with a different suffix .spec.ts. For example, items.component.spec.ts in Listing 5-20 is the test suite file for the items component with name items.component.ts.

Listing 5-20. items.components.spec.ts

```
import { async, ComponentFixture } from '@angular/core/testing';

import { ItemsComponent } from './items.component';
import { ItemComponent } from '../item/item.component';
import { TimeAgoPipe } from '../time-ago/time-ago.pipe';
import { TestUtils } from '../../../testing/test-utils';
import { By } from '@angular/platform-browser';

describe('ItemsComponent', () => {
  let component: ItemsComponent;
  let fixture: ComponentFixture<ItemsComponent>;

  beforeEach(async(() => {
    TestUtils.beforeEachCompiler([ItemsComponent,
    ItemComponent, TimeAgoPipe])
      .then(compiled => {
```

```
    fixture = compiled.fixture;
    component = compiled.instance;
  });
}));

it('should display a list of items', () => {
  component.items = [{
    id: 1,
    title: 'Test item 1',
    url: 'http://www.example.com/test1',
    by: 'user1',
    time: 1478576387,
    score: 242,
  }, {
    id: 2,
    title: 'Test item 2',
    url: 'http://www.example.com/test2',
    by: 'user2',
    time: 1478576387,
    score: 100,
  }];
  fixture.detectChanges();
  const debugElements = fixture.debugElement.queryAll(By.
  css('h2'));
  expect(debugElements.length).toBe(2);
  expect(debugElements[0].nativeElement.textContent).
  toContain('Test item 1');
  expect(debugElements[1].nativeElement.textContent).
  toContain('Test item 2');
});
```

```
it('should display no items', () => {
  component.items = [];
  fixture.detectChanges();
  const debugElement = fixture.debugElement.query(By.css('p'));
  expect(debugElement).not.toBeNull();
  expect(debugElement.nativeElement.textContent).
  toContain('No items');
});
});
```

In Listing 5-20, we use the method describe() to create a new test suite. The method beforeEach() is used to add code to execute before execution of each spec. TestUtils used in beforeEach() is an important utility class; see Listing 5-21. The method beforeEachCompiler() takes a list of components and providers as the input arguments and uses the method configureIonicTestingModule() to configure the testing module. The testing module imports Ionic modules and adds Ionic providers. This is required to set up the runtime environment for Ionic. After the testing module is configured, the components are compiled. After the compilation, the method TestBed.createComponent() creates an instance of the first component and returns the component test fixture. In the test suite, the returned test fixture and component instance are used for verifications.

Listing 5-21. TestUtils

```
import { TestBed } from '@angular/core/testing';
import { FormsModule } from '@angular/forms';
import { IonicModule } from '@ionic/angular';
import { CUSTOM_ELEMENTS_SCHEMA } from '@angular/core';

export class TestUtils {
  static beforeEachCompiler(components: Array<any>, providers:
  Array<any> = []): Promise<{fixture: any, instance: any}> {
```

```
  return TestUtils.configureIonicTestingModule(components,
  providers)
  .compileComponents().then(() => {
    const fixture: any = TestBed.createComponent(components[0]);
    return {
      fixture,
      instance: fixture.componentInstance,
    };
  });
}

static configureIonicTestingModule(components: Array<any>,
providers: Array<any> = []): typeof TestBed {
  return TestBed.configureTestingModule({
    declarations: [
      ...components,
    ],
    schemas: [CUSTOM_ELEMENTS_SCHEMA],
    providers: [
      ...providers,
    ],
    imports: [
      FormsModule,
      IonicModule,
    ],
  });
  }
}
```

In Listing 5-20, we created two test specs. The first spec is to test that the list component can display a list of items. The array items contains two items, so there should be two rendered h2 elements for items' titles, and the text should match the corresponding item's value of the property title. The `fixture.debugElement.queryAll()` method queries all the elements matching the given predicate. The `By.css()` method creates a predicate using a CSS selector. We can use the property `nativeElement` to get the native DOM element from the query result. The second spec is to test that the list component displays correct message when no items are in the list. The property `items` is set to an empty array, so there should be a p element with text `No items`.

Run Tests

To run tests using Karma, we can use `npm run test` to start the testing. Karma launches the Chrome browser and runs the tests inside of the browser. The testing results will also be reported in the console. Figure 5-1 shows the UI of Karma 3.0.0 running on Chrome 68.

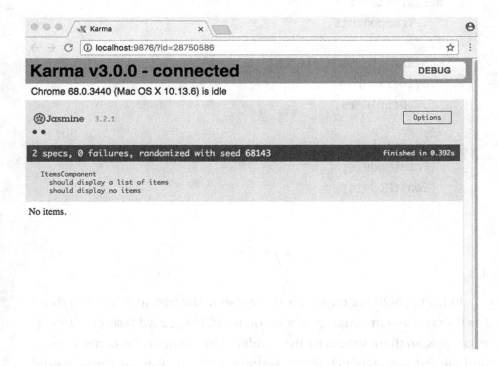

Figure 5-1. *Karma UI*

Clicking the **DEBUG** button in Figure 5-2 shows the debug page. In this page, we can see the results of all specs. We can also use Chrome Developer Tools to debug errors in the test scripts.

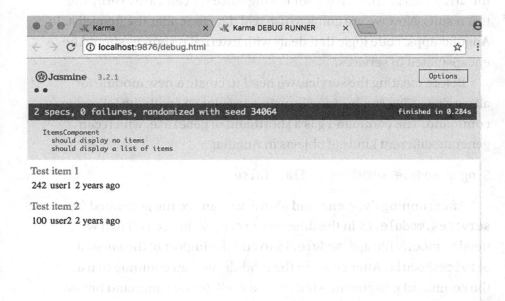

Figure 5-2. Karma debug UI

Note   Sometimes it is very hard to find causes of issues in unit tests. Below are some tips to make debugging of unit tests easier. Using `ng test --source-map=false` makes Angular generate detailed error messages. If you want to run a single test spec, just change the method `describe` to `fdescribe`, then only this test spec will be executed. We can also update the regular expression in `const context = require.context('./', true, /\.spec\.ts$/)` of `test.ts` to specify the test spec files to include.

Items Loading Service

When testing the items list component, we use hard-coded values for the array items. This is good for testing since we can easily verify the test results. Now we are going to use real data to render the items list. In Angular apps, code logic that deals with external resources should be encapsulated in services.

Before creating the service, we need to create a new module for all services. This can be done by using Angular CLI with the following command. The command g is a shorthand of generate, which can generate different kinds of objects in Angular.

```
$ ng g module services --flat false
```

After running the command above, we can see the generated file services.module.ts in the directory src/app/services. Then we need to modify file app.module.ts to add the import of the created ServicesModule. After creating the module, we can continue to use the command g to generate the service itself. In the command below, g service means generating a service, services/item is the path of the service to generate, -m services specifies the module to provide this service; --flat false means generating a separate directory for this service.

```
$ ng g service services/item -m services --flat false
```

After running the command above, we can see the generated files item.service.ts and item.service.spec.ts in the directory src/app/services/item. The file services.module.ts is also updated automatically to include this newly created service.

ItemService in Listing 5-22 has a single method load(offset, limit) to load a list of items. Because there can be many items, the method load() only loads a subset of items. Parameters offset and limit are used for pagination: offset specifies the position of the first loaded item in the whole items list, and limit specifies the number of loaded items. For example, load(0, 10) means loading the first 10 items.

Listing 5-22. ItemService

```
import { Injectable } from '@angular/core';
import { Observable, of } from 'rxjs';
import { Items } from '../../models/items';

@Injectable()
export class ItemService {

  load(offset: number, limit: number): Observable<Items> {
    return of({
      offset: 0,
      limit: 0,
      total: 0,
      results: [],
    });
  }
}
```

The return type of the load() method is Observable<Items>. Items is the model type we defined in Listing 5-2. It used to be just an alias of Item[], but now we update it to include more information related to pagination; see Listing 5-23. The type Items now has both properties offset and limit that match the parameters in the method load(). It also has the property total that represents the total number of items. The property total is optional, because in some cases the total number may not be available. The property results represents the actual array of items.

Listing 5-23. Updated Item model

```
import { Item } from './Item';
export interface Items {
  offset: number;
  limit: number;
  total?: number;
  results: Item[];
}
```

After we update the model Items, we also need to update code in the items list component and related test specs to use the new model.

ItemService uses decorator factory Injectable, so it'll be registered to Angular's injector and available for dependency injection to other components.

The return Observable<Items> of the method load() currently only emits an Items object with empty results. We'll improve the implementation to use the actual Hacker News API later.

Top Stories Page

Now we can create a new page in the Ionic app to show top stories using ItemsComponent and ItemService. This page is also the new index page. Each page has its own subdirectory. We continue to use Angular CLI for components generation. In Listing 5-24, we generate the module top-stories for the top stories page and the component top-stories for this page. You may notice the option --routing when creating the module top-stories. This option is for routing support with Angular Router. We'll discuss Angular Router in Chapter 8.

Listing 5-24. Generate modules and components

```
$ ng g module top-stories --routing
$ ng g component top-stories -m top-stories
```

After running the commands in Listing 5-24, all the required files for the top stories page are generated in the directory src/app/top-stories. We start from the file top-stories.component.ts. In Listing 5-25, the page class TopStoriesComponent implements the Angular interface OnInit. By implementing this interface, when TopStoriesComponent finishes initialization, the method ngOnInit() will be invoked automatically. The constructor of class TopStoriesPage takes one argument itemService of type ItemService. We use ItemService to load items and use ItemsComponent to display them.

TopStoriesPage class has a property items of type Items. The value of this property is passed to the ItemsComponent for rendering. In the method ngOnInit(), the method load() of ItemService is invoked. When the loading is finished, loaded items is set as the value of the property items. TopStoriesComponent class also implements the interface OnDestroy. In the method ngOnDestroy(), we use the method unsubscribe() of the Observable subscription to make sure resources are released.

Listing 5-25. top-stories.ts

```
import { Component, OnDestroy, OnInit } from '@angular/core';
import { Subscription } from 'rxjs';
import { Items } from '../../models/items';
import { ItemService } from '../../services/item/item.service';

@Component({
  selector: 'app-top-stories',
  templateUrl: './top-stories.component.html',
  styleUrls: ['./top-stories.component.scss']
})
export class TopStoriesComponent implements OnInit, OnDestroy {

  items: Items;
  private subscription: Subscription;
```

```
constructor(private itemService: ItemService) { }

ngOnInit() {
  this.subscription = this.itemService.load(0, 10).
  subscribe(items => this.items = items);
}

ngOnDestroy() {
  if (this.subscription) {
    this.subscription.unsubscribe();
  }
}
}
```

In the template file of Listing 5-26, `<app-items [items]="items">`
`</app-items>` creates the component `app-items` and binds the value of
the property `items` to the property `items` in `TopStoriesComponent` class.
Because loading items is asynchronous, the value of items is `undefined`
until the loading is finished successfully. The component `app-items`
already handles the case when the property is `undefined`.

Listing 5-26. top-stories.html

```
<ion-app>
  <ion-header>
    <ion-toolbar>
      <ion-title>Top Stories</ion-title>
    </ion-toolbar>
  </ion-header>
  <ion-content padding>
    <app-items [items]="items"></app-items>
  </ion-content>
</ion-app>
```

Test

Now we need to add a test suite for this page.

Items Loading Service Mock

To test the top stories page, we need a service that can load items and simulate different scenarios. The best solution is to create a service mock. ItemServiceMock in Listing 5-27 is the mock we use for ItemService. The implementation of the method load() in ItemServiceMock creates items based on input arguments offset and limit. With this service mock, we can generate any number of items.

Listing 5-27. ItemServiceMock

```
import { Injectable } from '@angular/core';
import { Observable } from 'rxjs';
import * as range from 'lodash.range';
import { Items } from '../model/Items';
import { Item } from '../model/Item';
import { ItemService } from '../services/ItemService';

@Injectable()
export class ItemServiceMock extends ItemService {
  load(offset?: number, limit?: number): Observable<Items> {
    const results: Item[] = range(offset, offset + limit).
    map(index => ({
      id: index,
      title: `Item ${index + 1}`,
      url: `http://www.example.com/item${index}`,
      by: `demo`,
      time: new Date().getTime() / 1000,
      score: index,
    }));
```

```
  return Observable.of({
    offset,
    limit,
    total: offset + limit,
    results,
  });
  }
}
```

Test Suite

When we used Angular CLI to generate the component of the top stories page, the test spec file is already generated with basic setup code to test it. We can use this spec file top-stories.component.spect.ts as the starting point to test this component. When using the method TestUtils. beforeEachCompiler() to configure the component, we need to register the ItemServiceMock as a provider. Here we use the Angular class provider. {provide: ItemService, useClass: ItemServiceMock} means the registered provider uses the default token ItemService but uses ItemServiceMock as the actual class. So TopStoriesComponent is injected with an instance of class ItemServiceMock.

The code of the test spec in Listing 5-28 is different from what's in Listing 5-20 for the spec of ItemsComponent. This is because TopStoriesPage uses an asynchronous service ItemService that makes testing more complicated.

At first, we need to use the method async() from Angular to wrap the testing function. The first fixture.detectChanges() invocation triggers the invocation of the method load() in ItemService. fixture. whenStable() returns a promise that waits for the returned observable of the method load() to emit values. In the resolve callback of the promise returned by whenStable(), the second fixture.detectChanges() invocation triggers ItemsComponent to update itself using the loaded items. At last, we verify the rendered DOM structure matches the expected result.

Listing 5-28. top-stories.spec.ts

```
import { ComponentFixture, async } from '@angular/core/testing';
import { By } from '@angular/platform-browser';
import { DebugElement } from '@angular/core';
import { TestUtil } from '../../test';
import { TopStoriesComponent } from './top-stories.component';
import { ItemsComponent } from '../../components/items/items.
      component';
import { ItemComponent } from '../../components/item/item.
      component';
import { TimeAgoPipe } from '../../pipes/TimeAgoPipe';
import { ItemService } from '../../services/ItemService';
import { ItemServiceMock } from '../../testing/ItemServiceMock';

let fixture: ComponentFixture<TopStoriesComponent> = null;
let component: any = null;

describe('top stories page', () => {

  beforeEach(async(() => TestUtils.beforeEachCompiler(
    [TopStoriesComponent, ItemsComponent, ItemComponent,
    TimeAgoPipe],
    [{provide: ItemService, useClass: ItemServiceMock}]
  ).then(compiled => {
    fixture = compiled.fixture;
    component = compiled.instance;
  })));

  it('should display a list of 10 items', async(() => {
    fixture.detectChanges();
    fixture.whenStable().then(() => {
      fixture.detectChanges();
```

```
    let debugElements = fixture.debugElement.queryAll(By.
    css('h2'));
    expect(debugElements.length).toBe(10);
    expect(debugElements[0].nativeElement.textContent).
    toContain('Item 1');
    expect(debugElements[1].nativeElement.textContent).
    toContain('Item 2');
  });
 }));
});
```

Now we have a top stories page that works with mock data. We continue to improve the implementation of ItemService to use the actual Hacker News API. The Hacker News API is a public Firebase database. We start from the Firebase basics.

Firebase Basics

Firebase is a product of Google. To create new Firebase projects, you need to have a Google account. Firebase projects can be created and managed using Firebase console (https://firebase.google.com/console/). Firebase offers two products for data persistence. The first one is the original Firebase Realtime Database, the second one is the new Cloud Firestore. These two products have different data models for persistence. Cloud Firestore offers richer features, better performance, and scalability. But Cloud Firestore is currently in beta. If you want to have a stable solution, Realtime Database is a better choice. If you want to try new features and a new data model, Cloud Firestore should be the choice. Firebase has a guide (https://firebase.google.com/docs/firestore/rtdb-vs-firestore) about how to choose between these two products. This book covers both products. Hacker News data is stored in the Realtime Database, so we use it to retrieve the data. The app's own data is stored in Cloud Firestore. We start from the Realtime Database.

Database Structure

Firebase Realtime Database has a unique database structure that is different from other databases. Each Firebase database is stored as a tree-like JSON object. This tree structure is very flexible for all kinds of data. You can organize the app's data in a way suitable for most of your apps. For an e-commerce app, its database can be organized as in Listing 5-29. The property products is a map of product id to its properties. The property customers is a map of customer id to its properties. The property orders is a map of order id to its properties.

Listing 5-29. Sample Firebase database

```
{
  "products": {
    "00001": {
      "name": "iPhone 6s plus",
      "price": 613.50
    },
    "00002": {
      "name": "LG Nexus 5",
      "price": 187.99
    }
  },
  "customers": {
    "00001": {
      "firstName": "Alex",
      "lastName": "Cheng",
      "email": "alex@example.com"
    }
  },
```

```
"orders": {
  "00001": {
    "customer": "00001",
    "items": {
      "00001": true,
      "00002": true
    },
    "shippingCost": 5.00
  }
}
}
```

Each data value in the database has a unique path to identify it. If you think of the whole JSON object as a file directory, then the path describes how to navigate from the root to a data value. For example, the path of the price of the product with id 00001 is /products/00001/price. The path /orders represents all orders. The path is used when reading or writing data, as well as configuring security rules.

Firebase JavaScript SDK

Firebase provides different SDKs for mobile and web apps to interact with its database. Ionic apps should use the web SDK (https://firebase. google.com/docs/web/setup).

To demonstrate the usage of Firebase JavaScript SDK, we use the e-commerce database as the example. The Firebase web SDK is a general library for all kinds of web apps. For Angular apps, AngularFire2 is a better choice that offers tight integration with Angular. In this section, we only discuss the usage of the general web SDK, which is very important to understand how Firebase works. AngularFire2 is used in the Ionic app and will be discussed later.

Setup

We use Firebase console to create a new project first. In the **Project Overview** page of your newly created Firebase project, clicking **Add Firebase to your web app** shows a dialog with code ready to be copied into the HTML file; see Figure 5-3.

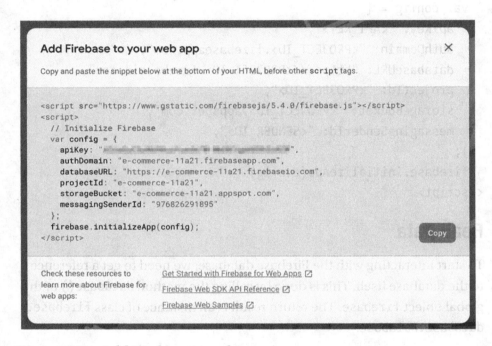

Figure 5-3. *Add Firebase to web app*

In Listing 5-30, we set different configuration properties for various Firebase features. PROJECT_ID is the id of the Firebase project.

- apiKey - Core Firebase app.

- authDomain - Firebase Authentication.

- databaseURL - Firebase Realtime Database.

- storageBucket - Firebase Storage.

- messagingSenderId - Firebase Cloud Messaging.

155

Listing 5-30. Set up Firebase web SDK

```
<script src="https://www.gstatic.com/firebasejs/5.4.0/firebasejs">
            </script>
<script>
  // Initialize Firebase
  var config = {
    apiKey: "<API_KEY>",
    authDomain: "<PROJECT_ID>.firebaseapp.com",
    databaseURL: "https://<PROJECT_ID>.firebaseio.com",
    projectId: "<PROJECT_ID>",
    storageBucket: "<PROJECT_ID>.appspot.com",
    messagingSenderId: "<SENDER_ID>",
  };
  firebase.initializeApp(config) ;
</script>
```

Read Data

To start interacting with the Firebase database, we need to get a reference to the database itself. This is done by calling the method `database()` of the global object `firebase`. The return result is an instance of class `firebase.database.Database`.

```
let database = firebase.database();
```

Once we get a reference to the Firebase database, we can use the method `ref(path)` of the object `database` to get a reference to the data specified by a given path. The return result `ref` is an instance of the class `firebase.database.Reference`.

```
let ref = database.ref('products');
```

Reading data from the Firebase database is done asynchronously using event listeners. After adding a listener of a certain event to the object ref, when the event is triggered, the listener will be invoked with related data. In Listing 5-31, a listener of the event value is added to the object ref using the method on(eventType, callback). When the data of path /products is changed, the event listener is invoked with a data snapshot taken at the time of the event. The event listener will also be triggered when the listener is attached to get the initial data.

Listing 5-31. Reading data

```
ref.on('value', function(snapshot) {
  console.log(snapshot.val());
});
```

The value of argument snapshot passed to the listener handler is a firebase.database.DataSnapshot object. It's an immutable object with different properties and methods to retrieve data from the snapshot. It represents the snapshot of data at the given path when the event occurs. This DataSnapshot object is only used for retrieving data. Modifying it won't change the value in the remote database. Table 5-1 shows the properties of DataSnapshot.

Table 5-1. *Properties of DataSnapshot*

Name	Description
key	Gets the key of this DataSnapshot, which is the last token in the path. For example, the key of the path /products/00001 is 00001.
ref	Gets the Reference object that created this DataSnapshot object.

157

Table 5-2 shows the methods of DataSnapshot.

Table 5-2. *Methods of DataSnapshot*

Name	Description
val()	Gets a JavaScript value of the data; could be a string, number, Boolean, array, or object. null means the DataSnapshot is empty.
exists()	Checks if this DataSnapshot contains any data. This method should be used instead of checking val() !== null.
forEach(action)	Invokes a function action for each child. The function receives the DataSnapshot object of each child as the argument.
child(childPath)	Gets a DataSnapshot object at the relative path specified by childPath.
hasChild(childPath)	Checks if data exists at the relative path specified by childPath.
hasChildren()	Checks if this DataSnapshot has any children.
numChildren()	Gets the number of children.
toJSON()	Returns the JSON serialized result of this object.

After an event listener of a Reference object is added, we can use the method off(eventType, callback) to remove the listener. To make sure all event listeners are correctly removed, for a certain event type on a certain reference, the number of invocation times of the method on() should match the number of invocation times of the method off(). Event listeners are not inherited. Removing an event listener on the parent node won't remove event listeners registered on its child nodes. Each event listener should be removed individually. Listing 5-32 shows three different ways to remove event listeners.

Listing 5-32.   Remove event listeners

```
ref.off('value', valueCallback); // Remove a single listener

ref.off('value'); // Remove all listeners of the event 'value'

ref.off(); // Remove all listeners for all events
```

Sometimes you may only need to retrieve the data once, so then the method once(eventType, callback) is a better choice than on(), because event listeners added using once() will only be triggered once and remove themselves after that. You don't need to worry about removing event listeners afterward.

There are five different type of events to listen to when reading data; see Table 5-3.

Table 5-3.   *Event types*

Name	Trigger condition	Arguments of listener function
value	Once with initial data and every time data changes.	DataSnapshot object.
child_added	Once for each initial child and every time a new child is added.	DataSnapshot object of the child added and key of its previous sibling child.
child_removed	Every time a child is removed.	DataSnapshot of the removed child.
child_changed	Every time a child's data changes.	DataSnapshot object of the child changed and key of its previous sibling child.
child_moved	When a child moves its position due to priority change.	DataSnapshot object of the child changed and key of its previous sibling child.

Listing 5-33 shows the examples of using these events.

Listing 5-33. Use events

```
let ref = database.ref('products');
ref.on('child_added', function(snapshot) {
  console.log('product added: ' + snapshot.val().name);
});

ref.on('child_removed', function(snapshot) {
  console.log('product removed: ' + snapshot.key);
});
```

Write Data

The reference object ref can also be used to write data. The method set(value, onComplete) replaces the data at the path of the current reference object. The method set() will override all data under that path, so be careful when using it. The method update(values, onComplete) selectively updates children data specified by relative paths in the value. Only children listed in the values will be replaced. The method update() supports updating multiple values. onComplete is the callback function to invoke after data changes are synchronized to the server. If you prefer to use Promise instead of callback functions, the return value of set() or update() is a firebase.Promise object that is similar to the standard Promise object. Corresponding events, for example, value and child_added, will be triggered after calling methods set() and update().

In Listing 5-34, the method set() replaces the whole data under the path products/00001, and the method update() only updates the property price.

Listing 5-34. Writing data

```
let ref = database.ref('products');

ref.child('00001').set({
  "name": "New iPhone 6s plus",
  "price": 699.99
});

ref.child('00001').update({
  "price": 639.99
});
```

The Reference object also has the method remove() to remove whole data at the given path, which is the same as using set(null).

If the data to store is a list of objects without meaningful business ids, we should use the method push(value, onComplete) to add a new object to the list. The method push() creates a unique value as the key of the object to add. It's not recommended to use sequence numbers as keys for objects in the list, as it causes synchronization problems in a distributed data system. The return value of the method push() is a new Reference object points to the newly created path. Listing 5-35 shows two different ways to use push().

Listing 5-35. Pushing data to list

```
let ref = database.ref('customers');
ref.push({
  "firstName": "Bob",
  "lastName": "Lee",
  "email": "bob@example.com"
});
```

```
ref.push().set({
  "firstName": "Bob",
  "lastName": "Lee",
  "email": "bob@example.com"
});
```

Query Data

The major disadvantage of reading data using event listeners on the Reference object is that the whole data at the given path will be read. This could affect performance for large objects or arrays. Sorting also cannot be done either. To filter and sort data under a given path, we can use other methods in the Reference object that return firebase.database.Query objects.

sort

Table 5-4 shows the methods for sorting. Listing 5-36 shows an example of sorting the products by price.

Table 5-4. *Methods for sorting*

Method	Description
orderByChild(path)	Orders by the value of specified child path.
orderByKey()	Orders by the value of child keys.
orderByValue()	Orders by the value of child values; only numbers, strings, and Booleans are supported.

Listing 5-36. Sort products by price

```
let ref = database.ref('products');
ref.orderByChild('price');
```

Filter

Table 5-5 shows the methods for filtering. In Listing 5-37, we sort the products by price first, then filter it to only return the first child.

Table 5-5. *Methods for filtering*

Method	Description
limitToFirst(limit)	Limits the number of returned items from the beginning of the ordered list of results.
limitToLast(limit)	Limits the number of returned items from the end of the ordered list of results.
startAt(value, key)	Sets the starting point of returned items in the ordered list of results. Only items with a value greater than or equal to the specified value or key will be included.
endAt(value, key)	Sets the ending point of returned items in the ordered list of results. Only items with a value less than or equal to the specified value or key will be included.
equalTo(value, key)	Sets the value to match for returned items in the ordered list of results. Only items with a value equal to the specified value or key will be included.

Listing 5-37. Filter to only return the first child

```
let ref = database.ref('products');
ref.orderByChild('price').limitToFirst(1);
```

The returned firebase.database.Query objects from filtering and sorting methods can be chained together to create complicated queries. There can be multiple filtering conditions, but only one sorting method is allowed.

Navigation

Given a `Reference` object, we can use it to navigate in the database tree. Table 5-6 shows the methods or properties for navigation. Listing 5-38 shows how to use these methods or properties.

Table 5-6. *Methods or properties for navigation*

Method	Description
child(path)	Gets the Reference object at the specified relative path.
parent	Gets the Reference object to its parent path.
root	Gets the Reference object to the database's root path.

Listing 5-38. Navigation

```
let ref = database.ref('products');
ref.child('00001');
// -> path is "/products/00001"
ref.parent;
// -> path is "/"
ref.root;
// -> path is "/"
```

Hacker News API

After understanding how to interact with Firebase database in JavaScript, we can now discuss how to integrate Hacker News API (https://github.com/HackerNews/API) in the app. The Hacker News API is just a public Firebase database at URL https://hacker-news.firebaseio.com/v0.

AngularFire2

In the last section, we discussed how to use the general Firebase JavaScript SDK. For Angular apps, a better choice is AngularFire2 (`https://github.com/angular/angularfire2`), which makes interacting with Firebase much easier. We use npm to install AngularFire2 packages.

```
$ npm i firebase @angular/fire
```

Now we need to add the AngularFire2 module into the Ionic app. The first step is to add the Firebase configuration to the file `src/environments/environment.ts`. The related object in Listing 5-39 only contains the property `databaseURL` that points to the Hacker News public database.

Listing 5-39. AngularFire2 configuration

```
export const environment = {
  production: false,
  firebase: {
    databaseURL: 'https://hacker-news.firebaseio.com',
  },
};
```

Then we need to configure the application module to import Firebase modules. In the `@NgModule` decorator, we need to add `AngularFireModule.initializeApp(environment.firebase)` and `AngularFireDatabaseModule` to the array of imported modules; see Listing 5-40. `AngularFireDatabaseModule` is the module for Realtime Database. More modules need to be imported when using other features provided by Firebase.

Listing 5-40. AppModule with AngularFire2 config

```
import { BrowserModule } from '@angular/platform-browser';
import { CUSTOM_ELEMENTS_SCHEMA, NgModule } from '@angular/core';

import { MyApp } from './app.component';

import { AngularFireModule } from '@angular/fire';
import { AngularFireDatabaseModule } from '@angular/fire/database';
import { environment } from '../environments/environment';

@NgModule({
  declarations: [
    MyApp,
  ],
  imports: [
    BrowserModule,
    AngularFireModule.initializeApp(environment.firebase),
    AngularFireDatabaseModule,
  ],
  bootstrap: [MyApp],
  schemas: [CUSTOM_ELEMENTS_SCHEMA],
  providers: []
})
export class AppModule {}
```

After importing the AngularFire2 modules, we can inject instances of AngularFireDatabase into components that need to interact with Firebase databases; see Listing 5-41. Methods related to Firebase databases are in the AngularFireDatabase object. To manipulate a list in the database, the method list() is used to get an AngularFireList object bound to the given path. The similar method object() should be used to get the AngularFireObject object to manipulate a single object bound to the given path. Both `AngularFireList` and `AngularFireObject` have the method `valueChanges()` to return an `Observable` object that contains the values. For `AngularFireList`, the value is a JSON array; for `AngularFireObject`, the value is a single JSON object.

Listing 5-41. Use AngularFire2 in components

```
import { Component } from '@angular/core';
import { Observable } from 'rxjs';
import { AngularFireDatabase } from '@angular/fire/database';
@Component({
  selector: 'app-component',
  templateUrl: 'app.component.html',
})
export class AppComponent {
  items: Observable<any[]>;
  constructor(private db: AngularFireDatabase) {
    this.items = this.db.list('/items').valueChanges();
  }
}
```

In the code below, a binding to path /products/00001 is created. The type of the variable product is Observable<any>.

```
let product = db.object('/products/00001').valueChanges();
```

To get the actual data, we use the Angular pipe `async` in the template to get the value.

```
<span>{{ (product | async)?.name }}</span>
```

`AngularFireObject` has methods `set()`, `update()`, and `remove()` to update the data, which have the same meaning as in the `Reference` object. The method `valueChanges()` of `AngularFireList` returns an

Observable<any[]>. We can use the directive *ngFor with the pipe async to display the results in the template. AngularFireList has the method push() to add new values to the list. AngularFireList also has the methods set(), update(), and remove() to update the list.

Hacker News API

Now we can implement the ItemService using Hacker News API. Hacker News doesn't have a single API to get the list of top stories. We need to use the path https://hacker-news.firebaseio.com/v0/topstories to get a list of ids of the top stories, then use those ids to get details of each story at path https://hacker-news.firebaseio.com/v0/item/${item_id}. For example, given the story id 9893412, the URL to get its details is https://hacker-news.firebaseio.com/v0/item/9893412. Listing 5-42 shows the sample JSON content of a story.

Listing 5-42. Sample JSON content of a story

```
{
  "by" : "Thorondor",
  "descendants" : 134,
  "id" : 9893412,
  "kids" : [ 9894173, 9893737, ..., 9893728, 9893803 ],
  "score" : 576,
  "text" : "",
  "time" : 1436987690,
  "title" : "The Icy Mountains of Pluto",
  "type" : "story",
  "url" : "https://www.nasa.gov/image-feature/the-icy-
  mountains-of-pluto"
}
```

Implement ItemService

Listing 5-43 shows the implementation of `ItemService` that uses Hacker News API. `this.db.list('/v0/topstories').valueChanges()` returns a `Observable<number[]>` instance. Each value in the `Observable<number[]>` is an array of all top stories ids. This array contains a large number of ids. Then we use the operator `map` to only select the subset of ids base on the value of parameters `offset` and `limit`. Each story id is mapped to an `Observable<Item>` using `this.db.object('/v0/item/' + id)`. `valueChanges()`. The result type of `ids.map(id => this.db.object` `('/v0/item/' + id).valueChanges())` is `Observable<Item>[]`. All these `Observable<Item>` objects are combined using the operator `combineLatest` to create an `Observable<Item[]>` object. The operator `mergeMap` is used to unwrap the inner `Observable<Observable<Item[]>>`, so the outer observable is still `Observable<Item[]>`. The final operator `map` creates the `Observable<Items>` from the `Observable<Item[]>` object.

Listing 5-43. ItemService

```
import { Injectable } from '@angular/core';
import { Observable, combineLatest } from 'rxjs';
import { map, mergeMap } from 'rxjs/operators';

import { Items } from '../../models/items';
import { AngularFireDatabase } from '@angular/fire/database';

@Injectable()
export class ItemService {
  constructor(private db: AngularFireDatabase) {}

  load(offset: number, limit: number): Observable<Items> {
    return this.db.list('/v0/topstories')
      .valueChanges()
        .pipe(
```

```
        map(ids => ids.slice(offset, offset + limit)),
        mergeMap((ids: any[]) => combineLatest(...(ids.map
        (id => this.db.object('/v0/item/' + id).valueChanges())))),
        map((items: any) => ({
            offset,
            limit,
            total: limit,
            results: items,
        }))
    );
  }

}
```

Alternative Model and Service Implementation

The current implementation of ItemService uses Observable operators to watch for changes in the Firebase database and emit values. However, some of those updates may not be necessary. When a story is updated, for example; when the score is updated; or new comments are added, a new Items object that contains all items is emitted from the Observable<Items> object and triggers an update of the whole UI. This is because the operator combineLatest emits a new combined value when any source Observable emits a value. This frequent UI update is not a good user experience. We can improve the performance by changing the data model.

Currently, we use Item[] in model Items to represent the items, which means all Item objects need to be resolved asynchronously before creating the Items object for the ItemsComponent to render. This makes users wait longer than expected. We can update the model Items to use Observable<Item>[] as the type of items; see Listing 5-44. Because each item is represented as its own Observable<Item> object, it can update itself separately. After updating the model, a new Items object is only emitted when the Observable of this.db.list('/v0/topstories').valueChanges() emits a new array of ids.

170

Listing 5-44. Updated model Items

```
import { Observable } from 'rxjs';
import { Item } from './Item';

export interface Items {
  offset: number;
  limit: number;
  total?: number;
  results: Observable<Item>[];
}
```

If we update the model, we can simplify the implementation of the ItemService; see Listing 5-45. After slicing the original array of item ids, the operator distinctUntilChanged is used to make sure that duplicate item ids won't be emitted to trigger unnecessary UI updates. Then the operator map is used to transform the array of item ids into an array of Observable<Item>.

Listing 5-45. Updated ItemService

```
import { Injectable } from '@angular/core';
import * as isEqual from 'lodash.isequal';
import { Observable } from 'rxjs';
import { map, distinctUntilChanged } from 'rxjs/operators';

import { Items } from '../../models/items';
import { AngularFireDatabase } from '@angular/fire/database';

@Injectable()
export class ItemService {
  constructor(private db: AngularFireDatabase) {}
```

```
load(offset: number, limit: number): Observable<Items> {
  return this.db.list('/v0/topstories')
    .valueChanges()
    .pipe(
      map(ids => ids.slice(offset, offset + limit)),
      distinctUntilChanged(isEqual),
      map((ids: any[]) => ids.map(id => this.db.object('/v0/
      item/' + id).valueChanges())),
      map((items: any) => ({
        offset,
        limit,
        total: limit,
        results: items,
      }))
    );
}

}
```

After updating the model, the implementation of ItemService can be simplified. However, it makes the implementation of ItemComponent complicated. As the type of the property item is changed from Item to Observable<Item>, ItemComponent needs to subscribe to the Observable and re-render itself when a new value is emitted. This can be done using the pipe async.

The changes to model and ItemComponent are an alternative way to implement the user story. However, this implementation violates one fundamental principle of designing components like ItemComponent. These components should only have pure rendering logic. The logic of handling Observables in ItemComponent makes it hard to test. This section only provides information about potential alternative implementations. The actual implementation of the example still uses the old model. The aforementioned performance issue will be solved by using state management frameworks in Chapter 6.

Further Improvements

When running this app, you may see the list of stories keeps updating itself. This causes some user experience issues. If the user is currently scrolling down the list of top stories and remote data is updated, then the list may be reordered to reflect the changes. This is annoying as the user's focus is lost. The list should only be refreshed explicitly by the user, for example, clicking a refresh button or pulling down the list to trigger the refresh. We also need to allow users to see more stories by implementing pagination.

To satisfy these requirements, we need to make changes to the ItemService. The current implementation of the method load() in ItemService returns a new Observable<Items> instance when invoked. This is unnecessary because we can reuse the same Observable<Items> instance for results of different queries. So we introduce a new method get() to retrieve the Observable<Items> instance. In Listing 5-46, the interface Query represents a query object for retrieving items. The properties offset and limit are used for pagination; refresh is used to indicate whether the list of story ids should be refreshed. The property queries is a RxJS Subject that acts as the communication channel between queries and result items. The method load() now emits a new Query object into the queries, which triggers the Observable<Items> to emit new Items object based on the value of the latest Query object.

Listing 5-46. Updated ItemService

```
import { Injectable } from '@angular/core';
import { combineLatest, merge, Observable, Subject } from 'rxjs';
import { filter, map, skip, switchAll, take, withLatestFrom }
from 'rxjs/operators';

import { Items } from '../../models/items';
import { Item } from '../../models/item';
```

```
import { AngularFireDatabase } from '@angular/fire/database';
import { Subject } from 'rxjs/Subject';
export interface Query {
  refresh?: boolean;
  offset: number;
  limit: number;
}

@Injectable()
export class ItemService {
  private queries: Subject<Query>;

  constructor(private db: AngularFireDatabase) {
    this.queries = new Subject<Query>();
  }

  load(query: Query) {
    this.queries.next(query);
  }

  get(): Observable<Items> {
    const rawItemIds = this.db.list<number>('/v0/topstories')
      .valueChanges();
    const itemIds = combineLatest(
      rawItemIds,
      this.queries
    ).pipe(
      filter(([ids, query]) => query.refresh),
      map(([ids, query]) => ids)
    );
    const selector = ({offset, limit}, ids) =>
      combineLatest(...(ids.slice(offset, offset + limit)
```

```
        .map(id => this.db.object<Item>('/v0/item/' + id).
        valueChanges()))
      ) as Observable<Items>;
    return merge(
      combineLatest(this.queries, itemIds).pipe(
        map(([query, ids]) => selector(query, ids).
        pipe(take(1)))
      ),
      this.queries.pipe(
        skip(1),
        withLatestFrom(itemIds, selector)
      )
    ).pipe(switchAll());
  }

}
```

The implementation of the method get() is a bit complicated, but it also shows the beauty of RxJS on how to simplify state management. rawItemIds is an Observable<number[]> object that represents the story ids. The method combineLatest() combines values from rawItemIds and queries to create an Observable of arrays with item ids and Query objects. The operator filter chained after combineLatest() is to make sure that values are only emitted when the property refresh is set to true in the Query object. This is to make sure the story ids are only updated when explicitly requested. Then we use the operator map to extract the ids from the array. Now the itemIds is an Observable of ids that emits the latest ids only when the property refresh is set to true.

The function selector is to combine a Query object and item ids to create Observable<Items> objects. This is done by using the similar approach as in the original implementation of ItemService

175

in Listing 5-25. By using the operator merge, we can get an
Observable<Observable<Items>> object. The merge is required to handle
the case that Observable itemIds may start emitting values after the
Observable queries has emitted the initial Query object. In this case, a single
withLatestFrom() doesn't work because the emitted value in Observable
itemIds can only be picked up when the Observable queries emits
another value. The operator combineLatest waits until both queries
and itemsId to emit at least one value, then combines the values using
the function selector. The operator take(1) means only the first value
is used. This handles the case when the initial query happens earlier than
the first emitted value of item ids. All the rest values come from the second
Observable. this.queries.pipe(skip(1), withLatestFrom(itemIds,
selector)) uses skip(1) to bypass the first value in queries, because the
first value is already captured in the first Observable object. For all of the
following values in queries, withLatestFrom() is used to combine Query
object and item ids using the function selector. The difference between
withLatestFrom and combineLatest is that withLatestFrom only emits a
new value when the source Observable emits a value. This can make sure
the result Observable only emits Items when a new query is received.

To load more stories, we can use the method load to send queries for
different pages. We just need to add a button to invoke the method. In
Listing 5-47, the new method doLoad() triggers the loading of items in the
next pages. The argument refresh is only true for the initial loading.

Listing 5-47. Load more stories

```
export class TopStoriesComponent implements OnInit, OnDestroy {
    items: Items;
    private subscription: Subscription;
    private offset = 0;
    private limit = 10;
```

```
constructor(private itemService: ItemService) { }

ngOnInit() {
  this.subscription = this.itemService.get().subscribe(items
  => this.items = items);
  this.doLoad(true);
}

ngOnDestroy() {
  if (this.subscription) {
    this.subscription.unsubscribe();
  }
}

doLoad(refresh: boolean) {
  this.itemService.load({
    offset: this.offset,
    limit: this.limit,
    refresh,
  });
  this.offset += this.limit;
}

}
```

Figure 5-4 shows the top stories page with a button to load more stories.

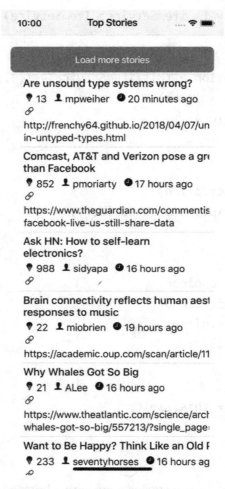

Figure 5-4. *Top stories page with load button*

Pagination and Refresh

Now we can add the UI for pagination and refresh. To build the UI, we need to add buttons to the page.

Button

Ionic provides the component ion-button for buttons. There are three types of buttons based on the value of the attribute fill. The default value is solid except inside of a toolbar, where the default value is clear.

- Solid style - Button with filled background, enabled by setting the attribute fill to solid.

- Outline style - Button with transparent background and borders, enabled by setting the attribute fill to outline.

- Clear style - Button with transparent background and no borders, enabled by setting the attribute fill to clear.

To change the color of a button, use the attribute color to specify the color. Possible colors are light, medium, dark, primary, secondary, tertiary, success, warning, and danger. By default, the color primary is used.

For buttons with borders, we can add the attribute round to make them use round borders. For layout purposes, we can use the attribute expand to make a button take 100% of its parent's width. The attribute expand can take two values: block for full-width buttons, fill for full-width buttons without left and right borders. To change the size of a button, add the attribute size to a button with values small, default, or large. The attribute type sets the type of buttons with possible values button, submit, and reset.

The component ion-button has four slots. The slot icon-only is used when the button only contains an icon. The default slot is for the content displayed in the button. The slots start and end are positioned before and after the default slot, respectively.

Pagination

Now we can add the pagination and refresh to the top stories page. We add the HTML markup to show the buttons in the top-stories.component.html file; see Listing 5-48.

Listing 5-48. Add pagination buttons

```
<ion-app>
  <ion-header>
    <ion-toolbar>
      <ion-title>Top Stories</ion-title>
    </ion-toolbar>
  </ion-header>
  <ion-content padding>
    <div>
      <ion-button color="light" [disabled]="!hasPrevious()"
      (click)="previous()">
        <ion-icon name="arrow-back" slot="start"></ion-icon>
        Prev
      </ion-button>
      <ion-button [disabled]="!canRefresh()" (click)="refresh()">
        <ion-icon name="refresh" slot="icon-only"></ion-icon>
      </ion-button>
      <ion-button color="light" [disabled]="!hasNext()"
      (click)="next()">
        <ion-icon name="arrow-forward" slot="end"></ion-icon>
        Next
      </ion-button>
    </div>
    <app-items [items]="items"></app-items>
  </ion-content>
</ion-app>
```

The file `top-stories.component.ts` is also updated to use the new methods of `ItemService` and includes action handlers for pagination and refresh buttons; see Listing 5-49. The value of the property `offset` is the index of the first loaded item in the whole list. We use `offset` to determine if the previous or next button should be enabled. Pagination is done by updating the value of `offset` and invoking the method `doLoad()`.

Listing 5-49. Updated TopStories

```
export class TopStoriesComponent implements OnInit, OnDestroy {
  items: Items;
  private subscription: Subscription;
  private offset = 0;
  private limit = 10;

  constructor(private itemService: ItemService) { }

  ngOnInit() {
    this.subscription = this.itemService.get().subscribe
    (items => this.items = items);
    this.doLoad(true);
  }

  ngOnDestroy() {
    if (this.subscription) {
      this.subscription.unsubscribe();
    }
  }

  hasPrevious(): boolean {
    return this.offset > 0;
  }

  previous(): void {
    if (!this.hasPrevious()) {
```

```
      return;
    }
    this.offset -= this.limit;
    this.doLoad(false);
  }

  hasNext(): boolean {
    return this.items != null && (this.offset + this.limit) <
    this.items.total;
  }

  next() {
    if (!this.hasNext()) {
      return;
    }
    this.offset += this.limit;
    this.doLoad(false);
  }

  canRefresh(): boolean {
    return this.items != null;
  }

  refresh() {
    if (!this.canRefresh()) {
      return;
    }
    this.offset = 0;
    this.doLoad(true);
  }

  private doLoad(refresh: boolean) {
    this.itemService.load({
      offset: this.offset,
      limit: this.limit,
```

```
        refresh,
    });
  }
}
```

Figure 5-5 shows the top stories page with buttons for pagination and refresh.

Figure 5-5. *Top stories page with pagination and refresh*

Advanced List

So far, we have implemented the top stories list with basic pagination and refresh support. But the current implementation is more like a traditional web app instead of a mobile app. Mobile apps have their own UI patterns. For pagination and refresh, it's better to use infinite scrolling and pull-to-refresh.

If infinite scrolling is enabled on the list, when the user scrolls down the list and nearly hits the bottom of the page, an action is triggered to load items of the next page. The user can continuously read through the list without clicking any buttons. Ionic provides built-in support for infinite scrolling with components `ion-infinite-scroll` and `ion-infinite-scroll-content`.

Pull-to-refresh is a very common feature in mobile apps. When displaying a list of items, a user can pull down the list and release, then the list will refresh to get the latest data. Ionic also provides built-in support for this feature with components `ion-refresher` and `ion-refresher-content`.

The component `ion-infinite-scroll` and `ion-refresher` follow the similar usage pattern. After adding these two components into the page, they invoke the provided callback functions when certain events happen, then wait for client code to notify them when the processing is finished. The components `ion-infinite-scroll-content` and `ion-refresher-content` are used to customize the feedback UI when the processing is still underway, respectively.

In Listing 5-50, `ion-refresher` is added to the top of the list of items, while `ion-infinite-scroll` is added to the bottom. For `ion-refresher`, we add a handler for the event `ionRefresh` and invoke the method `refresh()` with the current event object `$event` as the argument. The event object `$event` contains information about the event, especially the property `target` to get the component instance. The property `disabled` controls if the refresher is enabled or not. The default value of `disabled` is `true`, so a value `false` must be assigned to enable it. For the component `ion-infinite-scroll`, the event `ionInfinite` is handled using the method `load()`.

Listing 5-50. Add `ion-refresher` and `ion-infinite-scroll`

```
<ion-content padding>
  <ion-refresher slot="fixed" [disabled]="!canRefresh()"
  (ionRefresh)="refresh($event)">
    <ion-refresher-content></ion-refresher-content>
  </ion-refresher>
  <hnc-items [items]="items"></hnc-items>
  <ion-infinite-scroll [disabled]="!hasNext()" (ionInfinite)=
  "load($event)">
    <ion-infinite-scroll-content></ion-infinite-scroll-content>
  </ion-infinite-scroll>
</ion-content>
```

Listing 5-51 is the updated code of `top-stories.component.ts` to support infinite scrolling and pull-to-refresh. In the method `ngOnInit()`, when the `Observable<Items>` emits a new value, we need to check if it's a refresh request or normal loading request. For refresh requests, we simply assign the value `Items` to `this.items`. For a normal loading request, we need to merge the items from the value `Items` with those items already contained in `this.items`, so new items are displayed below the old items. The property `refresh` is newly added to model `Items` with the value coming from the property `refresh` in the `Query` object.

In the method `load()`, the instance of current `ion-infinite-scroll` component is saved to `this.infiniteScrollComponent`. When the loading of items is completed, the method `complete()` of `infiniteScrollComponent` must be called to stop the loading spinner. That's the reason to have method `notifyScrollComplete()` called in the subscription logic of `Observable<Items>`. The method `refresh()` also has the same logic to save the instance of the current `ion-refresher` component. We also call the method `notifyRefreshComplete()` to stop the spinner for refresh queries.

Listing 5-51. Updated TopStories

```
import { Component, OnDestroy, OnInit } from '@angular/core';
import { Subscription } from 'rxjs';
import * as concat from 'lodash.concat';
import { Items } from '../../models/items';
import { ItemService } from '../../services/item/item.service';

@Component({
  selector: 'app-top-stories',
  templateUrl: './top-stories.component.html',
  styleUrls: ['./top-stories.component.scss']
})
export class TopStoriesComponent implements OnInit, OnDestroy {

  items: Items;
  private subscription: Subscription;
  private offset = 0;
  private limit = 10;
  private infiniteScrollComponent: any;
  private refresherComponent: any;

  constructor(private itemService: ItemService) { }

  ngOnInit() {
    this.subscription = this.itemService.get().subscribe(items => {
      if (items.refresh) {
        this.items = items;
        this.notifyRefreshComplete();
      } else {
        this.items = {
          ...this.items,
          results: concat(this.items.results, items.results),
        };
```

```
      this.notifyScrollComplete();
    }
  });
  this.doLoad(true) ;
}

ngOnDestroy() {
  if (this.subscription) {
    this.subscription.unsubscribe();
  }
}

load(event) {
  this.infiniteScrollComponent = event.target;
  if (this.hasNext()) {
    this.next();
  }
}

hasNext(): boolean {
  return this.items != null && (this.offset + this.limit) <
  this.items.total;
}

next() {
  if (!this.hasNext()) {
    return;
  }
  this.offset += this.limit;
  this.doLoad(false);
}

canRefresh(): boolean {
  return this.items != null;
}
```

```
refresh(event) {
  this.refresherComponent = event.target;
  if (this.canRefresh()) {
    this.doRefresh();
  }
}

doRefresh() {
  this.offset = 0;
  this.doLoad(true);
}

private doLoad(refresh: boolean) {
  this.itemService.load({
    offset: this.offset,
    limit: this.limit,
    refresh,
  });
}

private notifyScrollComplete(): void {
  if (this.infiniteScrollComponent) {
    this.infiniteScrollComponent.complete();
  }
}

private notifyRefreshComplete(): void {
  if (this.refresherComponent) {
    this.refresherComponent.complete();
  }
}
}
```

As shown in Listing 5-51, we need to have a reference to the component `ion-infinite-scroll` to invoke its method `complete`. There is another way to provide the loading action without dealing with the component reference. This is done with the method `waitFor` of the component. This method accepts a `Promise` object as the action to call. When the action is finished, the method `complete` is invoked automatically. In Listing 5-52, the method `doLoad` is the action to call.

Listing 5-52. Use waitFor to complete action

```
<ion-infinite-scroll (ionInfinite)="load($event.detail.
waitFor(doLoad()))">
  <ion-infinite-scroll-content></ion-infinite-scroll-content>
</ion-infinite-scroll>
```

Customization

We can also customize the behaviors of the components `ion-infinite-scroll` and `ion-refresher`.

ion-infinite-scroll

By default, Ionic shows a platform-specific spinner when the infinite scrolling action is still in progress. We can customize the spinner and text displayed using the component `ion-infinite-scroll-content`. `ion-infinite-scroll-content` has two properties: `loadingSpinner` to set the spinner style, possible values are `lines`, `lines-small`, `bubbles`, `circles`, `crescent`, and `dots`; `loadingText` to set the text to display. Spinners are created using the component `ion-spinner`. In Listing 5-53, we configure the `ion-infinite-scroll` to use different a spinner and text.

Listing 5-53. ion-infinite-scroll customization

```
<ion-infinite-scroll-content
  loadingSpinner="circles"
  loadingText="Loading...">
</ion-infinite-scroll-content>
```

The `ion-infinite-scroll` also has the property `threshold` to control when to trigger the `ionInfinite` events. The value of the property `threshold` can be a percentage or absolute pixel value. When the current scrolling position reaches a specified threshold, the event `ionInfinite` is triggered. The default value of the threshold is 15%. It's recommended to provide a relatively large value for `threshold` so that the loading operation can have enough time to finish to provide the user with a smooth reading experience.

ion-refresher

We can use the property `pullMin` of `ion-refresher` to control the distance that the user needs to pull down before the event `ionRefresh` can be triggered. If the user keeps pulling down and reaches the distance specified in the property `pullMax`, the event `ionRefresh` is triggered automatically even though the user doesn't release yet. The default value of `pullMin` and `pullMax` is 60 and `pullMin + 60`, respectively.

Like `ion-infinite-scroll-content`, the component `ion-refresher-content` also provides several properties to control the style of `ion-refresher`. Listing 5-54 shows an example of customizing the `ion-refresher`.

- `pullingIcon` - Ionic icon to display when the user begins to pull down.

- `pullingText` - Text to display when the user begins to pull down.

- refreshingSpinner - A spinner to display when
  refreshing. Possible values are the same as the property
  loadingSpinner of ion-infinite-scroll-content.

- refreshingText - Text to display when refreshing.

Listing 5-54. ion-refresher customization

```
<ion-refresher-content
  pullingIcon="arrow-dropdown"
  pullingText="Pull to refresh"
  refreshingSpinner="bubbles"
  refreshingText="Loading...">
</ion-refresher-content>
```

Testing

As usual, we need to add test specs for infinite scrolling and pull-to-refresh features. In Listing 5-55, two new specs are added to existing top-stories. component.spec.ts. In the first test spec, the component is the instance of TopStoriesPage. We invoke component.next() directly to simulate the items loading triggered by scrolling. We check that there should be 20 items displayed. In the second test spec, we use component.next() to load more items, then use component.doRefresh() to simulate the refreshing event. We check that the number of items should be 10 after the refresh.

Listing 5-55. Test for scrolling and refresh

```
let fixture: ComponentFixture<TopStoriesComponent> = null;
let component: any = null;

describe('top stories page', () => {

  it('should show more items when scrolling down', async(() => {
    fixture.detectChanges();
```

```
  fixture.whenStable().then(() => {
    fixture.detectChanges();
    component.next();
    fixture.detectChanges();
    fixture.whenStable().then(() => {
      let debugElements = fixture.debugElement.queryAll(By.
      css('h2'));
      expect(debugElements.length).toBe(20);
      expect(debugElements[10].nativeElement.textContent).
      toContain('Item 11');
    });
  });
}));

it('should show first 10 items when refresh', async(() => {
  fixture.detectChanges();
  fixture.whenStable().then(() => {
    fixture.detectChanges();
    component.next();
    fixture.detectChanges();
    fixture.whenStable().then(() => {
      let debugElements = fixture.debugElement.queryAll
      (By.css('h2'));
      expect(debugElements.length).toBe(20);
      expect(debugElements[10].nativeElement.textContent).
      toContain('Item 11');
      component.doRefresh();
      fixture.detectChanges();
      fixture.whenStable().then(() => {
        let debugElements = fixture.debugElement.queryAll
        (By.css('h2'));
        expect(debugElements.length).toBe(10);
```

```
        expect(debugElements[0].nativeElement.textContent).
        toContain('Item 1');
      });
    });
  });
 }));
});
```

Loading and Error

All the code so far only deals with successful scenarios. An app should be robust and be ready to handle all kinds of expected or unexpected errors. For the app to be more responsive and user friendly, we also need to add loading indicators when the app is performing certain actions that require server interactions.

Loading Indicators

When the user triggers the refresh of the top stories page, a loading indicator should be displayed. Ionic provides a built-in loading component that renders spinner and text in a modal dialog.

In the ItemService, when a new Query object is received, we should immediately emit an Items object to represent the loading event and trigger the display of the loading indicator. When the items loading is finished, the subsequent Items object is emitted and triggers the dismissal of the loading indicator. We add a new Boolean property loading to the model Items.

In the updated implementation of ItemService of Listing 5-56, we use another Observable<Items> instance loadings to emit all loading events. The Items objects in the observable loadings all have property loading set to true. They are emitted when the subject queries receives

Query objects with the property refresh set to true. The returned
Observable<Items> object of the method ItemService.get() is the merge
of the observable loadings and existing observable items.

Listing 5-56. Updated ItemService

```
@Injectable()
export class ItemService {

  get(): Observable<Items> {
    // code omitted
    const loadings = this.queries
      .pipe(
        filter(v => v.refresh),
        map(query => ({
          loading: true,
          offset: query.offset,
          limit: query.limit,
          results: [],
        }))
      );
    // code omitted
    return merge(loadings, items);
  }
}
```

LoadingController and Loading

In the top-stories.component.ts file of Listing 5-57, we use
LoadingController from Ionic Angular to show the loading indicator.
LoadingController is an Angular service that can be injected into the
constructor of TopStoriesComponent. Under the hood, LoadingController
is a thin wrapper of Ionic component ion-loading-controller. All the

methods in `LoadingController` delegate to the same methods in
`ion-loading-controller`. This is a common pattern in Ionic Angular.
We'll see the usage of similar services later. `LoadingController` is
responsible for creating new instances of `ion-loading` elements of
type `HTMLIonLoadingElement`. In the method `showLoading()`, a new
instance of the `HTMLIonLoadingElement` is created using the method
`LoadingController.create()`, then it's displayed using the method
`HTMLIonLoadingElement.present()`. In the method `hideLoading()`,
`HTMLIonLoadingElement.dismiss()` is used to dismiss the loading
indicator. Once a `Loading` component is dismissed, it cannot be used
anymore, that is, you cannot make it display again. A new instance must be
created every time.

In the subscription logic of `Observable<Items>`, if the current `Items`
object represents a loading event, we just show the loading indicator and
return. Otherwise, the existing loading indicator is dismissed, and items are
rendered. The methods in `LoadingController` and `HTMLIonLoadingElement`
return `Promise` objects.

Listing 5-57. Updated TopStories

```
import { LoadingController } from '@ionic/angular';

export class TopStoriesComponent implements OnInit, OnDestroy {
  private loading: HTMLIonLoadingElement;

  constructor(private itemService: ItemService, private
  loadingCtrl: LoadingController) { }

  ngOnInit() {
    this.subscription = this.itemService.get().subscribe(items => {
      if (items.loading) {
        this.showLoading();
        return;
      }
```

```
      this.hideLoading();
      // code omitted
    });
    this.doLoad(true);
  }

  // code omitted

  private showLoading(): Promise<void> {
    return this.hideLoading().then(() => {
      return this.loadingCtrl.create({
        message: 'Loading...',
      }).then(loading => {
        this.loading = loading;
        return this.loading.present();
      });
    });
  }

  private hideLoading(): Promise<void> {
    if (this.loading) {
      return this.loading.dismiss().then(() => null);
    }
    return Promise.resolve(null);
  }
}
```

In the current implementation, when a refresh query is issued, the loading indicator is always displayed. In fact, except for the first-time loading, all the other refresh requests finish immediately. The first loading request needs to wait until the top stories ids to be retrieved. But all the subsequent refresh requests just use the latest retrieved top stories ids, even though these ids may not be up to date. We can only show the loading indicator for the first time.

We just need to change `loadings` to emit only one single value; see Listing 5-58.

Listing 5-58. Emit only one loading event

```
const loadings = of({
  loading: true,
  offset: 0,
  limit: 0,
  results: [],
});
```

Testing

To verify that the loading indicators are displayed and dismissed as expected, we need to add test specs for this scenario. The test spec is different than previous specs as it uses spies from Jasmine.

At first, we need to update the method `get()` of `ItemServiceMock` to emit the loading event. This can be done easily with RxJS operator `startWith`; see Listing 5-59.

Listing 5-59. ItemServiceMock to emit loading event

```
@Injectable()
export class ItemServiceMock extends ItemService {
  get(): Observable<Items> {
    return this.queries.pipe(
      map(query => ({
        refresh: query.refresh,
        offset: query.offset,
        limit: query.limit,
        total: query.offset + query.limit + 1,
        results: generateItems(query.offset, query.limit),
```

```
    } as Items)),
    startWith({
      loading: true,
      offset: 0,
      limit: 0,
      results: [],
    })
  );
  }
}
```

To verify that a Loading component is created by the LoadingController and displayed, we need to use test doubles for both components Loading and LoadingController. As in Listing 5-60, loadingStub is a Promise object that resolved to a simple object with two properties present and dismiss. The values of these two properties are Jasmine spy objects created using jasmine.createSpy(). loadingControllerStub is an object for LoadingController that has the method create() to always return the same loadingStub object.

Listing 5-60. Create Jasmine spy objects

```
const loadingStub = Promise.resolve({
  present: jasmine.createSpy('present').and.returnValue
  (Promise.resolve()),
  dismiss: jasmine.createSpy('dismiss').and.returnValue
  (Promise.resolve()),
});

const loadingControllerStub = {
  create: jasmine.createSpy('loading').and.returnValue
  (loadingStub),
};
```

These two test doubles are declared as value providers when invoking the method `TestUtils.beforeEachCompiler()`. The property `useValue` means all the instances of `LoadingController` use the same object `loadingControllerStub`. During the testing, the class `TopStoriesComponent` uses `loadingControllerStub.create()` to create a new `Loading` component and get the object `loadingStub` as the result. All the calls to methods `present` and `dismiss` are captured by the `loadingStub` object and this information is available for verifications.

```
{provide: LoadingController, useValue: loadingControllerStub}
```

In Listing 5-61, we first get the Angular injector using `fixture.debugElement.injector`, then get the `loadingControllerStub` object using the injector by looking up the token `LoadingController`. We can verify that the method `loadingControllerStub.create()` has been called once to create the loading component. For the created loading component, methods `present` and `dismiss` should also be called once.

Listing 5-61. Test spec for loading

```
it('should display loading indicators', async(() => {
  const loadingController = fixture.debugElement.injector.
  get(LoadingController);
  fixture.detectChanges();
  expect(loadingController.create).toHaveBeenCalledTimes(1);
  expect(loadingController.create().present).
  toHaveBeenCalledTimes(1);
  expect(loadingController.create().dismiss).
  toHaveBeenCalledTimes(1);
  fixture.whenStable().then(() => {
    fixture.detectChanges();
    let debugElements = fixture.debugElement.queryAll
    (By.css('h2'));
```

```
    expect(debugElements.length).toBe(10);
  });
}));
```

Error Handling

To handle errors in the Observables, we can add an error handler in the subscriber. For the Observable<Items> of top stories ids, when an error occurs, the observable object is terminated. We need to create a new Observable<Items> object to retry the loading. We can move the code in the method ngOnInit() into a separate method init() and invoke this method upon errors; see Listing 5-62.

Listing 5-62. Error handling

```
export class TopStoriesComponent implements OnInit {
  constructor(private toastCtrl: ToastController) {}

  ngOnInit(): void {
    this.init();
  }

  init(): void {
    this.itemService.get().subscribe(items => {
    }, error => {
      this.showError();
      this.init();
    });
    this.doLoad(true);
  }
}
```

Toast

Ionic has a built-in component to show toast notifications. We can use `ToastController` to create new toast notifications. The instance of `ToastController` is injected into `TopStoriesComponent` as the property `toastCtrl`. The usage of `ToastController` is similar to `LoadingController`. We need to use the method `create()` to create a new instance of `HTMLIonToastElement` first, then use its method `present()` and `dismiss()` to show and hide the toast, respectively. The method `showError()` in Listing 5-63 creates a toast and shows it.

Listing 5-63. Show error toast notifications

```
private showError() {
  this.toastCtrl.create({
    message: 'Failed to load items, retry now...',
    duration: 3000,
    showCloseButton: true,
  }).then(toast => toast.present());
}
```

When creating a new toast notification using the method `create()`, we can pass an object to configure the toast notification. The following configuration properties are supported.

- `message` - Message to display.

- `duration` - Number of milliseconds before the toast is dismissed.

- `position` - Position to show the toast; possible values are `top`, `middle`, and `bottom`.

- `showCloseButton` - Whether to show a button to close the toast.

- `closeButtonText` - Text of the close button.

- `dismissOnPageChange` - Whether to dismiss the toast when navigating to a different page.

- `cssClass` - Extra CSS classes to add to the toast.

The created toast object also has methods `present()` and `dismiss()` to show and dismiss it, respectively. When the toast is created with the property `duration` set, then it's not required to call the method `dismiss()` explicitly. The toast dismisses itself after the configured duration time elapsed.

Testing

To test the error handling, we need the `ItemService` to generate errors. We use a Jasmine spy to control the return values of the method `get()` of `ItemService` using Jasmine's method `returnValues()`; see Listing 5-64. The first return value is an `Observable` object that only throws an error. The second return value is a normal `Observable` object with items. When the test runs, the first request to load items will fail, so we verify that the error toast notification is displayed. Then we verify that the second loading is triggered automatically and renders the items correctly.

Listing 5-64. Test spec for error handling

```
it('should handle errors', async(() => {
  const itemService = fixture.debugElement.injector.
get(ItemService);
  spyOn(itemService, 'get')
    .and.returnValues(
      throwError(new Error('boom!')),
      of({
        refresh: true,
```

```
        offset: 0,
        limit: 10,
        results: generateItems(0, 10),
      })
    );
  const toastController = fixture.debugElement.injector.
  get(ToastController);
  fixture.detectChanges();
  fixture.whenStable().then(() => {
    fixture.detectChanges();
    expect(toastController.create).toHaveBeenCalledTimes(1);
    expect(toastController.create().present).
    toHaveBeenCalledTimes(1);
    let debugElements = fixture.debugElement.queryAll
    (By.css('h2'));
    expect(debugElements.length).toBe(10) ;
  });
}));
```

Summary

This longest chapter lays the groundwork for implementing various user stories in the app. It shows how to organize a user story implementation as components and services and use Jasmine and Karma to test them. Firebase basics and API are also covered. When using the Ionic 4 list component to display top stories, we also demonstrate the advanced features like infinite scrolling and pull-to-refresh. Loading indicators and error handling are also added. After this chapter, you should know how to implement a well-organized and tested user story. In the next chapter, we'll discuss a different way to manage states using NgRx.

CHAPTER 6

State Management with NgRx

When implementing the user story to list top stories in the last chapter, the actual data is stored in RxJS observables. Although the implementation in the ItemService is very concise, it's not very easy to understand, especially the usage of different RxJS operators. The combination of RxJS operators can be very complicated, which makes the debugging and testing very hard. It's better to use explicit state management in the app. We'll use NgRx for state management.

The Importance of State Management

You may wonder why the concept of state management is introduced in this chapter. Let's start with a brief history of web applications. In the early days of the Internet era, the web pages were very simple. They just displayed static content and offered very limited user interactions. With the prevalence of Web 2.0 (https://en.wikipedia.org/wiki/Web_2.0), web apps have evolved to take on more responsibility. Some business logic has shifted from the server-side to the browser-side. A typical example is the Gmail web app. These kinds of web apps may have complicated page flows and offer rich user interactions. Since these web apps usually have only one web page, they are called Single Page Applications, or SPAs. Ionic apps are a typical example of SPAs.

© Fu Cheng 2018

F. Cheng, *Build Mobile Apps with Ionic 4 and Firebase*,
https://doi.org/10.1007/978-1-4842-3775-5_6

After complicated logic is added to the front end, we need to manage the state inside of web apps. For typical SPAs, there are three kinds of states to manage.

- Global state: This state contains global data shared by all pages, including system configurations and metadata. This state is usually populated from the server-side when the app is loaded and rarely changes during the whole life cycle of the app.

- State to share between pages and components. This state is necessary for collaboration between different pages and components. States can be passed between different pages using the router, while components can share states using ancestor components or custom events.

- Internal state for components. Some components may have complicated user interactions or back-end communications, so they need to manage their own state. For example, a complex form needs to enable/disable form controls based on user input or results of validation logic.

With all these kinds of states, we can manage them in an ad hoc fashion. For example, we can simply use global objects for the global state and use component properties for the internal state. This approach works well for simple projects, but for most real-world projects, it makes it hard for developers to figure out the data flow between different components. A state may be modified in many different places and have weird bugs related to time. Error diagnosis and bug fixing could be nightmares for future maintainers when dealing with tightly coupled components.

The trend is to use a global store as the single source of an app state. This is the Flux architecture (https://facebook.github.io/flux/)

promoted by Facebook. There are several libraries that implement this architecture or its variants, including Redux (`https://redux.js.org/`) and NgRx used in this chapter.

Introduction to NgRx

NgRx (`https://github.com/ngrx/platform`) is a set of reactive libraries for Angular. It has several libraries for different purposes.

- @ngrx/store – State management with RxJS for Angular applications.

- @ngrx/effects – Side effects to model actions that may change an application state.

- @ngrx/entity – Entity state adapter to manage records.

- @ngrx/router-store – Integrate with Angular Router for @ngrx/store.

- @ngrx/store-devtools – Dev tools for store instrumentation and time traveling debugging.

- @ngrx/schematics – Scaffolding library for Angular applications.

We'll use @ngrx/store, @ngrx/effects, @ngrx/entity, and @ngrx/store-devtools in this chapter. @ngrx/store is inspired by the popular library Redux. Below are the basic concepts to understand @ngrx/store.

- Store – Store is a single immutable data structure that contains the whole state of the application.

- Actions – The state stored in the store can only be changed by actions. An action has a mandatory type and an optional payload.

- Reducers – Reducers are pure functions that change the state based on different actions. A reducer function takes the current state and the action as the input and returns the new state as the output. The output will become the new state and is the input of the next reducer function call.

- Selectors – Components use selectors to select the pieces of data from the whole state object for rendering.

When the application's state is managed by the NgRx store, components use data from the state object in the store to render their views. Components can dispatch actions to the store based on user interactions. These actions run through all reducers and compute the next state in the store. The state changes trigger the updates in the components to render with the updated data. Store is the single source of truth of the application's state. It's also very clear to track the changes to the state as all changes must be triggered by actions. With the powerful time-traveling debugging support of the @ngrx/store-devtools, it's possible to go back to the time after any previous action and view the state at that particular time. By checking the state, it's much easier to find the cause of bugs.

With an internal state separated out from components, components are much easier to implement and test. The view of a component is only determined by its input properties. We can easily prepare different inputs to verify its view in unit tests.

The global state in the store can be viewed as a big object graph. It's typical for large applications to divide the state object by features, where each feature manages one part of the whole state object. It's a common practice to organize features as Angular modules. Components can select any data from the state object for rendering. When the selected state changes, components are re-rendered automatically.

As we mentioned before, actions trigger state changes by running reducers. There are other actions that may have side effects. For example, loading data from the server may dispatch new actions to the store. If the data is loaded successfully, a new action with loaded data is dispatched. However, if an error occurred during the loading, a new action with the error is dispatched. NgRx uses effects to handle these kinds of actions. Effects subscribe to all actions dispatched to the store and perform certain tasks when some types of actions are observed. The execution results of these tasks are actions that are also dispatched to the store. In the data loading example, the effect may use Angular `HttpClient` to perform the request and return different types of actions based on the response.

Use NgRx

Now we are going to update the implementation of the top stories page with NgRx.

The first step is to define the state object for the application. This is usually an iterative progress. Properties in the state object may be added and removed during the whole development life cycle. It's typical to divide the state object by features. The state of each feature depends on the requirements of components. For the top stories page, we'll have two features. The first feature `items` is for all loaded items. This is because items are shared by different pages in the application. The second feature `topStories` is for the top stories page itself. The state of this feature contains ids of all top stories and pagination data.

When using NgRx, we have a convention for directory structure. TypeScript files of actions, reducers, and effects are put into the directories `actions`, `reducers`, and `effects`, respectively. Each module may have its own set of actions, reducers, and effects. The final application state is composed of states from all the modules.

Items Feature

Let's start from the state of the feature items.

Define State

As shown in Listing 6-1, the interface State is the state for the feature items. It's defined in the file src/app/reducers/items.ts. It extends from EntityState in @ngrx/entity. You can think of EntityState as a database table. Each entity in the EntityState is corresponding to a row in the table and each entity must have a unique id. EntityState already defines two properties: ids and entities. The property ids contains all ids of the entities. The property entities is a map from entity ids to the actual entity objects. Two more properties are added to State. The property loading represents the loading status of items, while the property error contains errors if loading fails.

Listing 6-1. State of the feature items

```
export interface State extends EntityState<Item> {
  loading: boolean;
  error: any;
}
```

Create Actions

The state for items is easy to define. Now we move to the actions. As shown in Listing 6-2, we define three actions in the enum ItemActionTypes in the file src/app/actions/items.ts. The action Load means starting the loading of items; LoadSuccess means items are loaded successfully; LoadFail means items have failed to load. Actions must have a property type to specify their types. Types are used to distinguish different actions.

Actions can also have optional payloads as the data sent with them. Actions in NgRx all implement the interface Action. The read-only property type is the type defined in the enum ItemActionTypes. If an action has a payload, the payload is defined as the only parameter in the constructor. The action Load has the payload of type number[ ] to specify the ids of items to load. LoadSuccess has the payload of type Item[ ] to specify the loaded items. The last action LoadFail has the payload type of any to specify the error that occurred during the loading. The type ItemActions is the union type of these three action types.

Listing 6-2. Actions of the feature items

```
import { Action } from '@ngrx/store';
import { Item } from '../models/item';

export enum ItemActionTypes {
  Load = '[Items] Load',
  LoadSuccess = '[Items] Load Success',
  LoadFail = '[Items] Load Fail',
}

export class Load implements Action {
  readonly type = ItemActionTypes.Load;

  constructor(public payload: number[]) {}
}

export class LoadSuccess implements Action {
  readonly type = ItemActionTypes.LoadSuccess;

  constructor(public payload: Item[]) {}
}
```

```
export class LoadFail implements Action {
  readonly type = ItemActionTypes.LoadFail;

  constructor(public payload: any) {}
}

export type ItemActions = Load | LoadSuccess | LoadFail;
```

Create Reducers

After defining the state and actions, we can create reducers. For each action defined, the reducer function needs to have logic to handle it. A reducer function takes two parameters: the first parameter is the current state; the second parameter is the action. The return result is the next state. If a reducer function doesn't know how to handle an action, it should return the current state. When the reducer function runs for the first time, there is no current state. We also need to define the initial state.

As shown in Listing 6-3, because the feature state in Listing 6-1 extends from EntityState in @ngrx/entity, we can use the function createEntityAdapter to create an EntityAdapter object that has several helper functions to manage the state. To create the adapter, we need to provide an object with two properties: the property selectId is the function to extract the id from the entity object; sortComparer is the comparer function to sort the entities if sorting is required. Here we use false to disable the sorting. The function getInitialState creates the initial state for the EntityState with initial values for additional properties loading and error.

For the function reducer, the parameter state has the default value initialState. The type of the parameter action is the union type ItemActions defined in Listing 6-2, so only actions related to items are accepted. The actual logic in the reducer function depends on the type of actions. For the action Load, we update the property loading to true.

For the action LoadSuccess, we use the function upsertMany provided by EntityAdapter to insert or update the loaded items. The property loading is also set to false to indicate that the loading is completed. The property error is set to null to clear any previous error. For action LoadingFail, we set the property error to be the error object in the action's payload. The property loading is also set to false. States should be immutable, so the reducer function should always return a new state object.

Listing 6-3. Reducer of items

```
export const adapter: EntityAdapter<Item> = createEntity
Adapter<Item>({
  selectId: (item: Item) => item.id,
  sortComparer: false,
});

export const initialState: State = adapter.getInitialState({
  loading: false,
  error: null,
});

export function reducer(
  state = initialState,
  action: ItemActions,
): State {
  switch (action.type) {
    case ItemActionTypes.Load: {
      return {
        ...state,
        loading: true,
      };
    }
```

```
case ItemActionTypes.LoadSuccess: {
  return adapter.upsertMany(action.payload, {
    ...state,
    loading: false,
    error: null,
  });
}
case ItemActionTypes.LoadFail: {
  return {
    ...state,
    loading: false,
    error: action.payload,
  };
}
default: {
  return state;
}
}
}
```

Add Effects

The actual logic of loading items is implemented in the effect.
In Listing 6-4, ItemEffects in the file src/app/effects/items.ts is a
service with two dependencies. The object of type Actions represents
the Observable of all actions dispatched to the store. Effects are
observables of actions decorated with @Effect, so the type of effects is
Observable<Action>. For the effect loadItems$, we use the function pipe
to provide a series of operators to operate on the observable actions. The
operator ofType is used to filter only actions of type Load; the operator map
extracts items ids from the action payload; the operator combineLatest

inside of the operator mergeMap combines Item objects for each item id and transforms them into action LoadSuccess or LoadFail. The logic to load items is similar to the ItemService.

Listing 6-4. Effects of items

```
@Injectable()
export class ItemsEffects {
  constructor(private actions$: Actions, private db:
  AngularFireDatabase) {}

  @Effect()
  loadItems$: Observable<Action> = this.actions$.pipe(
    ofType(ItemActionTypes.Load),
    map((action: Load) => action.payload),
    mergeMap((ids: number[]) =>
      combineLatest(
        ids.map(id => this.db.object('/v0/item/' + id).
        valueChanges().pipe(take(1)))
      ).pipe(
        map((items: Item[]) => new LoadSuccess(items)),
        catchError(error => of(new LoadFail(error))),
    ))
  );
}
```

With the effect loadItems$, the action Load triggers actions LoadSuccess or LoadFail.

Note   It's a convention for variables of Observables to use $ as the name suffix.

Top Stories Feature

To load items, we need to dispatch actions Load with ids of items. These ids are loaded from the Hacker News API of top stories ids. We also need to manage the state of top stories ids.

Define the State

The State in Listing 6-5 is similar to the state for items in Listing 6-1. The property ids represents ids of all top stories, while properties loading and error are for loading and error status, respectively.

Listing 6-5. State of top stories

```
export interface State {
  ids: number[];
  loading: boolean;
  error?: any;
}
```

Create Actions

We also have actions defined for top stories ids; see Listing 6-6. The actions LoadSuccess and LoadFail in the enum TopStoriesActionTypes have the same meanings as in the enum ItemActionTypes. Based on the requirements, there are two types of loading for top stories. The first type is to load all top stories ids from the API, which is specified as the action Refresh; the second type is to load more stories ids that have been retrieved, which is specified as the action LoadMore. The action Refresh is triggered when the user is pulling down the list to refresh, while the action LoadMore is triggered when the user is scrolling the list to view more stories. The payload of each action is very easy to understand.

Listing 6-6. Actions of top stories

```
import { Action } from '@ngrx/store';

export enum TopStoriesActionTypes {
  Refresh = '[Top Stories] Refresh',
  LoadMore = '[Top Stories] Load More',
  LoadSuccess = '[Top Stories] Load Success',
  LoadFail = '[Top Stories] Load Fail',
}

export class Refresh implements Action {
  readonly type = TopStoriesActionTypes.Refresh;
}

export class LoadMore implements Action {
  readonly type = TopStoriesActionTypes.LoadMore;
}

export class LoadSuccess implements Action {
  readonly type = TopStoriesActionTypes.LoadSuccess;

  constructor(public payload: number[]) {}
}

export class LoadFail implements Action {
  readonly type = TopStoriesActionTypes.LoadFail;

  constructor(public payload: any) {}
}

export type TopStoriesActions = Refresh | LoadMore |
LoadSuccess | LoadFail;
```

Create Reducers

The reducer function of top stories ids is shown in Listing 6-7. The implementation is straightforward. The action LoadMore is not included in this reducer function. This is because the action LoadMore doesn't have an effect on the state of top stories ids. It will be processed in the reducer function for pagination.

Listing 6-7. Reducer of top stories

```
const initialState: State = {
  ids: [],
  loading: false,
  error: null,
};

export function reducer(
  state = initialState,
  action: TopStoriesActions,
): State {
  switch (action.type) {
    case TopStoriesActionTypes.Refresh:
      return {
        ...state,
        loading: true,
      };
    case TopStoriesActionTypes.LoadSuccess:
      return {
        loading: false,
        ids: action.payload,
        error: null,
      };
```

```
  case TopStoriesActionTypes.LoadFail:
    return {
      ...state,
      loading: false,
      error: action.payload,
    };
  default: {
    return state;
  }
 }
}
```

Pagination

The top stories page needs to maintain the pagination state. The state and reducer function for pagination is shown in Listing 6-8. The state has three properties: offset, limit, and total. The page size is set to 10. For the action Refresh, the property offset is set to 0; for the action LoadMore, the property offset is increased by the page size; for the action LoadSuccess, the property total is updated with the number of stories.

Listing 6-8. State and reducer function for pagination

```
export const pageSize = 10;

const initialState: State = {
  offset: 0,
  limit: pageSize,
  total: 0,
};
```

```
export function reducer(
  state = initialState,
  action: TopStoriesActions,
): State {
  switch (action.type) {
    case TopStoriesActionTypes.Refresh:
      return {
        ...state,
        offset: 0,
        limit: pageSize,
      };
    case TopStoriesActionTypes.LoadMore:
      const offset = state.offset + state.limit;
      return {
        ...state,
        offset: offset < state.total ? offset : state.offset,
      };
    case TopStoriesActionTypes.LoadSuccess:
      return {
        ...state,
        total: action.payload.length,
      };
    default: {
      return state;
    }
  }
}
```

Add Effects

The last piece is the effect to load ids of top stories. Listing 6-9 shows the effect `TopStoriesEffects`. Comparing to `ItemsEffects` in Listing 6-4, the constructor of `TopStoriesEffects` has an extra parameter of type `Store<fromTopStories.State>`. This is because `TopStoriesEffects` needs to access the state in the store to perform its tasks. The type `fromTopStories.State` describes the state for the module top stories. `TopStoriesEffects` has two effects. The first effect `loadTopStories$` is responsible for loading ids of top stories from Hacker News API. The loading is triggered by the action `TopStoriesActionTypes.Refresh`. When the loading succeeds, two actions are dispatched to the store. The first action is the `topStoriesActions.LoadSuccess` shown in Listing 6-6, and the second action is the `itemActions.Load` shown in Listing 6-2 to trigger the loading of items in the first page. The second effect `loadMore$` is responsible for triggering the loading of items of the action `TopStoriesActionTypes.LoadMore`. This effect uses the operator `withLatestFrom` to get the current state from the store, then extracts ids of top stories and pagination status from the state, and finally dispatches the action `itemActions.Load`. The `Store` in NgRx is also an `Observable` object. This is the first time we see the structure of the global state object. We'll discuss the structure soon. Effects are only executed after actions run through all reducers. When the effect `loadMore$` is executed, the reducer function in Listing 6-8 already updates the pagination state to the next page.

Listing 6-9. Effects of top stories

```
import { Injectable } from '@angular/core';
import { Observable, of } from 'rxjs';
import { Action, Store } from '@ngrx/store';
import { Actions, Effect, ofType } from '@ngrx/effects';
import { TopStoriesActionTypes } from '../actions/top-stories';
import { catchError, map, mergeMap, switchMap, take,
withLatestFrom } from 'rxjs/operators';
```

```
import { AngularFireDatabase } from '@angular/fire/database';
import * as fromTopStories from '../reducers';
import { pageSize } from '../reducers/pagination';
import * as itemActions from '../actions/items';
import * as topStoriesActions from '../actions/top-stories';

@Injectable()
export class TopStoriesEffects {
  constructor(private actions$: Actions,
              private store: Store<fromTopStories.State>,
              private db: AngularFireDatabase) {}

  @Effect()
  loadTopStories$: Observable<Action> = this.actions$.pipe(
    ofType(TopStoriesActionTypes.Refresh),
    switchMap(() =>
      this.db.list('/v0/topstories').valueChanges()
        .pipe(
          take(1),
          mergeMap((ids: number[]) => of<Action>(
            new topStoriesActions.LoadSuccess(ids),
            new itemActions.Load(ids.slice(0, pageSize)))),
          catchError(error => of(new topStoriesActions.
          LoadFail(error))),
        )
    )
  );

  @Effect()
  loadMore$: Observable<Action> = this.actions$.pipe(
    ofType(TopStoriesActionTypes.LoadMore),
    withLatestFrom(this.store),
```

```
    map(([action, state]) => {
      const {
        pagination: {
          offset,
          limit,
        },
        stories: {
          ids,
        }
      } = state.topStories;
      return new itemActions.Load(ids.slice(offset,
      offset + limit));
    })
  );
}
```

The reducer functions in Listings 6-3, 6-7, and 6-8 only deal with a subset of the global state. The global state is a hierarchical composition of states at different levels. It's common to have the file index.ts in directory reducers to compose the state for a module. Listing 6-10 shows the state and reducers of the top stories module. The interface TopStoriesState is the composite of state with states from ids of top stories and pagination. The interface State includes states from the feature items and TopStoriesState. For TopStoriesState, fromTopStories.State, and fromPagination.State both have their reducer functions. ActionReducerMap is the map from states to reducer functions, which is commonly used to combine states and corresponding reducers.

Listing 6-10. State and reducers of top stories

```
import * as fromRoot from '../../reducers';
import * as fromTopStories from './top-stories';
import * as fromPagination from './pagination';
import * as fromItems from './items';

export interface TopStoriesState {
  stories: fromTopStories.State;
  pagination: fromPagination.State;
}

export interface State extends fromRoot.State {
  items: fromItems.State;
  topStories: TopStoriesState;
}

export const reducers: ActionReducerMap<TopStoriesState> = {
  stories: fromTopStories.reducer,
  pagination: fromPagination.reducer,
};
```

Selectors

After finishing the states, actions, and reducers, we need to update the components to interact with the store. Components get data from the store for the view and may dispatch actions to the store. A component is usually interested in a subset of the global state. We use the selectors provided by NgRx to select states from the store. Selectors are functions that define how to extract data from the state. Selectors can be chained together to reuse the selection logic. One important characteristic of selector functions is that they memorize results to avoid unnecessary computations. Selector functions are typically defined in the same file as the reducer functions.

Listing 6-11 shows the selector functions for the feature items. The function getItemsState is the selector to select the root state for the feature. It's created using the function createFeatureSelector from NgRx. The state of the feature items uses the EntityState from @ngrx/entity. We can use the adapter created in Listing 6-3 to create selectors. The selector getItemEntities selects the entities map from the state. The selectors getLoading and getError select the property loading and error from the state, respectively.

Listing 6-11. Selectors of the feature items

```
export const getItemsState = createFeatureSelector<State>
('items');

export const {
  selectEntities: getItemEntities,
} = adapter.getSelectors(getItemsState);

export const getLoading = (state: State) => state.loading;

export const getError = (state: State) => state.error;
```

We also create selectors for ids of top stories; see Listing 6-12. These three selectors, getIds, getLoading, and getError are very easy to understand.

Listing 6-12. Selectors of top stories

```
export const getIds = (state: State) => state.ids;

export const getLoading = (state: State) => state.loading;

export const getError = (state: State) => state.error;
```

With these simple selectors in Listings 6-11 and 6-12, we can define complicated selectors to use in components; see Listing 6-13.

- getTopStoriesState selects the root state of the feature topStories.

- getPaginationState selects the state of pagination.

- getStoriesState selects the state of ids of top stories.

- getStoryIds selects ids of top stories.

- getDisplayItems selects the items to display by combining the results from getStoryIds, getItemEntities, and getPaginationState.

- isItemsLoading selects the loading state of items.

- getItemsError selects the error of loading items.

- isTopStoriesLoadings selects the loading state of ids of top stories.

- getTopStoriesError selects the error of loading ids.

- getError selects the first error that occurred when loading items or ids.

The function createSelector chains selectors together to get the final result. For a selector, if the upstream selectors changed, it will be reevaluated.

Listing 6-13. Selectors for components

```
export const getTopStoriesState =
createFeatureSelector<TopStoriesState>('topStories');

export const getPaginationState = createSelector(
  getTopStoriesState,
  state => state.pagination,
);
```

```
export const getStoriesState = createSelector(
  getTopStoriesState,
  state => state.stories,
);

export const getStoryIds = createSelector(
  getStoriesState,
  fromTopStories.getIds,
);

export const getDisplayItems = createSelector(
  getStoryIds,
  getItemEntities,
  getPaginationState,
  (ids, entities, pagination) => {
    return {
      results: ids.slice(0, pagination.offset + pagination.
      limit).map(id => entities[id]),
    };
  }
);

export const isItemsLoading = createSelector(
  getItemsState,
  fromItems.getLoading,
);

export const getItemsError = createSelector(
  getItemsState,
  fromItems.getError,
);
```

```
export const isTopStoriesLoading = createSelector(
  getStoriesState,
  fromTopStories.getLoading,
);

export const getTopStoriesError = createSelector(
  getStoriesState,
  fromTopStories.getError,
);

export const getError = createSelector(
  getTopStoriesError,
  getItemsError,
  (e1, e2) => e1 || e2,
);
```

Update Components

Now we can update the TopStoriesComponent to use NgRx; see Listing 6-14.
The implementation is completely different from the previous one using
ItemService. TopStoriesComponent is injected with the Store from NgRx.
TopStoriesComponent defines different Observables using different selectors.
The observable items$ created by store.pipe(select(fromTopStories.
getDisplayItems)) uses the selector getDisplayItems to select the items to
display; itemsLoading$ represents the loading state of items; idsLoading$
represents the loading state of ids of top stories; errors$ represents errors.
For the values in itemsLoading$, the function notifyScrollComplete
is invoked to notify ion-infinite-scroll to complete. For the values in
idsLoading$, functions showLoading or hideLoading are invoked to show or
hide the loading spinner. For the values in errors$, the function showError
is invoked to show the toast displaying error messages. The function doLoad
dispatches the action topStoriesActions.Refresh or topStoriesActions.
LoadMore depends on the type of loading.

TopStoriesComponent also uses the change detection strategy
ChangeDetectionStrategy.OnPush to trigger the UI changes more
efficiently.

Listing 6-14. Updated TopStoriesComponent using NgRx

```
import { ChangeDetectionStrategy, Component, OnDestroy, OnInit }
from '@angular/core';
import { from, Observable, Subscription } from 'rxjs';
import { select, Store } from '@ngrx/store';
import { Items } from '../models/items';
import { LoadingController, ToastController } from
'@ionic/angular';

import * as fromTopStories from './reducers';
import * as topStoriesActions from './actions/top-stories';
import { filter, concatMap } from 'rxjs/operators';

@Component({
  selector: 'app-top-stories',
  changeDetection: ChangeDetectionStrategy.OnPush,
  templateUrl: './top-stories.component.html',
  styleUrls: ['./top-stories.component.scss']
})
export class TopStoriesComponent implements OnInit, OnDestroy {

  items$: Observable<Items>;
  private itemsLoading$: Observable<boolean>;
  private idsLoading$: Observable<boolean>;
  private errors$: Observable<any>;
  private infiniteScrollComponent: any;
  private refresherComponent: any;
  private loading: HTMLIonLoadingElement;
  private subscriptions: Subscription[];
```

```
constructor(private store: Store<fromTopStories.State>,
            private loadingCtrl: LoadingController,
            private toastCtrl: ToastController) {
  this.items$ = store.pipe(select(fromTopStories.
  getDisplayItems));
  this.itemsLoading$ = store.pipe(select(fromTopStories.
  isItemsLoading));
  this.idsLoading$ = store.pipe(select(fromTopStories.
  isTopStoriesLoading));
  this.errors$ = store.pipe(select(fromTopStories.getError),
  filter(error => error != null));
  this.subscriptions = [];
}

ngOnInit() {
  this.subscriptions.push(this.itemsLoading$.
  subscribe(loading => {
    if (!loading) {
      this.notifyScrollComplete();
    }
  }));
  this.subscriptions.push(this.idsLoading$.
  pipe(concatMap(loading => {
    return loading ? from(this.showLoading()) : from(this.
    hideLoading());
  })).subscribe());
  this.subscriptions.push(this.errors$.pipe(concatMap(error
  => from(this.showError(error))))).subscribe());
  this.doLoad(true);
}
```

```
ngOnDestroy(): void {
  this.subscriptions.forEach(subscription => subscription.
  unsubscribe());
}

load(event) {
  this.infiniteScrollComponent = event.target;
  this.doLoad(false);
}

refresh(event) {
  this.refresherComponent = event.target;
  this.doLoad(true);
}

doLoad(refresh: boolean) {
  if (refresh) {
    this.store.dispatch(new topStoriesActions.Refresh());
  } else {
    this.store.dispatch(new topStoriesActions.LoadMore());
  }
}

private notifyScrollComplete(): void {
  if (this.infiniteScrollComponent) {
    this.infiniteScrollComponent.complete();
  }
}

private notifyRefreshComplete(): void {
  if (this.refresherComponent) {
    this.refresherComponent.complete();
  }
}
```

```
private showLoading(): Promise<void> {
  return this.hideLoading().then(() => {
    return this.loadingCtrl.create({
      content: 'Loading...',
    }).then(loading => {
      this.loading = loading;
      return this.loading.present();
    });
  });
}

private hideLoading(): Promise<void> {
  if (this.loading) {
    this.notifyRefreshComplete();
    return this.loading.dismiss().then(() => null);
  }
  return Promise.resolve();
}

private showError(error: any): Promise<void> {
  return this.toastCtrl.create({
    message: `An error occurred: ${error}`,
    duration: 3000,
    showCloseButton: true,
  }).then(toast => toast.present());
}
}
```

After using Observable<Items> as the type of items, we need to update
the template as below.

```
<app-items [items]="items$ | async"></app-items>
```

To enable NgRx for the top stories module, we need to import some modules in TopStoriesModule. In Listing 6-15 of the file top-stories.module.ts, StoreModule.forFeature('topStories', topStoriesReducers) creates the module for the feature topStories with the reducers map defined in Listing 6-10. EffectsModule. forFeature([TopStoriesEffects, ItemsEffects]) creates the module for effects.

Listing 6-15. Import NgRx modules

```
import { CUSTOM_ELEMENTS_SCHEMA, NgModule } from
'@angular/core';
import { CommonModule } from '@angular/common';

import { TopStoriesRoutingModule } from './top-stories-routing.
module';
import { TopStoriesComponent } from './top-stories.component';

import { reducers as topStoriesReducers } from './reducers';
import { StoreModule } from '@ngrx/store';
import { TopStoriesEffects } from './effects/top-stories';
import { EffectsModule } from '@ngrx/effects';

@NgModule({
  imports: [
    CommonModule,
    TopStoriesRoutingModule,
    StoreModule.forFeature('topStories', topStoriesReducers),
    EffectsModule.forFeature([TopStoriesEffects]),
  ],
  declarations: [TopStoriesComponent],
  schemas: [CUSTOM_ELEMENTS_SCHEMA],
})
export class TopStoriesModule { }
```

NgRx modules for the feature items will be added to the root module. There are other NgRx modules that need to be imported in the root module. Listing 6-16 shows the code added to the file `app.module.ts`. Here we use `StoreModule.forRoot(reducers)` and `EffectsModule.forRoot([ItemsEffects])` for the root module. `StoreDevtoolsModule.instrument` is used to import the module of NgRx devtools from @ngrx/store-devtools.

Listing 6-16. Import NgRx modules in the root module

```
import { reducers } from './reducers';
import { StoreModule } from '@ngrx/store';
import { EffectsModule } from '@ngrx/effects';
import { StoreDevtoolsModule } from '@ngrx/store-devtools';
import { ItemsEffects } from './effects/items';

@NgModule({
  declarations: [
    MyApp,
  ],
  imports: [
    StoreModule.forRoot(reducers),
    StoreDevtoolsModule.instrument({
      name: 'NgRx HNC DevTools',
      logOnly: environment.production,
    }),
    EffectsModule.forRoot([ItemsEffects]),
  ],
})
export class AppModule {}
```

Unit Testing

We need to add unit tests for reducer functions and effects. Unit tests for reducer functions are easy to write, as reducer functions are pure functions. We just need to create the current state object, then call the reducer function with actions, and finally verify the result state. Listing 6-17 is the example of testing a reducer function for the feature items. In this test spec, we create three mock items: item1, item2, and item3. The initial state contains item1 and item2. In the first spec, after a Load action, the property loading should be true. In the second spec, the action is LoadSuccess with item3 as the payload, and item3 should be added to the entities. In the third spec, the action is LoadFail with an error object, and the property error should match the action's payload. The last spec verifies the selector to get the loading state.

Listing 6-17. Unit tests of the reducer function

```
import * as fromItems from './items';
import { reducer } from './items';
import { Load, LoadFail, LoadSuccess } from '../actions/items';
import { createMockItem } from '../models/item';

describe('ItemsReducer', () => {
  const item1 = createMockItem(1);
  const item2 = createMockItem(2);
  const item3 = createMockItem(3);

  const initialState: fromItems.State = {
    ids: [item1.id, item2.id],
    entities: {
      [item1.id]: item1,
      [item2.id]: item2,
    },
    loading: false,
    error: null,
  };
```

235

```
it('should set the loading state', () => {
  const action = new Load([item3.id]);
  const result = reducer(initialState, action);
  expect(result.loading).toBe(true);
});

it('should set the loaded items', () => {
  const action = new LoadSuccess([item3]);
  const result = reducer(initialState, action);
  expect(result.loading).toBe(false);
  expect(result.ids).toContain(item3.id);
  expect(result.entities[item3.id]).toEqual(item3);
});

it('should set the fail state', () => {
  const error = new Error('load fail');
  const action = new LoadFail(error);
  const result = reducer(initialState, action);
  expect(result.loading).toBe(false);
  expect(result.error).toEqual(error);
});

it('should select the the loading state', () => {
  const result = fromItems.getLoading(initialState);
  expect(result).toBe(false);
});
});
```

Testing effects is harder than reducer functions. Listing 6-18 is the unit test for ItemsEffects. To test this effect, we need to provide mocks for services Actions and AngularFireDatabase. TestActions is the mock for Actions that allows setting the dispatched actions, while dbMock is a mock object for AngularFireDatabase with the property object as a

Jasmine spy. This is because `ItemsEffects` uses the method `object` of `AngularFireDatabase`, so we need to provide mock implementation for this method.

In the first test spec for the success case, the dispatched action is a `Load` action with two ids. The expected action is a `LoadSuccess` with two loaded items. The Jasmine spy for the method `object` is updated to return different items based on the ids to load. The Jasmine function `callFake` provides the implementation of the spied method. Here we use the library jasmine-marbles (`https://www.npmjs.com/package/jasmine-marbles`) to easily create observables with specified values. For example, `hot('-a', { a: action })` creates a hot observable that emits the action, `cold('-b', { b: item })` creates a cold observable that emits the item. The second test spec is similar to the first one, expecting that the Jasmine spy returns an `Observable` with error when loading items, so the expected action is a `LoadFail` with the provided error as the payload.

Listing 6-18. Unit test of effects

```
import { Actions } from '@ngrx/effects';
import { AngularFireDatabase } from '@angular/fire/database';
import { EMPTY, Observable } from 'rxjs';
import { cold, hot } from 'jasmine-marbles';
import { TestBed } from '@angular/core/testing';
import { ItemsEffects } from './items';
import { Load, LoadFail, LoadSuccess } from '../actions/items';
import { createMockItem } from '../models/item';

export class TestActions extends Actions {
  constructor() {
    super(EMPTY);
  }
}
```

```
  set stream(source: Observable<any>) {
    this.source = source;
  }
}

export function getActions() {
  return new TestActions();
}

describe('ItemsEffects', () => {
  let db: any;
  let effects: ItemsEffects;
  let actions$: TestActions;

  const item1 = createMockItem(1);
  const item2 = createMockItem(2);

  beforeEach(() => {
    const dbMock = {
      object: jasmine.createSpy('object'),
    };
    TestBed.configureTestingModule({
      providers: [
        ItemsEffects,
        { provide: Actions, useFactory: getActions },
        { provide: AngularFireDatabase, useValue: dbMock },
      ],
    });

    db = TestBed.get(AngularFireDatabase);
    effects = TestBed.get(ItemsEffects);
    actions$ = TestBed.get(Actions);
  });
```

```
describe('loadItem$', () => {
  it('should return a LoadSuccess with items, on success', ()
  => {
    const action = new Load([1, 2]);
    const completion = new LoadSuccess([item1, item2]);

    actions$.stream = hot('-a', { a: action });
    db.object = jasmine.createSpy('object').and.callFake
    (path => {
      const id = parseInt(/\/v0\/item\/(\d+)/.exec(path)[1], 10);
      const item = id === 1 ? item1 : item2;
      return {
        valueChanges: () => cold('-b', { b: item }),
      };
    });
    const expected = cold('--c', { c: completion });
    expect(effects.loadItems$).toBeObservable(expected);
  });

  it('should return a LoadFail with error, on error', () => {
    const action = new Load([1, 2]);
    const error = 'Error';
    const completion = new LoadFail(error);

    actions$.stream = hot('-a', { a: action });
    db.object = jasmine.createSpy('object').and.callFake
    (path => {
      return {
        valueChanges: () => cold('-#', {}, error),
      };
    });
    const expected = cold('--c', { c: completion });
    expect(effects.loadItems$).toBeObservable(expected);
```

```
    });
  });
});
```

Use @ngrx/store-devtools

We already configured @ngrx/store-devtools in the app module. To view the state and actions in the store, we need to install the Redux Devtools Extension (`https://github.com/zalmoxisus/redux-devtools-extension/`) on Chrome or Firefox. This extension provides powerful features for debugging. Figure 6-1 shows the screenshot of the extension.

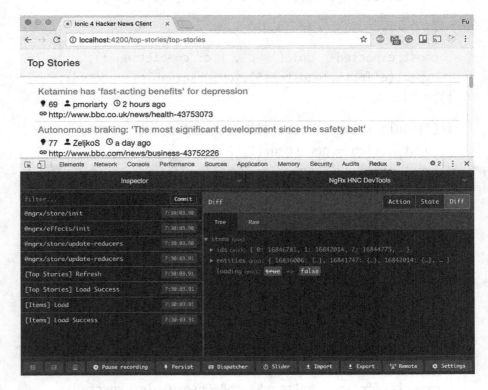

Figure 6-1. *Use Redux Devtools Extension*

Summary

State management is an important part of any nontrivial applications. With the prevalence of Redux, developers are already familiar with concepts related to state management. NgRx is the best choice for state management of Angular applications. This chapter covers concepts like state, actions, reducers, effects, and selectors in NgRx and updates the top stories page to use NgRx to manage the state. In the next chapter, we'll implement the user story to view web pages of top stories.

CHAPTER 7

View Story

After we finish the `TopStoriesComponent` to list top stories, we are going to allow users to view the actual web pages of stories. In this chapter, we'll use Cordova InAppBrowser plugin to view web pages.

A Simple Solution

The basic solution is quite simple. We just need to use the standard HTML `<a>` elements in the item's template. As in Listing 7-1, we added the `<a>` element with the attribute `href` set to `item.url`. The old `div` element that contains the URL is removed.

Listing 7-1. Use <a> for a story's URL

```
<h2 class="title">
  <a [href]="item.url">{{ item.title }}</a>
</h2>
```

When we run the code inside of an emulator or a device, clicking the title opens the platform's default browser and shows the web page. On Android, the user can use the back button to return to the app; while on the iOS platform, the user can use the back button on the top left of the status bar to return to the app.

© Fu Cheng 2018
F. Cheng, *Build Mobile Apps with Ionic 4 and Firebase*,
https://doi.org/10.1007/978-1-4842-3775-5_7

In-App Browser

Using `<a>` elements is a valid solution for opening links in the app, but it has one major disadvantage in that the user needs to leave the app to read the stories in the browser and return to the app after that. This creates a bad user experience for interrupting the user's normal flow. Another disadvantage is that we cannot customize the behaviors of the opened browser windows. A better solution is to use the Cordova InAppBrowser plugin (`https://cordova.apache.org/docs/en/latest/reference/cordova-plugin-inappbrowser/`).

To use Cordova plugins in Ionic apps, Ionic creates a library Ionic Native (`https://ionicframework.com/docs/v2/native/`) as a wrapper for Cordova plugins. The package `@ionic-native/core` is already installed when the app is created from the starter template.

Installation

Cordova plugins can be installed using either the command `ionic cordova plugin add` or `cordova plugin add`. The plugins files are installed into the directory `plugins`. Version 3.0.0 of `cordova-plugin-inappbrowser` is used in the project.

```
$ ionic cordova plugin add cordova-plugin-inappbrowser --save
```

After the plugin `inappbrowser` is installed in the app, we also need to install the package `@ionic-native/in-app-browser`.

```
$ npm i @ionic-native/in-app-browser
```

To use this plugin, we need to import the module `InAppBrowser` and make it as a provider in the `AppModule`. Then we can inject `InAppBrowser` into components.

Open a URL

To open the story's web page, we can create a new instance of `InAppBrowserObject` or use the static method `InAppBrowser.create(url, target, options)`. The constructor of `InAppBrowserObject` has the same parameters as the method `create()`. `url` is the URL to open. `target` is the target to load the URL with following possible values:

- `_self` - If the URL is in the white list, it opens in the `WebView`, otherwise it opens in the `InAppBrowser`.

- `_blank` - Opens in the `InAppBrowser`.

- `_system` - Opens in the system web browser.

The parameter `options` is a string to configure the on/off status for different features in `InAppBrowser`. Different platforms have their own supported options. `location` is the only option that is supported on all platforms. The option `location` can be set to `yes` or `no` to show or hide the browser's location bar. The default value of `options` is `location=yes`. Options for different features are separated by commas, for example, `location=no,hidden=yes`.

Some common options are:

- `hidden` - When set to `yes`, the browser is created and loads the page, but it's hidden. We need to use the method `InAppBrowser.show()` to show it.

- `clearcache` - When set to `yes`, the browser's cookie cache is cleared before opening the page.

- `clearsessioncache` - When set to `yes`, the browser's session cookie cache is cleared before opening the page.

In Listing 7-2, we add a new method openPage() in the ItemComponent to open a given URL. The URL is opened using target _blank. Creating a new InAppBrowser opens the URL and shows it by default.

Listing 7-2. Open page

```
import { Component, Input } from '@angular/core';
import { Item } from '../../model/Item';
import { InAppBrowserObject } from ' @ionic-native/in-app-
browser/ngx';

@Component({
  selector: 'app-item',
  templateUrl: 'item.component.html',
})
export class ItemComponent {
  @Input() item: Item;
  openPage(url: string): void {
    new InAppBrowserObject(url, '_blank');
  }
}
```

It's not a good practice to put the actual page opening logic in the ItemComponent. As we mentioned before, we should encapsulate this kind of logic in services. We create a new OpenPageService to encapsulate the logic of opening pages. The new service is created using Angular CLI.

```
$ ng g service services/open-page -m services --flat false
```

Listing 7-3 shows the implementation of OpenPageService. OpenPageService uses the function create of the inject instance of InAppBrowser to create a new browser object of type InAppBrowserObject. We only allow at most one InAppBrowserObject to be opened at the same time, so the existing browser is closed before opening a new page.

246

Listing 7-3. OpenPageService

```
import { Injectable } from '@angular/core';
import { InAppBrowser, InAppBrowserObject } from
'@ionic-native/in-app-browser/ngx';

@Injectable()
export class OpenPageService {
  private inAppBrowserObject: InAppBrowserObject;

  constructor(private inAppBrowser: InAppBrowser) {}

  open(url: string) {
    if (this.inAppBrowserObject) {
      this.inAppBrowserObject.close();
      this.inAppBrowserObject = null;
    }
    this.inAppBrowserObject = this.inAppBrowser.create(url,
    '_blank');
  }
}
```

When the user clicks an item in the list, the function open of
OpenPageService needs to be invoked with the item's URL. This is done
by using Angular's EventEmitter. In Listing 7-4, the property toOpen is an
EventEmitter with the decorator Output. openPage is the handler of the
click event to emit the URL of the item.

Listing 7-4. Updated ItemComponent

```
export class ItemComponent {
  @Input() item: Item;
  @Output() toOpen = new EventEmitter<string>();
```

```
openPage(url: string) {
  this.toOpen.emit(url);
}
}
```

Below is the updated template to add the handler.

```
<h2 class="title" (click)="openPage(item.url)">{{ item.title
}}</h2>
```

The same EventEmitter is also required in the ItemsComponent. This is because Angular custom events emitted by EventEmitters don't bubble up. Below is the updated template of ItemsComponent.

```
<app-item [item]="item" (toOpen)="openPage($event)"></app-item>
```

In the TopStoriesComponent, the event handler of toOpen is added; see Listing 7-5. We simply call the function open of OpenPageService.

Listing 7-5. Event handler of toOpen

```
openUrl(url) {
  this.openPageService.open(url);
}
```

The template file is also updated to add the event handler.

```
<app-items [items]="items$ | async" (toOpen)="openUrl($event)">
</app-items>
```

Events

InAppBrowserObject has different events to listen on.

- loadstart – Fired when the InAppBrowserObject starts to load a URL.

- `loadstop` – Fired when the `InAppBrowserObject` finishes loading a URL.

- `loaderror` – Fired when an error occurred when the `InAppBrowserObject` is loading a URL.

- `exit` - Fired when the `InAppBrowserObject` is closed.

To add listeners on a certain event, we can use the method `on(event)` of `InAppBrowserObject` object. The method `on()` returns an `Observable < InAppBrowserEvent>` object that emits event objects when subscribed. Unsubscribing the `Observable` removes the event listener.

With these events, we can have fine-grained control over web page loading in the `InAppBrowserObject` to improve user experiences. For example, we can make the `InAppBrowserObject` hidden when it's loading the page and show it after the loading is completed.

Alerts

We can use components `ion-loading-controller` and `ion-loading` to show a message when the page is still loading. The component `ion-loading` only supports adding spinners and texts, but we need to add a cancel button in the loading indicator to allow users to abort the operation. In this case, we should use Ionic components `ion-alert-controller` and `ion-alert`.

The usage of components `ion-alert-controller` and `ion-alert` is like `ion-loading-controller` and `ion-loading`. The component `ion-alert-controller` has the same method `create()` to create `ion-alert` components, but the options are different. The component `ion-alert` has the same methods `present()` and `dismiss()` to show and hide the alert, respectively.

The method create() supports following options.

- header – The header of the alert.

- subHeader – The subheader of the alert.

- message – The message to display in the alert.

- cssClass – Space-separated extra CSS classes.

- inputs – An array of inputs.

- buttons – An array of buttons.

- backdropDismiss – Whether the alert should be dismissed when the user taps on the backdrop.

Alerts can include different kinds of inputs to gather data from the user. Supported inputs are text boxes, radio buttons, and checkboxes. Inputs can be added by specifying the option inputs in the method create(). The following properties can be used to configure an input.

- type – The type of the input. Possible values are text, radio, checkbox, tel, number, and other valid HTML5 input types.

- name – The name of the input.

- placeholder – The placeholder of the input.

- label – The label of the input, for radio buttons and checkboxes.

- value – The value of the input.

- checked – Whether the input is checked or not.

- id – The id of the input.

- disabled – Whether the input is disabled or not.

- handler – The handler function for the input.

- min – Minimal value of the input.

- max – Maximal value of the input.

Buttons can also be added using the option buttons. Buttons can have the following properties.

- text – The text of the button.

- handler – The expression to evaluate when the button is pressed.

- cssClass – Space-separated extra CSS classes.

- role – The role of the button – can be null or cancel. When backdropDismiss is set to true and the user taps on the backdrop to dismiss the alert, then the handler of the button with cancel role is invoked.

A Better Solution

We can now create a better implementation that combines the InAppBrowserObject events and alerts to give users more feedback and control over opening web pages. In Listing 7-6, the options when creating a new InAppBrowserObject instance is location=no,hidden=yes, which means the location bar is hidden and the browser window is initially hidden. We subscribe to all four different kinds of events: loadstart, loadstop, loaderror, and exit. In the handler of the event loadstart, an ion-alert is created and presented with the button to cancel the loading. In the handler of the event loadstop, we hide the alert and use the method show() of InAppBrowserObject to show the browser window. In the handler of the event loaderror, we create a toast notification and show it. In the handler of the event exit, we unsubscribe all subscriptions to the event observables and use the method close() of InAppBrowserObject to close the browser window.

The handler of the cancel button is the method `cancel()` of OpenPageService, so when the cancel button is tapped, the loading alert is dismissed and the browser window is closed.

The RxJS Subscription class has the method `add()` to add child subscriptions. These child subscriptions are unsubscribed when the parent subscription is unsubscribed. We can use only one Subscription object to manage subscriptions to four different events.

Listing 7-6. Updated OpenPageService

```
import { Injectable } from '@angular/core';
import { InAppBrowser, InAppBrowserEvent, InAppBrowserObject }
from '@ionic-native/in-app-browser';
import { AlertController, ToastController } from
'@ionic/angular';
import { Subscription } from 'rxjs';

@Injectable()
export class OpenPageService {
  private browser: InAppBrowserObject;
  private loading: HTMLIonAlertElement;
  private subscription: Subscription;

  constructor(private inAppBrowser: InAppBrowser,
              private alertCtrl: AlertController,
              private toastCtrl: ToastController) {}

  open(url: string) {
    this.cancel().then(() => {
      this.browser = this.inAppBrowser.create(url, '_blank',
      'location=no,hidden=yes');
      this.subscription = this.browser.on('loadstart').
      subscribe(() => this.showLoading());
```

```
    this.subscription.add(this.browser.on('loadstop').
    subscribe(() => {
      this.hideLoading().then(() => this.browser.show());
    }));

    this.subscription.add(this.browser.on('loaderror').
    subscribe(event => this.handleError(event)));

    this.subscription.add(this.browser.on('exit').
    subscribe(() => this.cleanup()));
  });
}

private showLoading(): Promise<void> {
  return this.alertCtrl.create({
    header: 'Opening...',
    message: 'The page is loading. You can press the Cancel
    button to stop it.',
    enableBackdropDismiss: false,
    buttons: [
      {
        text: 'Cancel',
        handler: this.cancel.bind(this),
      }
    ],
  }).then(loading => {
    this.loading = loading;
    return loading.present();
  });
}

private hideLoading(): Promise<boolean> {
  if (this.loading) {
    return this.loading.dismiss();
```

```
    } else {
      return Promise.resolve(true);
    }
  }

  private cancel(): Promise<boolean> {
    return this.hideLoading().then(this.cleanup.bind(this));
  }

  private handleError(event: InAppBrowserEvent): Promise<void> {
    return this.showError(event).then(this.cleanup.bind(this));
  }

  private showError(event: InAppBrowserEvent): Promise<void> {
    return this.hideLoading().then(() => {
      return this.toastCtrl.create({
        message: `Failed to load the page. Code: ${event.code},
        Message: ${event.message}`,
        duration: 3000,
        showCloseButton: true,
      }).then(toast => toast.present());
    });
  }

  private cleanup() {
    if (this.subscription) {
      this.subscription.unsubscribe();
      this.subscription = null;
    }
    if (this.browser) {
      this.browser.close();
      this.browser = null;
    }
  }
}
```

The new implementation gives users a better experience when viewing web pages. Figure 7-1 shows the alert when a page is opening.

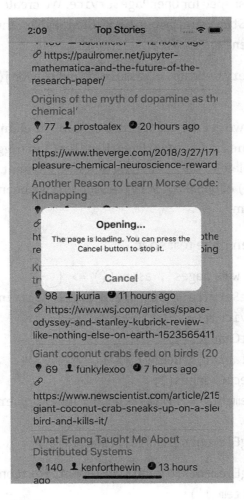

Figure 7-1. *Opening page*

Testing

We need to add test spec for OpenPageService. We create a test stub object openPageServiceStub using jasmine spy, then register the stub object as the provider of OpenPageService.

```
const openPageServiceStub = jasmine.createSpyObj('openPage',
['open']);
```

In Listing 7-7, we get the debugElement of the h2 element in the first item and use the method triggerEventHandler() to trigger the click event, which simulates a user's clicking of the h2 element. We then verify the method open() of openPageServiceStub to have been called with the URL of the first item.

Listing 7-7. Open page test spec

```
it('should open web pages', async(() => {
  const openPageService = fixture.debugElement.injector.
get(OpenPageService);
  fixture.detectChanges();
  fixture.whenStable().then(() => {
    fixture.detectChanges();
    let debugElements = fixture.debugElement.queryAll(By.
    css('h2'));
    expect(debugElements.length).toBe(10);

    expect(debugElements[0].nativeElement.textContent).
    toContain('Item 1');
    debugElements[0].triggerEventHandler('click', null);
    expect(openPageService.open)
      .toHaveBeenCalledWith('http://www.example.com/item0');
  });
}));
```

Summary

In this chapter, we implemented the user story to view stories. We used the plugin InAppBrowser to allow users to view the web pages inside of the app itself. Events of InAppBrowser are used to control its behavior. By using Ionic 4 Alerts, we can create a smooth experience for users to view web pages. In the next chapter, we'll implement the user story to view comments of stories.

CHAPTER 8

View Comments

So far, we have focused on the top stories page, which is also the index page of the app. Now we need to add new pages to show comments of a story and replies to a comment. Before adding those pages, we need to talk about page navigation in Ionic with Angular Router. In this chapter, we'll first discuss Angular Router and then implement the page to show comments and replies.

Angular Router

Ionic apps are Single Page Applications, or SPAs, so there is no page reload after the initial page loading. To archive the similar effect as normal page navigation, a router watches the changes in the URL and updates the view. Angular Router is the built-in routing solution for Angular applications.

We first create a new module and a new component for the new page using the command below.

```
$ ng g module comments --flat false --routing true
$ ng g component comments-list -m comments
```

When creating the module, we pass the option `--routing true` to let Angular CLI create a new routing module. The file of the routing module is `comments-routing.module.ts`. In Listing 8-1, the variable `routes` defines the routes for the comments module. This module only has one component `CommentsListComponent`, so it's mapped to the empty path. The function `RouterModule.forChild` creates the router module to import.

© Fu Cheng 2018
F. Cheng, *Build Mobile Apps with Ionic 4 and Firebase*,
https://doi.org/10.1007/978-1-4842-3775-5_8

Listing 8-1. Routing module for comments

```
import { NgModule } from '@angular/core';
import { Routes, RouterModule } from '@angular/router';
import { CommentsListComponent } from './comments-list.
component';

const routes: Routes = [
  { path: ", component: CommentsListComponent },
];

@NgModule({
  imports: [RouterModule.forChild(routes)],
  exports: [RouterModule]
})
export class CommentsRoutingModule { }
```

After defining the routing for the comments module, we need to
add the routing to the root module. In the root routing module of the
file app-routing.module.ts in Listing 8-2, three routing mappings
are defined. The first one with path top-stories is mapped to the
TopStoriesModule, while the second one with path comments/:id is
mapped to CommentsModule. :id in the path is a routing parameter, so it
matches URLs like comments/123 or comments/456. The parameter's value
can be extracted to be used in the component. The property loadChildren
means this module is lazily loaded. The module is only loaded when the
route path is accessed for the first time. Lazy loading of routes can reduce
the initial bundle size and improve performance. If the user only views
the top stories page, then the comments module is never loaded. The
last empty path is matched when the user accesses the root URL, which
is redirected to path /top-stories. The function RouterModule.forRoot
accepts extra options to configure the router. The property useHash means
using a URL hash like http://localhost:4200/#/top-stories or http://
localhost:4200/#/comments/123.

Listing 8-2. Root routing module

```
import { NgModule } from '@angular/core';
import { Routes, RouterModule } from '@angular/router';

const routes: Routes = [
  { path: 'top-stories', loadChildren: 'app/top-stories/top-
  stories.module#TopStoriesModule' },
  { path: 'comments/:id', loadChildren: 'app/comments/comments.
  module#CommentsModule' },
  { path: ', redirectTo: '/top-stories', pathMatch: 'full' },
];

@NgModule({
  imports: [RouterModule.forRoot(routes, {
    useHash: true,
  })],
  exports: [RouterModule]
})
export class AppRoutingModule { }
```

We can also configure Angular Router to work with NgRx. By using @ngrx/router-store to connect Angular Router with the NgRx store, we can access a router state in the store. The store dispatches different kinds of actions when navigation changes. NgRx already provides the reducer function to work with Angular Router. We just need to integrate it with the store. Listing 8-3 shows the file app/reducers/index.ts for the root module.

In Listing 8-3, RouterStateUrl is the state for routing. The property url is the current URL, params is the routing parameters; queryParams is the query parameters. CustomRouterStateSerializer is a custom implementation of RouterStateSerializer that serializes RouterStateSnapshot objects to custom format. This is because RouterStateSnapshot contains a lot of information about the current routing state. Generally, we don't need all of these data, and large data may have performance issues. CustomRouterStateSerializer only extracts RouterStateUrl objects. fromRouter.RouterReducerState<RouterStateUrl> defines the state of the router, while fromRouter.routerReducer is the provided reducer function from @ngrx/router-store.

Listing 8-3. Connect Angular Router to NgRx store

```
import { ActionReducerMap } from '@ngrx/store';
import { Params, RouterStateSnapshot } from '@angular/router';
import { RouterStateSerializer } from '@ngrx/router-store';
import * as fromItems from './items';
import * as fromRouter from '@ngrx/router-store';

export interface RouterStateUrl {
  url: string;
  params: Params;
  queryParams: Params;
}

export class CustomRouterStateSerializer
  implements RouterStateSerializer<RouterStateUrl> {
  serialize(routerState: RouterStateSnapshot): RouterStateUrl {
    let route = routerState.root;

    while (route.firstChild) {
      route = route.firstChild;
    }

    const { url, root: { queryParams } } = routerState;
    const { params } = route;
    return { url, params, queryParams };
  }
}
```

262

```
export interface State {
  router: fromRouter.RouterReducerState<RouterStateUrl>;
  items: fromItems.State;
}

export const reducers: ActionReducerMap<State> = {
  router: fromRouter.routerReducer,
  items: fromItems.reducer,
};
```

We need to update the root module to import NgRx modules for the router. In Listing 8-4, `StoreRouterConnectingModule.forRoot` connects the router to the store. The property `stateKey` specifies the key for route data in the state. We also need to declare `CustomRouterStateSerializer` as the provider of `RouterStateSerializer`.

Listing 8-4. Import NgRx router module

```
import { RouterStateSerializer, StoreRouterConnectingModule }
from '@ngrx/router-store';

@NgModule({
  declarations: [
    MyApp,
  ],
  imports: [
    StoreModule.forRoot(reducers),
    StoreRouterConnectingModule.forRoot({
      stateKey: 'router',
    }),
  ],
```

```
  providers: [
    { provide: RouterStateSerializer, useClass:
    CustomRouterStateSerializer },
  ]
})
export class AppModule {}
```

Comment Model

Now we are going to implement the page to display comments for each top story. For each comment, we also want to show its replies. We'll create a new comments page. Clicking the comments icon of an item in the top stories page triggers the navigation to the comments page. In the comments page, clicking the replies icon navigates to the comments page again but shows the replies to this comment.

Stories and comments are all items in Hacker News API. They can both have children items, which can be comments or replies. The data structure is recursive, so we can use the same comments page to show both comments and replies.

For the model Item, we add three new properties related to comments.

- text – The text of the comment.

- descendants – The number of descendants of this item. For stories, this is the number of comments; for comments, this is the number of replies.

- kids – The array of ids of descendants of this item. For stories, this is the array of comments ids; for comments, this is the array of replies ids.

View Comments

Even though stories and comments are both items, the components to display them are different. The comment component needs to show the text instead of titles and links. We have separate components to render comments and lists of comments.

We use the Angular CLI to generate stub code of the two components. These components are put into the same components module as ItemsComponent and ItemComponent.

```
$ ng g component components/comment
$ ng g component components/comments
```

Comment Component

Listing 8-5 shows the template of the CommentComponent. We use binding of the property innerHTML to display the content of item.text because item.text contains HTML markups. We check the property item.kids for replies to this comment. If a comment has replies, the number of replies is displayed. The property routerLink of the ion-button specifies the link to navigate. Because the comments link requires the id, ['/comments', item.id] is the way to provide the id as the parameter.

Listing 8-5. Template of CommentComponent

```
<div *ngIf="item">
  <div [innerHTML]="item.text"></div>
  <div>
    <span>
      <ion-icon name="person"></ion-icon>
      {{ item.by }}
    </span>
```

```
  <span>
    <ion-icon name="time"></ion-icon>
    {{ item.time | timeAgo }}
  </span>
  <ion-button *ngIf="item.kids" [fill]="'clear'"
  [routerLink]="['/comments', item.id]">
    <ion-icon slot="icon-only" name="chatboxes"></ion-icon>
    {{ item.kids.length }}
  </ion-button>
  </div>
</div>
<div *ngIf="!item">
  Loading...
</div>
```

The CommentComponent in Listing 8-6 only has one Input binding of
type Item.

Listing 8-6. CommentComponent

```
import { Component, Input } from '@angular/core';
import { Item } from '../../models/item';

@Component({
  selector: 'app-comment',
  templateUrl: './comment.component.html',
  styleUrls: ['./comment.component.scss']
})
export class CommentComponent {
  @Input() item: Item;
}
```

Comments Component

The template of CommentsComponent is also like the ItemsComponent; see Listing 8-7.

Listing 8-7. Template of CommentsComponent

```
<ion-list *ngIf="items && items.length > 0">
  <ion-item *ngFor="let item of items">
    <app-comment [item]="item"></app-comment>
  </ion-item>
</ion-list>
<p *ngIf="items && items.length === 0">
  No items.
</p>
<p *ngIf="!items">
  Loading...
</p>
```

The code of CommentsComponent is also like the ItemsComponent; see Listing 8-8.

Listing 8-8. CommentsComponent

```
import { Component, Input } from '@angular/core';
import { Items } from '../../models/items';

@Component({
  selector: 'app-comments',
  templateUrl: './comments.component.html',
  styleUrls: ['./comments.component.scss']
})
export class CommentsComponent {
  @Input() items: Items;
}
```

ItemComponent Changes

We also need to update the ItemComponent to display the number of comments and allows users to view the comments; see Listing 8-9. The same property routerLink is used to navigate to the comments page.

Listing 8-9. Updated template of ItemComponent

```
<ion-button *ngIf="item.kids" [fill]="'clear'"
[routerLink]="['/comments', item.id]">
  <ion-icon slot="icon-only" name="chatboxes"></ion-icon>
  {{ item.kids.length }}
</ion-button>
```

State Management

Now we start adding the logic to show comments and replies. We still use NgRx to manage the state of comments page. Since comments and replies are all items, we can reuse the state for the feature items to store comments and replies.

Actions

Listing 8-10 shows the actions for the comments page. The action Select means selecting the comment to view. The payload is the item id. The action LoadMore means loading more comments or replies. The action LoadSuccess means the loading of an item is successful. This action is required because the user may access the comments page directly, so it's possible that the comment has not been loaded yet, so we need the loading action. Payload types of these actions are straightforward.

Listing 8-10. Comments actions

```
import { Action } from '@ngrx/store';
import { Item } from '../../models/item';

export enum CommentsActionTypes {
  Select = '[Comments] Select',
  LoadMore = '[Comments] Load More',
  LoadSuccess = '[Comments] Load Success',
}

export class Select implements Action {
  readonly type = CommentsActionTypes.Select;

  constructor(public payload: number) {}
}

export class LoadMore implements Action {
  readonly type = CommentsActionTypes.LoadMore;
}

export class LoadSuccess implements Action {
  readonly type = CommentsActionTypes.LoadSuccess;

  constructor(public payload: Item) {}
}

export type CommentsActions = Select | LoadMore | LoadSuccess;
```

Reducers

The first reducer function is for selected comments; see Listing 8-11. The state only contains one property `selectedItemId` to contain the id of selected item. This property is updated when the action `LoadSuccess` is dispatched.

Listing 8-11. Reducer function for selected comments

```
import { CommentsActions, CommentsActionTypes } from
'../actions/comments';
export interface State {
  selectedItemId: number;
}
const initialState: State = {
  selectedItemId: null,
};
export function reducer(
  state = initialState,
  action: CommentsActions,
) {
  switch (action.type) {
    case CommentsActionTypes.LoadSuccess:
      return {
        ...state,
        selectedItemId: action.payload.id,
      };
    default: {
      return state;
    }
  }
}
export const getSelectedItemId = (state: State) => state.
selectedItemId;
```

Because there may be many comments or replies, the pagination is still required. In Listing 8-12, the state and reducer functions are similar to those ones in the top stories page. The difference is that the total number of items is determined by the length of property kids.

Listing 8-12. Reducer for pagination

```
import { CommentsActions, CommentsActionTypes } from
'../actions/comments';

export interface State {
  offset: number;
  limit: number;
  total: number;
}

export const pageSize = 20;

const initialState: State = {
  offset: 0,
  limit: pageSize,
  total: 0,
};

export function reducer(
  state = initialState,
  action: CommentsActions,
): State {
  switch (action.type) {
    case CommentsActionTypes.LoadMore:
      const offset = state.offset + state.limit;
      return {
        ...state,
        offset: offset < state.total ? offset : state.offset,
      };
```

```
case CommentsActionTypes.LoadSuccess: {
  return {
    ...state,
    total: (action.payload.kids && action.payload.kids.
    length) || 0,
  };
}
default: {
  return state;
}
}
}
```

The final reducer map and selectors are listed in Listing 8-13. The most important selector is getSelectedItemChildren, which will be used by the comments component to select the items to display. Here we use the selector getItemEntities from the feature items to select loaded items.

Listing 8-13. Reducer map and selectors

```
import * as fromRoot from '../../reducers';
import * as fromComments from './comments';
import * as fromPagination from './pagination';
import { ActionReducerMap, createFeatureSelector,
createSelector } from '@ngrx/store';
import { getItemEntities } from '../../reducers/items';

export interface CommentsState {
  comments: fromComments.State;
  pagination: fromPagination.State;
}
```

```
export interface State extends fromRoot.State {
  comments: CommentsState;
}

export const reducers: ActionReducerMap<CommentsState> = {
  comments: fromComments.reducer,
  pagination: fromPagination.reducer,
};

export const getCommentsFeatureState = createFeatureSelector
<CommentsState>('comments');

export const getCommentsState = createSelector(
  getCommentsFeatureState,
  state => state.comments,
);

export const getPaginationState = createSelector(
  getCommentsFeatureState,
  state => state.pagination,
);

export const getSelectedItemId = createSelector(
  getCommentsState,
  fromComments.getSelectedItemId,
);

export const getSelectedItem = createSelector(
  getItemEntities,
  getSelectedItemId,
  (entities, id) => entities[id],
);
```

```
export const getSelectedItemChildren = createSelector(
  getSelectedItem,
  getItemEntities,
  getPaginationState,
  (item, entities, pagination) => {
    return item ? (item.kids || []).slice(0, pagination.offset +
    pagination.limit)
      .map(id => entities[id]) : [];
  }
);
```

Effects

NgRx effects are also required for loading the comments. In Listing 8-14, the effect loadComment$ handles the action Select. After the item is loaded, it dispatches three actions as the result. The first action itemActions. LoadSuccess updates the items store with the loaded item; the second action commentsActions.LoadSuccess selects the item to view; the third action itemActions.Load triggers the loading of comments or replies. The effect loadMore$ handles the action LoadMore. It gets the state from the store and dispatches the action itemActions.Load with the ids from the selected item's property kids.

Listing 8-14. Effects

```
@Injectable()
export class CommentsEffects {
  constructor(private actions$: Actions,
              private store: Store<fromComments.State>,
              private db: AngularFireDatabase) {

  }
```

```
@Effect()
loadComment$: Observable<Action> = this.actions$.pipe(
  ofType(CommentsActionTypes.Select),
  switchMap((action: commentsActions.Select) =>
    this.db.object(`/v0/item/${action.payload}`).valueChanges()
      .pipe(
        take(1),
        mergeMap((item: Item) => of<Action>(
          new itemActions.LoadSuccess([item]),
          new commentsActions.LoadSuccess(item),
          new itemActions.Load((item.kids || []).slice(0,
          pageSize))))
      )
  )
);

@Effect()
loadMore$: Observable<Action> = this.actions$.pipe(
  ofType(CommentsActionTypes.LoadMore),
  withLatestFrom(this.store),
  map(([action, state]) => {
    const {
      items: { entities },
      comments: {pagination: { offset, limit },
      comments: { selectedItemId }}
    } = state;
    const ids = entities[selectedItemId].kids || [];
    return new itemActions.Load(ids.slice(offset, offset +
    limit));
  })
);
}
```

Connect Component to the Store

After we finish the store-related code, the last step is to connect the component with the store. The comments component uses the same infinite scrolling as in the top stories page. Listing 8-15 shows the template of the component. The component ion-button renders a back arrow that can be used to go back to the previous URL.

Listing 8-15. Template of the comments component

```
<ion-header>
  <ion-toolbar>
    <ion-buttons slot="start">
      <ion-button (click)="goBack()">
        <ion-icon slot="icon-only" name="arrow-back">
        </ion-icon>
      </ion-button>
    </ion-buttons>
    <ion-title>Comments</ion-title>
  </ion-toolbar>
</ion-header>
<ion-content padding>
  <app-comments [items]="items$ | async"></app-comments>
  <ion-infinite-scroll (ionInfinite)="load($event)">
    <ion-infinite-scroll-content></ion-infinite-scroll-content>
  </ion-infinite-scroll>
</ion-content>
```

Listing 8-16 shows the code of the component. The constructor parameter of type ActivatedRoute is provided by Angular Router to access the current activated route. We can get the route parameters from ActivatedRoute. The return value of this.route.params is an Observable<Params> object. When the parameters change, a new Params object is emitted. In this case, we need to dispatch an action `Select` to trigger the loading of comments or replies. The method `goBack` uses the `Location` object to go back to the previous URL.

Listing 8-16. CommentsListComponent

```
import { ChangeDetectionStrategy, Component, OnInit, OnDestroy
} from '@angular/core';
import { ActivatedRoute } from '@angular/router';
import { Location } from '@angular/common';

import * as fromItems from '../reducers/items';
import * as fromComments from './reducers';
import * as commentsActions from './actions/comments';
import { select, Store } from '@ngrx/store';
import { Observable, Subscription } from 'rxjs';
import { Items } from '../models/items';
import { map } from 'rxjs/operators';

@Component({
  selector: 'app-comments-list',
  changeDetection: ChangeDetectionStrategy.OnPush,
  templateUrl: './comments-list.component.html',
  styleUrls: ['./comments-list.component.scss']
})
export class CommentsListComponent implements OnInit, OnDestroy
{
  items$: Observable<Items>;
  private itemsLoading$: Observable<boolean>;
  private infiniteScrollComponent: any;
  private subscriptions: Subscription[];

  constructor(private route: ActivatedRoute,
              private store: Store<fromComments.State>,
              private location: Location) {
```

277

```
    this.items$ = store.pipe(select(fromComments.
    getSelectedItemChildren));
    this.itemsLoading$ = store.pipe(select(fromItems.
    isItemsLoading));
    this.subscriptions = [];
  }

  ngOnInit() {
    this.subscriptions.push(this.itemsLoading$.
    subscribe(loading => {
      if (!loading) {
        this.notifyScrollComplete();
      }
    }));
    this.subscriptions.push(this.route.params.pipe(
      map(params => new commentsActions.Select(parseInt(params.
      id, 10)))
    ).subscribe(this.store));
  }

  ngOnDestroy(): void {
    this.subscriptions.forEach(subscription => subscription.
    unsubscribe());
  }

  load(event) {
    this.infiniteScrollComponent = event.target;
    this.store.dispatch(new commentsActions.LoadMore());
  }

  goBack(): void {
    this.location.back();
  }
```

```
private notifyScrollComplete(): void {
  if (this.infiniteScrollComponent) {
    this.infiniteScrollComponent.complete();
  }
 }
}
```

Figure 8-1 shows the screenshot of the comments page.

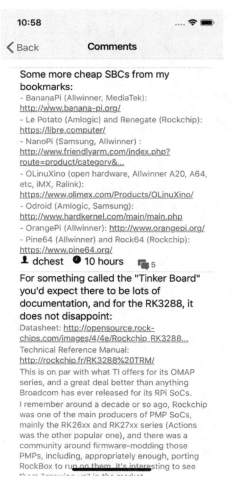

Figure 8-1. *Comments page*

Summary

In this chapter, we implemented the user story to view comments of stories. We used Angular Router to implement the transition from the top stories page to the comments page. The comments page also uses NgRx to manage the state. In the next chapter, we'll discuss user management with Firebase.

CHAPTER 9

User Management

So far, all the implemented user stories in the app are public and available to all users; now we are going to implement some personalized user stories of the app. Before adding personalization features, we need to add basic support for user management. Implementing user management is a task we must do, but it's a tedious task for developers. Although there are a lot of high-quality open source libraries in different programming languages to handle user authentication, we still need to integrate those libraries with app code and manage back-end storage. It's also very common for an app to allow users to log in using third-party providers, for example, Google or Facebook. To support this scenario, more libraries need to be integrated, which makes user management a harder task to finish.

Firebase provides an easy integration with user authentication for the web and mobile apps. Firebase manages user authentication data, so we don't need to manage the storage ourselves. Firebase also supports logging in with third-party providers, including Google, Facebook, Twitter, and GitHub.

To support user management, we need to add UI for users to sign up and log in. This requires us to use form controls and other UI components. After reading this chapter, you should know how to integrate Firebase user management with Ionic apps. We start from these Ionic UI controls.

© Fu Cheng 2018
F. Cheng, *Build Mobile Apps with Ionic 4 and Firebase*,
https://doi.org/10.1007/978-1-4842-3775-5_9

Ionic UI Controls

To gather users' information, we need to use different input controls, including standard HTML form elements like inputs, checkboxes, radio buttons and selects; and components designed for mobile platforms, like toggles or ranges. Ionic provides out-of-box components with beautiful styles for different requirements.

Inputs

The component `ion-input` is for different types of inputs. This component supports the following properties.

- `type` – The type of the input. Possible values are `text`, `password`, `email`, `number`, `search`, `tel`, or `url`. The default type is `text`.

- `value` – The value of the input.

- `placeholder` – The placeholder of the input.

- `disabled` – Whether the input is disabled or not.

- `clearInput` – Whether to show the icon that can be used to clear the text.

- `clearOnEdit` – Whether to clear the input when the user starts editing the text. If the type is `password`, the default value is `true`; otherwise the default value is `false`.

- `accept` – If the type is file, this property specifies a comma-separated list of content types of files accepted by the server.

- `autocapitalize` – Whether the text should be automatically capitalized. The default value is `none`.

- `autocomplete` – Whether the value should be automatically completed by the browser. The default value is `off`.

- `autocorrect` – Whether auto-correction should be enabled. The default value is `off`.

- `autofocus` –Whether the control should have input focus when the page loads.

- `debounce` – The amount of time in milliseconds to wait to trigger the event `ionChange` after each keystroke. The default value is 0.

- `inputmode` – The hint for the browser for the keyboard to display.

- `max` – The maximum value.

- `maxlength` – The maximum number of characters that the user can enter.

- `min` – The minimum value.

- `minlength` – The minimum number of characters that the user can enter.

- `step` – The increment at which a value can be set. This property is used with `min` and `max`.

- `multiple` – Whether the user can enter multiple values. It only applies when the type is `email` or `file`.

- `name` – Name of the control.

- `pattern` – A regular expression to check the value.

- `readonly` – Whether the value can be changed by the user.

- `required` – Whether the value is required.

- `spellcheck` – Whether to check the spelling and grammar.

- `size` – The initial size of the control.

`ion-input` also supports following events.

- `ionBlur` – Fired when the input loses focus.

- `ionFocus` – Fired when the input has focus.

- `ionChange` – Fired when the value has changed.

- `ionInput` – Fired when a keyboard input occurred.

Below is a basic sample of using `ion-input`.

```
<ion-input type="text" [(ngModel)]="name" name="name"
required></ion-input>
```

Checkbox

The component `ion-checkbox` creates checkboxes with Ionic styles. It has the following properties.

- `color` - The color of the checkbox. Only predefined color names like `primary` and `secondary` can be used.

- `checked` - Whether the checkbox is checked. The default value is `false`.

- `disabled` - Whether the checkbox is disabled. The default value is `false`.

`ion-checkbox` also supports the event `ionChange` that fired when the value of the checkbox is changed.

Below is a basic sample of using `ion-checkbox`.

```
<ion-checkbox [(ngModel)]="enabled"></ion-checkbox>
```

Radio Buttons

Radio buttons can be checked or unchecked. Radio buttons are usually grouped together to allow the user to make selections. A radio button is created using the component `ion-radio`. `ion-radio` supports properties `color`, `checked`, and `disabled` with the same meaning as the `ion-checkbox`. `ion-radio` also has a property `value` to set the value of the radio button. `ion-radio` supports the event `ionSelect` that fired when it's selected.

A radio buttons group is created by the component `ion-radio-group`, then all the descendant `ion-radio` components are put into the same group. Only one radio button in the group can be checked at the same time. In Listing 9-1, we create a group with three radio buttons.

Listing 9-1. Radio buttons groups

```
<ion-radio-group>
  <ion-list>
    <ion-list-header>
      Traffic colors
    </ion-list-header>
    <ion-item>
      <ion-label>Red</ion-label>
      <ion-radio slot="start" value="red"></ion-radio>
    </ion-item>
    <ion-item>
      <ion-label>Green</ion-label>
      <ion-radio slot="start" value="green"></ion-radio>
    </ion-item>
```

```
  <ion-item>
    <ion-label>Blue</ion-label>
    <ion-radio slot="start" value="blue"></ion-radio>
  </ion-item>
</ion-list>
</ion-radio-group>
```

Figure 9-1 shows the screenshot of the radio buttons.

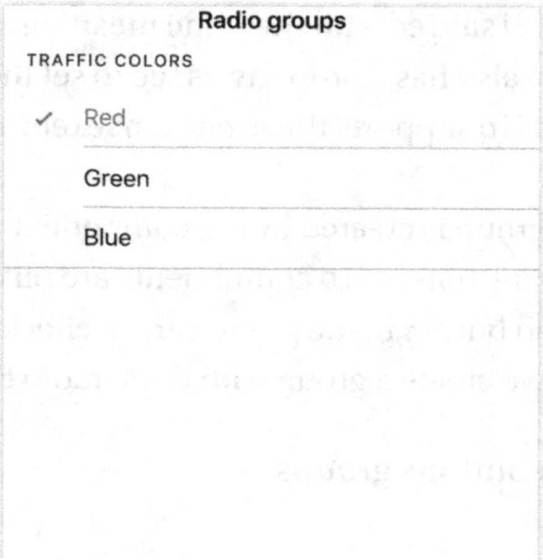

Figure 9-1. *Radio buttons*

Selects

The component ion-select is similar to the standard HTML <select> element, but its UI is more mobile friendly. The options of ion-select are specified using ion-select-option. If the ion-select only allows a single selection, each ion-select-option is rendered as a radio button in the group. If the ion-select allows multiple selections, then each ion-select-option is rendered as a checkbox. Options can be presented using alerts or action sheets. Below are configuration options for ion-select.

- `multiple` – Whether the `ion-select` supports multiple selections.

- `disabled` – Whether the `ion-select` is disabled.

- `interface` – The interface to display the `ion-select`. Possible values are `alert`, `popover`, and `action-sheet`. The default value is `alert`.

- `interfaceOptions` – Additional options passed to the interface.

- `okText` – The text to display for the OK button.

- `cancelText` – The text to display for the cancel button.

- `placeholder` – The text to display when no selection.

- `selectedText` – The text to display when selected.

`ion-select` also supports the following events.

- `ionChange` – Fired when the selection has changed.

- `ionCancel` – Fired when the selection was canceled.

- `ionBlur` – Fired when the select loses focus.

- `ionFocus` – Fired when the select has focus.

The `ion-select` in Listing 9-2 renders a single selection select.

Listing 9-2. Single selection select

```
<ion-select placeholder="Select a color">
  <ion-select-option value="red">Red</ion-select-option>
  <ion-select-option value="green" selected>Green</ion-select-
  option>
  <ion-select-option value="blue">Blue</ion-select-option>
</ion-select>
```

Figure 9-2 show the screenshot of a single selection select. Only one option can be selected at the same time.

Figure 9-2. *Single selection*

The `ion-select` in Listing 9-3 allows multiple selections. The `ion-select-options` don't have a property `value` to set the value, so the value will be the text value.

Listing 9-3. Multiple selections select

```
<ion-select multiple="true" placeholder="Select browsers">
  <ion-select-option>IE</ion-select-option>
  <ion-select-option selected>Chrome</ion-select-option>
  <ion-select-option selected>Firefox</ion-select-option>
</ion-select>
```

Figure 9-3 shows the screenshot of a multiple-selections select. The checkboxes before the options allow multiple selections.

Figure 9-3. *Multiple selection*

The `ion-select` in Listing 9-4 uses an action sheet to display options.

Listing 9-4. Use action sheet to display

```
<ion-select interface="action-sheet" placeholder="your
response">
  <ion-select-option>Yes</ion-select-option>
  <ion-select-option>No</ion-select-option>
  <ion-select-option>Maybe</ion-select-option>
</ion-select>
```

289

Figure 9-4 shows the screenshot of using an action sheet to display options.

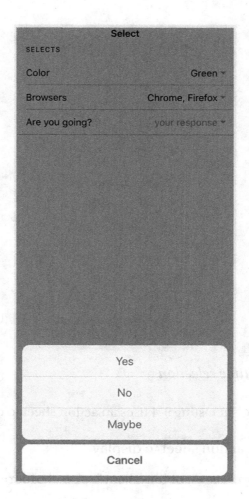

Figure 9-4. *Use action sheet*

Toggles

Like checkboxes, toggles represent Boolean values but are more user friendly on the mobile platforms. `ion-toggle` supports the same properties and events as `ion-checkbox`. See the code below for a sample of `ion-toggle`.

```
<ion-toggle [(ngModel)]="enabled"></ion-toggle>
```

Ranges

Range sliders allow users to select from a range of values by moving the knobs. By default, a range slider has one knob to select only one value. It also supports using dual knobs to select a lower and upper value. Dual knobs range sliders are perfect controls for choosing ranges, that is, a price range for filtering.

The component `ion-range` has the following properties. Standard properties, including `color` and `disabled`, are omitted.

- `min` and `max` - Set the minimum and maximum integer value of the range. The default values are 0 and 100, respectively.

- `step` - The value granularity of the range that specifies the increasing or decreasing values when the knob is moved. The default value is 1.

- `snaps` - Whether the knob snaps to the nearest tick mark that evenly spaced based on the value of `step`. The default value is `false`.

- `pin` - Whether to show a pin with current value when the knob is pressed. The default value is `false`.

- debounce - How many milliseconds to wait before triggering the ionChange event after a change in the range value. The default value is 0.

- dualKnobs - Whether to show two knobs. The default value is false.

To add labels to either side of the slider, we can use the property slot of the child components of the ion-range. Labels can be texts, icons, or any other components.

The ion-range in Listing 9-5 uses two icons as the labels.

Listing 9-5. Labels of ion-range

```
<ion-range min="1" max="5">
  <ion-icon name="sad" slot="start"></ion-icon>
  <ion-icon name="happy" slot="end"></ion-icon>
</ion-range>
```

The ion-range in Listing 9-6 sets the property step and snaps.

Listing 9-6. Step and snaps

```
<ion-range step="10" snaps="true" pin="true">
  <ion-label slot="start">Min</ion-label>
  <ion-label slot="end">Max</ion-label>
</ion-range>
```

The last ion-range in Listing 9-7 has double knobs.

Listing 9-7. Double knobs

```
<ion-range dual-knobs="true" min="0" max="10000">
  <ion-label slot="start">Low</ion-label>
  <ion-label slot="end">High</ion-label>
</ion-range>
```

Figure 9-5 shows the screenshot of ranges created in Listings 9-5, 9-6, and 9-7.

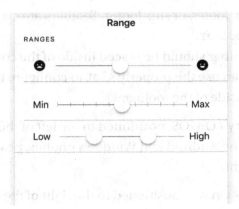

Figure 9-5. *Different kinds of ranges*

Labels

Labels can be used to describe different types of inputs. ion-label is the component for labels. It supports different ways to position the labels relative to the inputs using the property position.

- fixed - Labels are always displayed next to the inputs.

- floating - Labels will float above the inputs if inputs are not empty or have focus.

- stacked - Labels will always appear on the top of inputs.

We can add the property position to the ion-label to specify the position.

Toolbar

A toolbar is a generic container for text and buttons. It can be used as a header, sub-header, footer, or sub-footer. Toolbars are created using the component `ion-toolbar`.

Buttons in a toolbar should be placed inside of the component `ion-buttons`. We can use the property `slot` to configure the position of the `ion-buttons` inside of the toolbar.

- `secondary` - On iOS, positioned to the left of the content; on Android and Windows phones, positioned to the right.

- `primary` - On iOS, positioned to the right of the content; on Android and Windows phones, positioned to the far right.

- `start` - Positioned to the left of the content in LTR, and to the right in RTL.

- `end` - Positioned to the right of the content in LTR, and to the left in RTL.

In Listing 9-8, we have two `ion-buttons` at both sides of the `ion-title`.

Listing 9-8. Toolbar

```
<ion-app>
  <ion-header>
    <ion-toolbar>
      <ion-buttons slot="start">
        <ion-button>
          <ion-icon name="menu" slot="icon-only"></ion-icon>
        </ion-button>
      </ion-buttons>
```

```
  <ion-title>My App</ion-title>
  <ion-buttons slot="end">
    <ion-button>
      <ion-icon name="settings" slot="icon-only"></ion-icon>
    </ion-button>
  </ion-buttons>
</ion-toolbar>
</ion-header>
<ion-content padding>
  App content
</ion-content>
</ion-app>
```

Email and Password Login

The simplest way to add user management is to allow users to log in using an email and password. Firebase already provides built-in support for email and password authentication. Firebase manages storage of users' emails and passwords for the app. By using Firebase's JavaScript library, it's very easy to add email and password login. We first need to enable the email and password login for the Firebase project. In the **Authentication** section of the Firebase project, go to the **Sign-in method** tab and click **Email/Password** to enable it; see Figure 9-6. This is also the place to enable other third-party login methods.

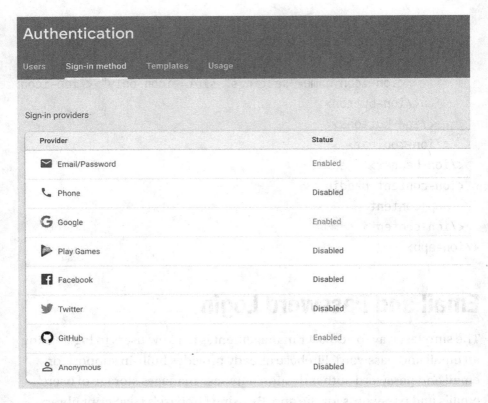

Figure 9-6. *Enable Email/Password login*

Model for User Management

We first create models required for authentication; see Listing 9-9. The interface `User` represents logged-in users. It has four properties: `uid`, `displayName`, `email`, and `photoURL`. The property `photoURL` is the URL of user's profile image. The interface `EmailPasswordPair` contains `email` and `password`, which is used for login requests. The interface `NewAccount` contains information for new users, which is used for sign-up requests.

Listing 9-9. Models for user management

```
export interface User {
  uid: string;
  displayName: string;
  email: string;
  photoURL?: string;
}

export interface EmailPasswordPair {
  email: string;
  password: string;
}

export interface NewAccount {
  name: string;
  email: string;
  password: string;
}
```

AuthService

As usual, we start with the service for authentication. AngularFire2 already supports authentication with Firebase using the service `AngularFileAuth`. In the previous implementation of the top stories page, we already use the injected `AngularFireDatabase` object to retrieve data from the Hacker News database. AngularFire2 simplifies the way to work with Firebase. Now we need to use AngularFire2 to integrate the authentication for our app. However, AngularFire2 doesn't provide a way to easily switch between different Firebase instances in the same app. The injected `AngularFireDatabase` instance can only easily access a single Firebase instance. To work around this limitation, we use the standard way of AngularFire2 instance to access the app's Firebase instance but use another way to manually create the `AngularFireDatabase` instance for Hacker News API.

In the current constructor of `TopStoriesEffects`, we simply use `db: AngularFireDatabase` to inject the instance of `AngularFireDatabase`. Now that we have two Firebase databases to work with, we need to distinguish between these two `AngularFireDatabase` instances. This is done by using a custom injection token for the Hacker News database. `HACKER_NEWS_DB` in Listing 9-10 is the injection token.

Listing 9-10. Injection token for Hacker News database

```
import { AngularFireDatabase } from '@angular/fire/database';
import { InjectionToken } from '@angular/core';

export const HACKER_NEWS_DB = new InjectionToken<AngularFire
Database>('Hacker News db');
```

In the app's root module, we need to declare the provider of this `AngularFileDatabase` instance. In Listing 9-11, we create a new `AngularFileDatabase` object and provide it with the token `HACKER_NEWS_DB`. The constructor of `AngularFireDatabase` requires five parameters.

1. An option object to configure AngularFire2. The object `environment.hackernews_db` only contains a single property `databaseURL` as we only use the database feature for Hacker News.

2. A name for the Firebase app.

3. The database URL. Since we already specified the database URL in the option object, we can use `null` here.

4. Angular platform id.

5. Angular `NgZone` object.

The values of the last two parameters need to be injected by the Angular injector. Here we use the Angular factory service provider to create the AngularFireDatabase instance.

Listing 9-11. Create AngularFileDatabase object

```
import { NgModule, NgZone, PLATFORM_ID } from '@angular/core';
import { HACKER_NEWS_DB } from './hackernews-db';

@NgModule({
  declarations: [
    MyApp,
  ],
  providers: [
    {
      provide: HACKER_NEWS_DB,
      useFactory: (platformId: Object, zone: NgZone) =>
        new AngularFireDatabase(environment.hackernews_db,
        'HackerNews', null, platformId, zone),
      deps: [PLATFORM_ID, NgZone]
    },
  ]
})
export class AppModule {
}
```

The constuctor of TopStoriesEffects needs to be updated to use @Inject(HACKER_NEWS_DB) private db: AngularFireDatabase for injection.

After updating the existing AngularFireDatabase instance to use a different injection token, we can use the default way to access the app's database. The Firebase configuration of this app is copied to the file environment.ts; see Listing 9-12.

Listing 9-12. Updated Firebase config

```
export const environment = {
  hackernews_db: {
    databaseURL: 'https://hacker-news.firebaseio.com',
  },
  app_db: {
    apiKey: '<API_KEY>',
    authDomain: '<PROJECT_ID>.firebaseapp.com',
    databaseURL: 'https://<PROJECT_ID>.firebaseio.com',
    storageBucket: '<PROJECT_ID>.appspot.com',
    projectId: '<PROJECT_ID>',
    messagingSenderId: '<SENDER_ID>',
  }
};
```

To use the authentication in Firebase, we also need to import the module `AngularFireAuthModule`. Listing 9-13 is the implementation of `AuthService`. The injected `AngularFireAuth` object is the primary object to interact with Firebase authentication. In the method `create`, the method `createUserAndRetrieveDataWithEmailAndPassword` creates a new user account and returns information about the created user. The method `login` uses `signInWithEmailAndPassword` to log in with an email and password. The method signInWithEmailAndPassword returns a `Promise<firebase.auth.UserCredential>` object, so we need to chain the returned `Promise` object with `result => result.user` to extract the `firebase.User` object. The method `logout` uses the method `signOut` to log out the current user. All these methods return `Promise` objects.

Listing 9-13. AuthService

```
import { Injectable } from '@angular/core';
import { AngularFireAuth } from '@angular/fire/auth';
import { EmailPasswordPair, NewAccount } from '../../models/user';
import * as firebase from 'firebase';

@Injectable()
export class AuthService {

  constructor(private afAuth: AngularFireAuth) { }

  create(user: NewAccount): Promise<firebase.User> {
    return this.afAuth.auth.createUserAndRetrieveDataWithEmail
    AndPassword(user.email, user.password)
      .then(result => result.user);
  }

  login(user: EmailPasswordPair): Promise<firebase.User> {
    return this.afAuth.auth.signInWithEmailAndPassword(user.
    email, user.password).then(result => result.user);
  }

  logout(): Promise<any> {
    return this.afAuth.auth.signOut();
  }
}
```

State Management

We continue to use NgRx to manage a state related to authentication.
We define different actions related to login, sign-up, and logout; see
Listing 9-14. For each group of actions, there are three actions for the
scenarios when the request is sent, success result is received, and failure

result is received, respectively. For example, the action Login means the login request with payload of type EmailPasswordPair; LoginSuccess means the login succeeds; LoginFailure means the login fails with an error as the payload.

Listing 9-14. Actions

```
import { Action } from '@ngrx/store';
import { User, EmailPasswordPair, NewAccount } from
'../../models/user';

export enum AuthActionTypes {
  Login = '[Auth] Login',
  LoginSuccess = '[Auth] Login Success',
  LoginFailure = '[Auth] Login Failure',
  Signup = '[Auth] Sign Up',
  SignupSuccess = '[Auth] SignUp Success',
  SignupFailure = '[Auth] SignUp Failure',
  Logout = '[Auth] Logout',
  LogoutSuccess = '[Auth] Logout Success',
  LogoutFailure = '[Auth] Logout Failure',
}

export class Login implements Action {
  readonly type = AuthActionTypes.Login;

  constructor(public payload: EmailPasswordPair) {}
}

export class LoginSuccess implements Action {
  readonly type = AuthActionTypes.LoginSuccess;

  constructor(public payload: User) {}
}
```

```
export class LoginFailure implements Action {
  readonly type = AuthActionTypes.LoginFailure;

  constructor(public payload: any) {}
}

export class Signup implements Action {
  readonly type = AuthActionTypes.Signup;

  constructor(public payload: NewAccount) {}
}

export class SignupSuccess implements Action {
  readonly type = AuthActionTypes.SignupSuccess;
}

export class SignupFailure implements Action {
  readonly type = AuthActionTypes.SignupFailure;

  constructor(public payload: any) {}
}

export class Logout implements Action {
  readonly type = AuthActionTypes.Logout;
}

export class LogoutSuccess implements Action {
  readonly type = AuthActionTypes.LogoutSuccess;
}

export class LogoutFailure implements Action {
  readonly type = AuthActionTypes.LogoutFailure;

  constructor(public payload: any) {}
}
```

```
export type AuthActions = Login | LoginSuccess | LoginFailure
  | Signup | SignupSuccess | SignupFailure
  | Logout | LogoutSuccess | LogoutFailure;
```

We also define states and related reducer functions. The state for the feature auth contains three sub-states. The first one is for the authentication status, which has properties loggedIn, user, and logoutError. This is used to control UI elements related to authentication. The second one is for the login page, which has properties loading and error. The last one is for the sign-up page, which also has the properties loading and error. The reducer functions for these three states are very simple and straightforward.

Listing 9-15 shows the state and reducer function for the authentication status. For the action LoginSuccess, the state property loggedIn is set to true, while the property user is set to the logged-in user.

Listing 9-15. Reducer for the authentication status

```
import { User } from '../../models/user';
import { AuthActions, AuthActionTypes } from '../actions/auth';

export interface State {
  loggedIn: boolean;
  user: User | null;
  logoutError: any;
}

export const initialState: State = {
  loggedIn: false,
  user: null,
  logoutError: null,
};
```

```
export function reducer(state = initialState, action:
AuthActions): State {
  switch (action.type) {
    case AuthActionTypes.LoginSuccess: {
      return {
        ...state,
        loggedIn: true,
        user: action.payload,
        logoutError: null,
      };
    }

    case AuthActionTypes.LogoutSuccess: {
      return initialState;
    }

    case AuthActionTypes.LogoutFailure: {
      return {
        ...state,
        logoutError: action.payload,
      };
    }

    default: {
      return state;
    }
  }
}

export const getLoggedIn = (state: State) => state.loggedIn;
export const getUser = (state: State) => state.user;
```

For the state and reducers of the login page and sign-up page, please refer to the full source code with this book.

Listing 9-16 show the state of the feature auth and its selectors. The AuthState is composed of the three aforementioned states. The ActionReducerMap is also a mapping from these three states to their reducers. Selectors are used by UI components to retrieve data from the states.

Listing 9-16. State and selectors of the feature auth

```
import {
  createSelector,
  createFeatureSelector,
  ActionReducerMap,
} from '@ngrx/store';
import * as fromRoot from '../../reducers';
import * as fromAuth from './auth';
import * as fromLoginPage from './login-page';
import * as fromSignupPage from './signup-page';

export interface AuthState {
  status: fromAuth.State;
  loginPage: fromLoginPage.State;
  signupPage: fromSignupPage.State;
}

export interface State extends fromRoot.State {
  auth: AuthState;
}

export const reducers: ActionReducerMap<AuthState> = {
  status: fromAuth.reducer,
  loginPage: fromLoginPage.reducer,
  signupPage: fromSignupPage.reducer,
};
```

```
export const selectAuthState = createFeatureSelector<AuthState>
('auth');

export const selectAuthStatusState = createSelector(
  selectAuthState,
  (state: AuthState) => state.status
);

export const getLoggedIn = createSelector(
  selectAuthStatusState,
  fromAuth.getLoggedIn
);

export const getUser = createSelector(selectAuthStatusState,
fromAuth.getUser);

export const selectLoginPageState = createSelector(
  selectAuthState,
  (state: AuthState) => state.loginPage
);

export const getLoginPageError = createSelector(
  selectLoginPageState,
  fromLoginPage.getError
);

export const getLoginPageLoading = createSelector(
  selectLoginPageState,
  fromLoginPage.getLoading
);

export const getSignupPageState = createSelector(
  selectAuthState,
  (state: AuthState) => state.signupPage
);
```

```
export const getSignupPageLoading = createSelector(
  getSignupPageState,
  fromSignupPage.getLoading
);

export const getSignupPageError = createSelector(
  getSignupPageState,
  fromSignupPage.getError
);
```

The actual logic related to sign-up, login, and logout is added to the AuthEffects in Listing 9-17. For effects login$, signup$, and logout$, the corresponding method in AuthService is invoked to perform the task and dispatch actions based on the result. Because all the methods in AuthService return Promise objects, we simply create new Observables from the Promise objects and use map or mergeMap to convert the results into actions. Errors are captured using catchError and converted to actions. For the effect loginSuccess$, the method navigate of Router is used to navigate to the path / after a successful login. The @Effect({dispatch: false}) means this effect doesn't dispatch actions to the store.

Listing 9-17. AuthEffects

```
@Injectable()
export class AuthEffects {
  constructor(private action$: Actions,
              private authService: AuthService,
              private router: Router) {
  }

  @Effect()
  login$ = this.action$.pipe(
    ofType(AuthActionTypes.Login),
    map((action: Login) => action.payload),
```

```
  mergeMap((pair: EmailPasswordPair) =>
    from(this.authService.login(pair))
      .pipe(
        mergeMap(user => of<Action>(new LoginSuccess(user))),
        catchError(error => of(new LoginFailure(error)))
      )
  )
);

@Effect()
signup$ = this.action$.pipe(
  ofType(AuthActionTypes.Signup),
  map((action: Signup) => action.payload),
  mergeMap((user: NewAccount) =>
    from(this.authService.create(user))
      .pipe(
        mergeMap(createdUser => of<Action>(new
        SignupSuccess(), new LoginSuccess(createdUser))),
        catchError(error => of(new SignupFailure(error)))
      )
  )
);

@Effect({dispatch: false})
loginSuccess$ = this.action$.pipe(
  ofType(AuthActionTypes.LoginSuccess),
  tap(() => this.router.navigate(['/']))
);

@Effect()
logout$ = this.action$.pipe(
  ofType(AuthActionTypes.Logout),
  mergeMap(() =>
```

```
    from(this.authService.logout())
      .pipe(
        map(user => new LogoutSuccess()),
        catchError(error => of(new LogoutFailure(error)))
      )
    )
  );
}
```

Sign-Up Page

Now we can create the sign-up page for users to create new accounts. The
sign-up page contains inputs for name, email, and password.

Let's start from the template of the sign-up component in Listing 9-18.
In the ion-header, we use the component ion-toolbar to show the title
and an ion-button to go back to the home page. In the component, we
use two-way bindings [(ngModel)] to bind ion-inputs to properties of the
user model object. #signupForm="ngForm" sets a reference to the ngForm
object with name signupForm, so we can access its state to set the enable
status of the sign-up button.

Listing 9-18. Template of the sign-up page

```
<ion-header>
  <ion-toolbar>
    <ion-buttons slot="start">
      <ion-button routerLink="/top-stories">
        <ion-icon slot="icon-only" name="home"></ion-icon>
      </ion-button>
    </ion-buttons>
    <ion-title>Create New Account</ion-title>
  </ion-toolbar>
</ion-header>
```

```
<ion-content padding>
  <form #signupForm="ngForm">
    <ion-list>
      <ion-item>
        <ion-label position="floating">Name</ion-label>
        <ion-input name="name" type="text" [(ngModel)]="name"
        required="true"></ion-input>
      </ion-item>
      <ion-item>
        <ion-label position="floating">Email</ion-label>
        <ion-input name="email" type="email"
        [(ngModel)]="email" required="true"></ion-input>
      </ion-item>
      <ion-item>
        <ion-label position="floating">Password</ion-label>
        <ion-input name="password" type="password"
        [(ngModel)]="password" required="true"></ion-input>
      </ion-item>
      <ion-item>
        <ion-button shape="round" size="default"
        [disabled]="signupForm.invalid || (loading$ | async)"
        (click)="signUp(signupForm.value)">Create</ion-button>
      </ion-item>
      <ion-item color="danger" *ngIf="error$ | async">
        <p>{{ error$ | async }}</p>
      </ion-item>
    </ion-list>
  </form>
</ion-content>
```

The component SignupPage in Listing 9-19 is very simple. The properties name, email, and password are used to bind inputs in the template. The Observable loading$ represents the loading status, and error$ represents errors that occurred in the sign-up. These two Observables controls the status of the login button and the ion-item to display errors, respectively. When the button is clicked, the action Signup is dispatched with values in the form.

Listing 9-19. SignupPage

```
import { Component } from '@angular/core';
import { Observable } from 'rxjs/Observable';
import { select, Store } from '@ngrx/store';
import * as fromAuth from '../reducers';
import { NewAccount } from '../../models/user';
import { Signup } from '../actions/auth';

@Component({
  selector: 'app-signup',
  templateUrl: './signup.component.html',
  styleUrls: ['./signup.component.scss']
})
export class SignupComponent {
  name: string;
  email: string;
  password: string;
  loading$: Observable<Boolean>;
  error$: Observable<any>;

  constructor(private store: Store<fromAuth.State>) {
    this.loading$ = this.store.pipe(select(fromAuth.
    getSignupPageLoading));
```

```
this.error$ = this.store.pipe(select(fromAuth.
getSignupPageError));
}

signUp(value: NewAccount) {
  this.store.dispatch(new Signup(value));
}
}
```

Figure 9-7 shows the screenshot of the sign-up page.

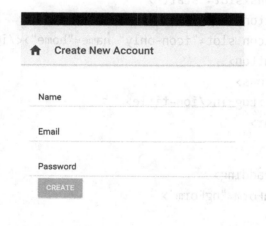

Figure 9-7. *Sign-up page*

Login Page

We create a new page for users to log in. This page contains the form for
users to input email and password, and a button to log in. It also contains a
button to show the sign-up page; see Listing 9-20.

Listing 9-20. Template of login page

```
<ion-header>
  <ion-toolbar>
    <ion-buttons slot="start">
      <ion-button routerLink="/top-stories">
        <ion-icon slot="icon-only" name="home"></ion-icon>
      </ion-button>
    </ion-buttons>
    <ion-title>Log In</ion-title>
  </ion-toolbar>
</ion-header>

<ion-content padding>
  <form #loginForm="ngForm">
    <ion-list>
      <ion-item>
        <ion-label position="floating">Email</ion-label>
        <ion-input name="email" type="email"
        [(ngModel)]="email" required="true"></ion-input>
      </ion-item>
      <ion-item>
        <ion-label position="floating">Password</ion-label>
        <ion-input name="password" type="password"
        [(ngModel)]="password" required="true"></ion-input>
      </ion-item>
```

```
    <ion-item>
      <ion-button shape="round" size="default"
      [disabled]="loginForm.invalid || (loading$ | async)"
      (click)="login(loginForm.value)">Log In</ion-button>
    </ion-item>
    <ion-item color="danger" *ngIf="error$ | async">
      <p>{{ error$ | async }}</p>
    </ion-item>
    <ion-item routerLink="/signup">
        <ion-icon name="person-add" slot="start"></ion-icon>
        Sign Up
    </ion-item>
  </ion-list>
  </form>
</ion-content>
```

The LoginPage in Listing 9-21 is similar to the SignupPage in Listing 9-19.
It has the properties email and password to bind the inputs in the page.
It also has Observables loading$ and error$ to control the components
status. When the button is clicked, the action Login is dispatched.

Listing 9-21. LoginPage

```
import { Component } from '@angular/core';
import * as fromAuth from '../reducers';
import { select, Store } from '@ngrx/store';
import { Observable } from 'rxjs/Observable';
import { EmailPasswordPair } from '../../models/user';
import { Login } from '../actions/auth';
```

```
@Component({
  selector: 'app-login',
  templateUrl: './login.component.html',
  styleUrls: ['./login.component.scss']
})
export class LoginComponent {
  email: string;
  password: string;
  loading$: Observable<Boolean>;
  error$: Observable<any>;

  constructor(private store: Store<fromAuth.State>) {
    this.loading$ = this.store.pipe(select(fromAuth.
    getLoginPageLoading));
    this.error$ = this.store.pipe(select(fromAuth.
    getLoginPageError));
  }

  login(value: EmailPasswordPair) {
    this.store.dispatch(new Login(value));
  }
}
```

Update User's Name

In the sign-up page, we asked the user to input both name and email, but when the user is logged in using email, the name was not displayed. This is because we didn't save the user's name after the sign-up. Firebase also stores the user's basic profile information, including the user's display name and the profile photo URL. We need to update the user's profile to set the display name after sign-up. In Listing 9-22, the method createUserAndRetrieveDataWithEmailAndPassword() creates a new user and returns a `Promise` with the new `firebase.auth.UserCredential` object. The property user of `firebase.auth.UserCredential` is the `firebase.User` object. Then the method `updateProfile()` of the `firebase.User` object is invoked to update the user's display name.

Listing 9-22. Update user name

```
@Injectable()
export class AuthService {

  constructor(private afAuth: AngularFireAuth) { }

  create(user: NewAccount): Promise<firebase.User> {
    return this.afAuth.auth.createUserAndRetrieveDataWithEmail
    AndPassword(user.email, user.password)
      .then(result => result.user.updateProfile({
        displayName: user.name,
        photoURL: null,
      }).then(() => result.user));
  }
}
```

Third-Party Login

It's tedious for users to register different accounts for various online services or apps. Many services or apps allow users to log in using existing accounts of popular third-party services, for example, Twitter or Facebook. Apart from the email/password authentication, Firebase provides support for common third-party providers, including Google, Twitter, Facebook, and GitHub. It's very easy to add support for logging in using third-party providers.

Before we can use those third-party service providers, we need to enable them in the Firebase console. In the **Sign-in method** tab of the **Authentication** section, we can enable all supported sign-in providers.

- Google sign-in can be enabled without additional settings.

- For Twitter sign-in, we need to register the app on Twitter and get the API key and secret for the app. When enabling Twitter sign-in, we need to fill the API key and secret. After it's enabled, we set `https://<auth_domain>/__/auth/handler` as the Callback URL for the Twitter app.

- Facebook sign-in is similar to Twitter sign-in; we also need to register the app on Facebook to get the app ID and secret to enable it. After enabling it, we also need to set the OAuth redirect URI to the same one as Twitter app's Callback URL.

- GitHub sign-in is also very similar. We first register the app on GitHub to get the client id and secret, then enable it in the Firebase console, and finally set the Authorization callback URL of the GitHub app.

Integrating Firebase third-party login with web apps is very easy. With the method `signInWithPopup`, a browser window is popped up to the provider's login page and asks the user to authorize the access. After the access is granted, the popup window is closed, and we can get the authentication information from the result. When we do the testing on browsers, this popup authentication method works fine. But when we try to run the app on emulators or devices, we find it failed with error code `auth/operation-not-supported-in-this-environment`. We need an additional configuration for Firebase authentication to run on the Cordova platform.

We first need to add an Android app and iOS app for the project in the Firebase console. Then we need to enable **Dynamic Links** in the Firebase console. If **Dynamic Links** is enabled, you should see the **Dynamic Link Domain** like xyz.app.goo.gl. The following Cordova plugins need to be installed for the project. Listing 9-23 shows the required plugins. For the last plugin cordova-plugin-customurlscheme, the variable URL_SCHEME should be the package ID of your app.

Listing 9-23. Required Cordova plugins

```
cordova plugin add cordova-plugin-buildinfo --save
cordova plugin add https://github.com/walteram/cordova-
universal-links-plugin.git --save
cordova plugin add cordova-plugin-browsertab --save
cordova plugin add cordova-plugin-inappbrowser --save
cordova plugin add cordova-plugin-customurlscheme --variable \
    URL_SCHEME=io.vividcode.ionic4.hnc --save
```

The configuration in Listing 9-24 needs to be added to the config.xml of Cordova. <DYNAMIC_LINK_DOMAIN> and <AUTH_DOMAIN> should be replaced with values for your app.

Listing 9-24. Cordova configurations

```
<universal-links>
  <host name="<DYNAMIC_LINK_DOMAIN>.app.goo.gl" scheme="https" />
  <host name="<AUTH_DOMAIN>.firebaseapp.com" scheme="https">
    <path url="/__/auth/callback" />
  </host>
</universal-links>
```

For Android applications, the following configuration should also be added to config.xml.

```
<preference name="AndroidLaunchMode" value="singleTask" />
```

After these configurations, we can integrate Firebase authentication in Cordova. Listing 9-25 shows the updated AuthService with the new method logInWithProvider. The type LoginProvider specifies the supported third-party service providers. The function createProvider creates the Firebase provider objects for login. In the method logInWithProvider, we use the method signInWithRedirect to log in using the provider. If the login is successful, the method getRedirectResult returns the firebase.auth.UserCredential object to get the authenticated user.

Listing 9-25. Log in with providers

```
export type LoginProvider = 'google' | 'facebook' | 'twitter' |
'github';

export const createProvider = (provider: LoginProvider) => {
  switch (provider) {
    case 'google': return new firebase.auth.GoogleAuthProvider();
    case 'facebook': return new firebase.auth.Facebook
    AuthProvider();
    case 'twitter': return new firebase.auth.Twitter
    AuthProvider();
    case 'github': return new firebase.auth.GithubAuthProvider();
  }
};

@Injectable()
export class AuthService {

  constructor(private afAuth: AngularFireAuth) { }

  logInWithProvider(provider: LoginProvider): Promise<firebase.
  User> {
```

```
    return this.afAuth.auth.signInWithRedirect(createProvider(p
    rovider))
      .then(() => firebase.auth().getRedirectResult())
      .then(result => result.user);
  }
}
```

We also need to add a new action for login with third-party providers and a new effect to handle the action. Listing 9-26 shows the updated template of the login page to include icons for different providers. The function `loginWithProvider` dispatches the action to log in with providers.

Listing 9-26. Updated login page

```
<ion-item>
  <ion-buttons>
    <ion-button (click)="loginWithProvider('google')"><ion-icon
    slot="icon-only" name="logo-googleplus"></ion-icon></ion-
    button>
    <ion-button (click)="loginWithProvider('facebook')">
    <ion-icon slot="icon-only" name="logo-facebook"></ion-icon>
    </ion-button>
    <ion-button (click)="loginWithProvider('twitter')">
    <ion-icon slot="icon-only" name="logo-twitter"></ion-icon>
    </ion-button>
    <ion-button (click)="loginWithProvider('github')">
    <ion-icon slot="icon-only" name="logo-github"></ion-icon>
    </ion-button>
  </ion-buttons>
</ion-item>
```

Listing 9-27 shows the new effect to handle the new action for login with third-party providers.

Listing 9-27. Effect to handle action for login with third-party providers

```
@Effect()
loginWithProvider$ = this.action$.pipe(
  ofType(AuthActionTypes.LoginWithProvider),
  map((action: LoginWithProvider) => action.payload),
  mergeMap((provider: LoginProvider) =>
    from(this.authService.logInWithProvider(provider))
      .pipe(
        mergeMap(user => of<Action>(new LoginSuccess(user),
        new favoritesActions.Load())),
        catchError(error => of(new LoginFailure(error)))
      )
  )
);
```

Figure 9-8 shows the screenshot of the final login page.

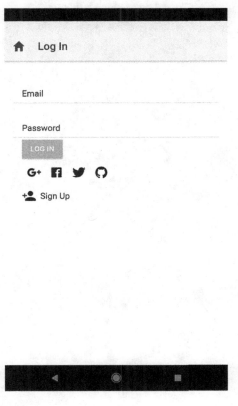

Figure 9-8. *Login page*

Summary

In this chapter, we discussed how to add user management to the example app with Firebase. For email/password login, we used Ionic 4 forms for users to sign up and log in. For third-party login, we used Cordova plugins to support login with service providers. In the next chapter, we'll implement the user story to manage users' favorites.

CHAPTER 10

Manage Favorites

After adding user management, we can now move to the next user story
that allows users to add stories to their favorites. Favorites data is stored
in the Firebase Cloud Firestore. We'll use AngularFire2 to interact with
Firestore. The favorites page is only accessible to authenticated users,
and we'll use authentication guard to protect this page. After reading this
chapter, you should know how to interact with Firebase Cloud Firestore.

Favorites Service

Favorites data is stored in the Firebase Cloud Firestore. Even though Cloud
Firestore is still in beta at the time of writing, it's still recommended for
you to give it a try. If you have used MongoDB or other document-oriented
databases before, you may find the concepts in Cloud Firestore are quite
familiar. Cloud Firestore stores data in documents, while documents are
stored in collections. A document is a lightweight record that contains
fields, which map to values. Collections can be nested to create a
hierarchical data structure.

The favorites data is stored in the collection `favorites`. Each
document in this collection has the ID matching a user's ID. These user
documents have a subcollection `items` that contains documents for
favorite items of the current user. Each document of the favorite items
collection has the ID matching the item's ID and a field `timestamp`

© Fu Cheng 2018
F. Cheng, *Build Mobile Apps with Ionic 4 and Firebase*,
https://doi.org/10.1007/978-1-4842-3775-5_10

representing the time when the favorite item is added. The `timestamp` is used to sort the favorite items to make sure newly added items appear first in the list. The path of a favorite item looks like `/favorites/<user_id>/items/<item_id>`.

AngularFire2 already has support for Cloud Firestore. We only need to import the module `AngularFirestoreModule`, then we can use the injected service `AngularFirestore` to interact with Cloud Firestore.

We start from the `FavoritesService` in Listing 10-1. The method `collection` returns the items collection for a user with a given `userId`. The method `add` adds a new item to the collection with a current timestamp. The method `remove` deletes an item from the collection. The method `list` returns the list of favorite items in the collection. `orderBy('timestamp', 'desc')` specifies that the items are sorted in descending order by timestamp.

Listing 10-1. FavoritesService

```
import { Injectable } from '@angular/core';
import { AngularFirestore } from '@angular/fire/firestore';
import { Favorite } from '../../models/favorite';

@Injectable()
export class FavoritesService {

  constructor(private afStore: AngularFirestore) {}

  add(userId: string, itemId: number): Promise<Favorite> {
    const timestamp = new Date().getTime();
    return this.collection(userId)
      .doc(`${itemId}`)
      .set({
        timestamp,
```

```
    }).then(() => ({
      itemId,
      timestamp,
    }));
}

remove(userId: string, itemId: number): Promise<void> {
  return this.collection(userId)
    .doc(`${itemId}`)
    .delete();
}

list(userId: string): Promise<Favorite[]> {
  return this.collection(userId)
    .orderBy('timestamp', 'desc')
    .get().then(snapshot => snapshot.docs.map(doc => ({
      itemId: parseInt(doc.id, 10),
      timestamp: doc.data()['timestamp'],
    })));
}

  private collection(userId: string) {
    return this.afStore.firestore.collection('favorites')
      .doc(userId)
      .collection('items');
  }
}
```

Favorite in Listing 10-2 is the type to describe a favorite item. It contains two properties: itemId and timestamp.

Listing 10-2. Favorite

```
export interface Favorite {
  itemId: number;
  timestamp: number;
}
```

State Management

NgRx is used to manage the state related to favorites. Listing 10-3 shows the actions that can change state. The action Load means loading the current user's favorite items. The action Add means adding an item to the favorite. The action Remove means removing an item from the favorite. These three actions all have two other actions to represent the results. The payload of these actions is straightforward.

Listing 10-3. Actions

```
import { Action } from '@ngrx/store';
import { Favorite } from '../../models/favorite';

export enum FavoritesActionTypes {
  Load = '[Favorites] Load',
  LoadSuccess = '[Favorites] Load Success',
  LoadFailure = '[Favorites] Load Failure',
  Add = '[Favorites] Add',
  AddSuccess = '[Favorites] Add Success',
  AddFailure = '[Favorites] Add Failure',
  Remove = '[Favorites] Remove',
  RemoveSuccess = '[Favorites] Remove Success',
  RemoveFailure = '[Favorites] Remove Failure',dt2fr56uk
}
```

```
export class Load implements Action {
  readonly type = FavoritesActionTypes.Load;
}

export class LoadSuccess implements Action {
  readonly type = FavoritesActionTypes.LoadSuccess;

  constructor(public payload: Favorite[]) {}
}

export class LoadFailure implements Action {
  readonly type = FavoritesActionTypes.LoadFailure;

  constructor(public payload: any) {}
}

export class Add implements Action {
  readonly type = FavoritesActionTypes.Add;

  constructor(public payload: number) {}
}

export class AddSuccess implements Action {
  readonly type = FavoritesActionTypes.AddSuccess;

  constructor(public payload: Favorite) {}
}

export class AddFailure implements Action {
  readonly type = FavoritesActionTypes.AddFailure;

  constructor(public payload: number) {}
}
```

```
export class Remove implements Action {
  readonly type = FavoritesActionTypes.Remove;

  constructor(public payload: number) {}
}

export class RemoveSuccess implements Action {
  readonly type = FavoritesActionTypes.RemoveSuccess;

  constructor(public payload: number) {}
}

export class RemoveFailure implements Action {
  readonly type = FavoritesActionTypes.RemoveFailure;

  constructor(public payload: number) {}
}

export type FavoritesActions = Load | LoadSuccess | LoadFailure
  | Add | AddSuccess | AddFailure
  | Remove | RemoveSuccess | RemoveFailure;
```

The state, reducer function, and selectors are shown in Listing 10-4. The interface FavoritesItem describes the favorite items. The property loading specifies whether the action to modify it is still in progress. For example, when removing a favorite item, the property loading is updated to true. This property is useful for UI to display the loading indicators. The state for favorites also uses EntityState from @ngrx/entity, just like the feature items. When creating the EntityAdapter, we provide the sortComparer to sort by the timestamp.

In the reducer function, we use different functions of the adapter to update the state. For the action LoadSuccess, loaded favorite items are added to the entities store; for the actions Add and Remove, the property loading is set to true; for the action AddSuccess, the added favorite item is saved and the property loading is set to false; for the action

RemoveFailure, only the property loading is set to false; for the actions RemoveSuccess and AddFailure, the favorite item is removed.

The function inFavorite returns a selector to check whether an item is in the favorite. The function getLoading returns a selector to check whether an item in in the loading status. The selector getFavoriteItems returns all favorite items.

Listing 10-4. State, reducer function, and selectors

```
import { FavoritesActions, FavoritesActionTypes } from
'../actions/favorites';
import { createEntityAdapter, EntityAdapter, EntityState } from
'@ngrx/entity';
import { createFeatureSelector, createSelector } from
'@ngrx/store';
import * as fromAuth from '../../auth/reducers';
import { getItemEntities } from '../../reducers/items';
import { FavoritesService } from '../services/favorites.
service';

export interface FavoritesItem {
  itemId: number;
  timestamp?: number;
  loading: boolean;
}

export const adapter: EntityAdapter<FavoritesItem> =
createEntityAdapter<FavoritesItem>({
  selectId: (item: FavoritesItem) => item.itemId,
  sortComparer: (item1, item2) => item2.timestamp - item1.
  timestamp,
});
```

```
export type State = EntityState<FavoritesItem>;

export interface FavoritesState {
  auth: fromAuth.State;
  favorites: State;
}

export const initialState: State = adapter.getInitialState();

export function reducer(state = initialState, action:
FavoritesActions) {
  switch (action.type) {
    case FavoritesActionTypes.LoadSuccess: {
      return adapter.upsertMany(action.payload.map(item => ({
        ...item,
        loading: false,
      })), state);
    }

    case FavoritesActionTypes.Add: {
      return adapter.addOne({
        itemId: action.payload,
        loading: true,
      }, state);
    }

    case FavoritesActionTypes.Remove: {
      return adapter.updateOne({
        id: action.payload,
        changes: {
          loading: true,
        },
      }, state);
    }
```

```
    case FavoritesActionTypes.AddSuccess:
      const favorite = action.payload;
      return adapter.updateOne({
        id: favorite.itemId,
        changes: {
          ...favorite,
          loading: false,
        },
      }, state);

    case FavoritesActionTypes.RemoveFailure: {
      return adapter.updateOne({
        id: action.payload,
        changes: {
          loading: false,
        },
      }, state);
    }

    case FavoritesActionTypes.RemoveSuccess:
    case FavoritesActionTypes.AddFailure: {
      return adapter.removeOne(action.payload, state);
    }

    default: {
      return state;
    }
  }
}

export const getFavoritesState = createFeatureSelector<State>
('favorites');
```

```
export const {
  selectEntities: selectFavoriteEntities,
  selectIds: selectFavorites,
} = adapter.getSelectors(getFavoritesState);

export const inFavorite = (itemId) => createSelector(
  selectFavoriteEntities,
  entities => entities[itemId] && !entities[itemId].loading
);

export const getLoading = (itemId) => createSelector(
  selectFavoriteEntities,
  entities => entities[itemId] && entities[itemId].loading
);

export const getFavoriteItems = createSelector(
  selectFavorites,
  selectFavoriteEntities,
  getItemEntities,
  (ids: number[], favorites, entities) =>
    ids.filter(id => favorites[id] && !favorites[id].loading)
      .map(id => entities[id])
);
```

The FavoritesEffects in Listing 10-5 uses FavoritesService to perform different actions. Because favorites data is stored for each user, we need to access the store to get the information of the current logged-in user. The effect load$ uses the method list to load all favorite items. Here we also need to dispatch an action itemsActions.Load to trigger the loading of those items. The effects add$ and remove$ use corresponding methods of FavoritesService and dispatch actions based on the results.

Listing 10-5. FavoritesEffects

```
@Injectable()
export class FavoritesEffects {
  constructor(private action$: Actions,
              private store: Store<fromAuth.State>,
              private favoritesService: FavoritesService) {
  }

  @Effect()
  load$ = this.action$.pipe(
    ofType(FavoritesActionTypes.Load),
    withLatestFrom(this.store),
    mergeMap(([action, state]) => {
      const {auth: {status: {user}}} = state;
      return from(this.favoritesService.list(user.uid)).pipe(
        mergeMap(favorites => of<Action>(
          new LoadSuccess(favorites),
          new itemsActions.Load(favorites.map(f => f.itemId))
        ))
      );
    })
  );

  @Effect()
  add$ = this.action$.pipe(
    ofType(FavoritesActionTypes.Add),
    withLatestFrom(this.store),
    mergeMap(([action, state]) => {
      const {auth: {status: {user}}} = state;
      const itemId = (action as Add).payload;
```

```
    return from(this.favoritesService.add(user.uid, itemId)).
    pipe(
      map(result => new AddSuccess(result)),
      catchError((error) => of(new AddFailure(itemId)))
    );
  })
);

@Effect()
remove$ = this.action$.pipe(
  ofType(FavoritesActionTypes.Remove),
  withLatestFrom(this.store),
  mergeMap(([action, state]) => {
    const {auth: {status: {user}}} = state;
    const itemId = (action as Remove).payload;
    return from(this.favoritesService.remove(user.uid,
    itemId)).pipe(
      map(() => new RemoveSuccess(itemId)),
      catchError((error) => of(new RemoveFailure(itemId)))
    );
  })
);
}
```

Favorite Toggle

In the top stories page, we need to add a control for each item to allow a user to add a story to the favorite or remove a story from the favorite. The component FavoriteToggleComponent in Listing 10-6 displays different icons based on the item's status in the favorites. The input property itemId is the id of the item to check. The property inFavorite specifies whether the item is in the favorite. The property loading specifies whether the action is still in progress. The EventEmitters toAdd and toRemove emit the item id when the user clicks the icon to toggle the favorite status.

Listing 10-6. FavoriteToggleComponent

```
import { Component, EventEmitter, Input, OnInit, Output } from
'@angular/core';

@Component({
  selector: 'app-favorite-toggle',
  templateUrl: './favorite-toggle.component.html',
  styleUrls: ['./favorite-toggle.component.scss']
})
export class FavoriteToggleComponent {
  @Input() itemId: number;
  @Input() inFavorite: boolean;
  @Input() loading: boolean;
  @Output() toAdd = new EventEmitter<number>();
  @Output() toRemove = new EventEmitter<number>();

  constructor() { }

  add() {
    this.toAdd.emit(this.itemId);
  }

  remove() {
    this.toRemove.emit(this.itemId);
  }
}
```

Listing 10-7 shows the template of the component FavoriteToggleComponent. The component displays different elements based on the values of input properties loading and inFavorite.

Listing 10-7. Template of FavoriteToggleComponent

```
<span>
  <ion-spinner *ngIf="loading"></ion-spinner>
  <ion-button fill="clear" *ngIf="!loading && inFavorite"
(click)="remove()">
    <ion-icon slot="icon-only" name="heart" color="danger">
    </ion-icon>
  </ion-button>
  <ion-button fill="clear" class="btnLike" *ngIf="!loading &&
  !inFavorite" (click)="add()">
    <ion-icon slot="icon-only" name="heart-empty"
    color="danger"></ion-icon>
  </ion-button>
</span>
```

The component FavoriteToggleComponent is very simple as it only has plain input properties. The actual logic to deal with the store is encapsulated in the component FavoriteToggleContainerComponent in Listing 10-8. FavoriteToggleContainerComponent only has one input property itemId. isLoggedIn$ is the observable of the user's login status using the selector fromAuth.getLoggedIn; inFavorite$ is the observable of the item's favorite status using the function fromFavorites.inFavorite to create the selector; loading$ is the observable of the item's loading status using the function fromFavorites.getLoading to create the selector. The methods add and remove dispatch actions with the item's id.

Listing 10-8. FavoriteToggleContainerComponent

```
import { Component, Input, OnInit } from '@angular/core';
import * as fromFavorites from '../../reducers';
import * as fromAuth from '../../../auth/reducers';
import { select, Store } from '@ngrx/store';
```

```
import { Observable } from 'rxjs/Observable';
import { Add, Remove } from '../../actions/favorites';

@Component({
  selector: 'app-favorite-toggle-container',
  templateUrl: './favorite-toggle-container.component.html',
  styleUrls: ['./favorite-toggle-container.component.scss']
})
export class FavoriteToggleContainerComponent implements OnInit {
  @Input() itemId: number;
  isLoggedIn$: Observable<boolean>;
  inFavorite$: Observable<boolean>;
  loading$: Observable<boolean>;

  constructor(private store: Store<fromFavorites.State>) {}

  ngOnInit() {
    this.isLoggedIn$ = this.store.pipe(select(fromAuth.
    getLoggedIn));
    this.inFavorite$ = this.store.pipe(select(fromFavorites.
    inFavorite(this.itemId)));
    this.loading$ = this.store.pipe(select(fromFavorites.
    getLoading(this.itemId)));
  }

  add() {
    this.store.dispatch(new Add(this.itemId));
  }

  remove() {
    this.store.dispatch(new Remove(this.itemId));
  }
}
```

Listing 10-9 shows the template of the component FavoriteToggleComponent. We simply use the pipe async to extract the values as properties for FavoriteToggleComponent.

Listing 10-9. Template of FavoriteToggleContainerComponent

```
<app-favorite-toggle *ngIf="isLoggedIn$ | async"
                     [itemId]="itemId"
                     [inFavorite]="inFavorite$ | async"
                     [loading]="loading$ | async"
                     (toAdd)="add()"
                     (toRemove)="remove()"></app-favorite-
                     toggle>
```

Favorites Page

The page to show favorite items is very simple. In Listing 10-10, we use the selector fromFavorites.getFavoriteItems to get all favorite items. In the method ngOnInit, we dispatch the action Load to load all favorite items.

Listing 10-10. Favorites page

```
@Component({
  selector: 'app-favorites-list',
  changeDetection: ChangeDetectionStrategy.OnPush,
  templateUrl: './favorites-list.component.html',
  styleUrls: ['./favorites-list.component.scss']
})
export class FavoritesListComponent implements OnInit {
  items$: Observable<Items>;
```

```
constructor(private store: Store<fromFavorites.State>) {
  this.items$ = store.pipe(select(fromFavorites.
  getFavoriteItems));
}

ngOnInit() {
  this.store.dispatch(new Load());
}
}
```

The template of the favorites page is also very simple; see Listing 10-11.

Listing 10-11. Template of favorites page

```html
<ion-header>
  <ion-toolbar>
    <ion-buttons slot="start">
      <ion-button routerLink="/top-stories">
        <ion-icon slot="icon-only" name="home"></ion-icon>
      </ion-button>
    </ion-buttons>
    <ion-title>Favorites</ion-title>
  </ion-toolbar>
</ion-header>
<ion-content padding>
  <app-items [items]="items$ | async"></app-items>
</ion-content>
```

The template of ItemComponent needs to be updated to include the component FavoriteToggleContainerComponent, see below.

```html
<app-favorite-toggle-container [itemId]="item.id">
</app-favorite-toggle-container>
```

Authentication Guards

The favorites page can only work when the user is logged in, so we can get the user id to retrieve the favorites data. If the user accesses the favorites page directly, we should redirect to the login page. This check can be done using authentication guards in Angular Router.

Listing 10-12 shows the AuthGuard to check for user login. AuthGuard implements the interface CanActivate from Angular Router. In the method canActivate, we use the selector fromAuth.getLoggedIn to get the login state. If the user is not logged in, we dispatch an action authActions. LoginRedirect to redirect the user to the login page.

Listing 10-12. AuthGuard

```
import { Injectable } from '@angular/core';
import { CanActivate } from '@angular/router';
import { Store, select } from '@ngrx/store';
import { Observable } from 'rxjs';
import { map, take } from 'rxjs/operators';
import * as authActions from '../actions/auth';
import * as fromAuth from '../reducers';

@Injectable()
export class AuthGuard implements CanActivate {
  constructor(private store: Store<fromAuth.State>) {}

  canActivate(): Observable<boolean> {
    return this.store.pipe(
      select(fromAuth.getLoggedIn),
      map(isAuthed => {
        if (!isAuthed) {
          this.store.dispatch(new authActions.LoginRedirect());
          return false;
        }
```

```
      return true;
    }),
    take(1)
  );
}
}
```

The action `LoginRedirect` is handled in the `AuthEffects`; see Listing 10-13. We use the method navigate of Router to navigate to the URL `/login`.

Listing 10-13. Handle login redirects

```
@Effect({ dispatch: false })
loginRedirect$ = this.action$.pipe(
  ofType(AuthActionTypes.LoginRedirect, AuthActionTypes.
  Logout),
  tap(() => {
    this.router.navigate(['/login']);
  })
);
```

In the root routing module, we use the property `canActivate` to specify the `AuthGuard` to protect this routing; see Listing 10-14.

Listing 10-14. Use AuthGuard

```
{ path: 'favorites',
  loadChildren: 'app/favorites-list/favorites-list.
  module#FavoritesListModule',
  canActivate: [AuthGuard]
}
```

Integration with Authentication

After finishing the state management of favorites data, we still need to deal with the integration with authentication. When a user is logged in, we need to load the favorites data. This is done by dispatching the action Load in effect login$ of AuthEffects. When a user is logged out, we need to clear the favorites data. This is done by adding a new action Clear with the reducer function to clear all entities in the favorites; see the updated reducer function in Listing 10-15. The action Clear is dispatched in the effect logout$ of AuthEffects.

Listing 10-15. Remove all favorites data

```
export function reducer(state = initialState, action:
FavoritesActions) {
  switch (action.type) {
    case FavoritesActionTypes.Clear: {
      return adapter.removeAll(state);
    }
  }
}
```

Figure 10-1 shows the screenshot of the top stories page with the icon for favorites.

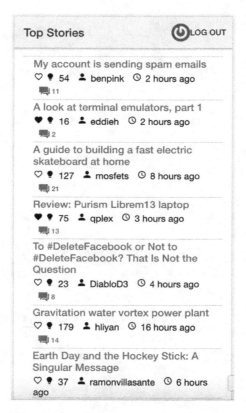

Figure 10-1. *Top stories page*

Summary

In this chapter, we implemented the user story to manage favorites, including adding stories into the favorites and removing stories from the favorites. Favorites data is stored in the Firebase Cloud Firestore. We implemented the service to interact with Firebase. We also created the page to list stories in the favorites. Since the favorites feature is only enabled when the user is logged in, we also discussed the integration with the authentication in this chapter. In the next chapter, we'll implement the user story to share stories.

CHAPTER 11

Share Stories

Now we move to the last user story on the list that allows users to share stories. In this chapter, we'll discuss the Ionic 4 card layout and grid layout. The Cordova Social Sharing plugin is used to share stories to social network services.

Card Layout

To allow users to share stories, we need to add a new button. If we add this button to the current UI, then all these UI components cannot fit into one line. We need a new layout for all those components. A good choice is the card layout.

Cards are created using the component `ion-card`. A card can have a header and content that can be created using `ion-card-header` and `ion-card-content`, respectively. Listing 11-1 shows a simple card with a header and content.

Listing 11-1. A simple card

```
<ion-card>
  <ion-card-header>
    Header
  </ion-card-header>
```

© Fu Cheng 2018
F. Cheng, *Build Mobile Apps with Ionic 4 and Firebase*,
https://doi.org/10.1007/978-1-4842-3775-5_11

```
<ion-card-content>
  Card content
</ion-card-content>
</ion-card>
```

In the `ion-card-content`, we can include different kinds of components. The component `ion-card-title` can be used to add title text to the content. The component `ion-card-subtitle` adds a subtitle to the content. Listing 11-2 shows a card with an image and a title.

Listing 11-2. A complex card

```
<ion-card>
  <ion-card-content>
    <img src="http://placehold.it/600x100?text=Item1">
    <ion-card-title>Item 1</ion-card-title>
    <ion-card-subtitle>Another item</ion-card-subtitle>
    <p>
      This is item 1.
    </p>
  </ion-card-content>
</ion-card>
```

See Figure 11-1 for the screenshot of the card in Listing 11-2.

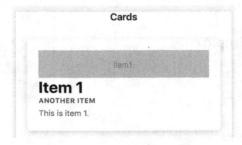

Figure 11-1. Card

After using the card layout, each item in the list is rendered as a card.

348

Grid Layout

In the item card, we need to display two or three buttons. These buttons should take up the same horizontal space of the line. This layout requirement can be easily archived by using the grid layout. The grid layout is implemented using the CSS3 flexbox layout (`https://css-tricks.com/snippets/css/a-guide-to-flexbox/`).

The grid layout uses three components: `ion-grid`, `ion-row`, and `ion-col`. `ion-grid` represents the grid itself, `ion-row` represents a row in the grid, `ion-col` represents a column in a row. Rows take up the full horizontal space in the grid and flow from top to bottom. Horizontal space of a row is distributed evenly across all columns in the row. Grid layout is based on a 12-column layout. We can also specify the width for each column using attributes from `col-1` to `col-12`. The number after `col-` is the number of columns it takes in the 12-column layout, for example, `col-3` means it takes 3/12 of the whole width. By default, columns in a row flow from the left to the right and are placed next to each. We can use the property `offset-*` to specify the offset from the left side. We can the same pattern as in `col-*` to specify the offset, for example, `offset-3` and `offset-6`. Columns can also be reordered using attributes `push-*` and `pull-*`. The attributes `push-*` and `pull-*` adjust the left and right of the columns, respectively. The difference between `offset-*` and `push-*` and `pull-*` is that `offset-*` changes the margin of columns, while `push-*` and `pull-*` change the CSS properties `left` and `right`, respectively.

For the alignment of rows and columns, we can add attributes like `align-items-start`, `align-self-start`, and `justify-content-start` to `ion-row` and `ion-col`. These attribute names are derived from flexbox CSS properties and values. For example, `align-items-start` means using `start` as the value of the CSS property `align-items`.

Listing 11-3 shows an example of using the grid layout to create the basic UI of a calculator.

Listing 11-3. Grid layout

```
<ion-grid>
  <ion-row>
    <ion-col><ion-button expand="full">1</ion-button></ion-col>
    <ion-col><ion-button expand="full">2</ion-button></ion-col>
    <ion-col><ion-button expand="full">3</ion-button></ion-col>
  </ion-row>
  <ion-row>
    <ion-col><ion-button expand="full">4</ion-button></ion-col>
    <ion-col><ion-button expand="full">5</ion-button></ion-col>
    <ion-col><ion-button expand="full">6</ion-button></ion-col>
  </ion-row>
  <ion-row>
    <ion-col><ion-button expand="full">7</ion-button></ion-col>
    <ion-col><ion-button expand="full">8</ion-button></ion-col>
    <ion-col><ion-button expand="full">9</ion-button></ion-col>
  </ion-row>
  <ion-row>
    <ion-col col-4><ion-button expand="full">0</ion-button>
    </ion-col>
    <ion-col col-8><ion-button expand="full"
    color="secondary">=</ion-button></ion-col>
  </ion-row>
</ion-grid>
```

Figure 11-2 shows the screenshot of Listing 11-3.

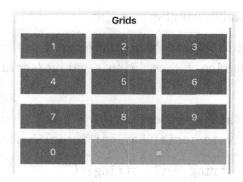

Figure 11-2. *A calculator UI using grid layout*

Sharing

We can use the Cordova plugin Social Sharing (https://github.com/ EddyVerbruggen/SocialSharing-PhoneGap-Plugin) to share stories via different channels. We need to install the plugin cordova-plugin-x-socialsharing using Cordova CLI and install the related Ionic Native package @ionic-native/social-sharing.

```
$ cordova plugin add cordova-plugin-x-socialsharing --save
$ npm i @ionic-native/social-sharing
```

We create the new SocialSharingService for the social sharing functionality; see Listing 11-4. It has a single method share(message: string, url: string) with the message for the sharing and the URL of the shared item. It simply calls the method share() from the SocialSharing object of the Ionic Native wrapper of this Cordova plugin. It pops up the platform-specific sharing sheet to do the sharing.

Listing 11-4. SocialSharingService

```
import { Injectable } from '@angular/core';
import { SocialSharing } from '@ionic-native/social-sharing/ngx';

@Injectable()
export class SocialSharingService {
  constructor(private socialSharing: SocialSharing) {}

  share(message: string, url: string) {
    this.socialSharing.share(message, null, null, url);
  }
}
```

Then we update the template of ItemComponent to include a new button to do the sharing; see Listing 11-5. We pass the item's title as the message to display. In the card for each item, we use three rows in the grid. The first row contains the item's title. The second row contains the item's score, author, and published time. The last row contains buttons for toggling favorites, sharing, and viewing comments.

Listing 11-5. Updated ItemComponent

```
<ion-card *ngIf="item">
  <ion-grid>
    <ion-row (click)="openPage(item.url)">
      <ion-col>
        <h2 class="title">{{ item.title }}</h2>
      </ion-col>
    </ion-row>
    <ion-row>
      <ion-col>
        <app-favorite-toggle-container [itemId]="item.id">
        </app-favorite-toggle-container>
      </ion-col>
```

```
    <ion-col>
      <ion-button [fill]="'clear'" (click)="share()">
        <ion-icon slot="icon-only" name="share"></ion-icon>
      </ion-button>
    </ion-col>
    <ion-col>
      <ion-button *ngIf="item.kids" [fill]="'clear'"
      [routerLink]="['/comments', item.id]">
        <ion-icon slot="icon-only" name="chatboxes">
        </ion-icon>
        {{ item.kids.length }}
      </ion-button>
    </ion-col>
  </ion-row>
  </ion-grid>
</ion-card>
<ion-card *ngIf="!item">
  <ion-card-header>Loading...</ion-card-header>
</ion-card>
```

Use SocialSharing Plugin

The method share(message, subject, file, url) of SocialSharing
actually takes four arguments:

- message - The message to share with.

- subject - The subject of the sharing.

- file - URL or local path to files or images. Can be an
  array for sharing multiple files or images.

- url - The URL to share.

The method share() uses the sharing sheet to let the user choose the sharing channels. We can also use other methods to directly share with specific social providers.

- shareViaTwitter(message, image, url) - Share to Twitter.

- shareViaFacebook(message, image, url) - Share to Facebook.

- shareViaInstagram(message, image) - Share to Instagram.

- shareViaWhatsApp(message, image, url) - Share to WhatsApp.

- shareViaSMS(message, phoneNumber) - Share via SMS.

- shareViaEmail(message, subject, to, cc, bcc, files) - Share via emails.

Or we can use the generic method shareVia(appName, message, subject, image, url) to share via any app. Because the sharing features depend on the native apps installed on a user's device, it's better to check whether the sharing feature is available first. The method canShareVia(appName, message, subject, image, url) does the check for a given app. For sharing via emails, the specific method canShareViaEmail() should be used for the check.

Figure 11-3 shows the final result of the top stories page.

Figure 11-3. *Final result of top stories page*

Figure 11-4 shows the screenshot of the sharing sheet. The available sharing features depend on the underlying platform. Since the emulator running the app doesn't install other apps, the number of sharing features is limited.

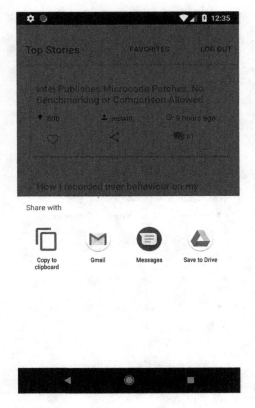

Figure 11-4. Sharing sheet

Summary

In this chapter, we implemented the user story to share Hacker News stories to social networking services. Since we need to add a new button for each story in the list to trigger the sharing action, we also used Ionic 4 card and grid layout to make the UI look better. In the next chapter, we'll discuss some common Ionic 4 components that are not used in the example app.

CHAPTER 12

Common Components

When implementing those user stories for the app, we already use many Ionic built-in components. There are still some Ionic components that are useful but not included in the app. We are going to discuss several important components, including action sheet, popover, slides, tabs, modal, and menu. After reading this chapter, you should know how to use these components.

Action Sheet

An action sheet is a special kind of dialog that lets user choose from a group of options. It's like the component `ion-alert` we mentioned before, but only buttons are allowed in an action sheet. It can also be used as menus. An action sheet contains an array of buttons. There are three kinds of buttons in action sheets: destructive, normal, or cancel. This can be configured by setting the property `role` to `destructive` or `cancel`. Destructive buttons usually represent dangerous actions, for example, deleting an item or canceling a pending request. Destructive buttons have different styles to clearly convey the message to the user, and they usually appear first in the array `buttons`. Cancel buttons always appear last in the array `buttons`.

© Fu Cheng 2018
F. Cheng, *Build Mobile Apps with Ionic 4 and Firebase*,
https://doi.org/10.1007/978-1-4842-3775-5_12

Just like alerts and loading indicators, there are two Ionic components for action sheets. The component `ion-action-sheet-controller` is responsible for creating, presenting, and dismissing action sheets. The component `ion-action-sheet` is the actual component displayed to the user. Action sheets are created using the method `create()` of `ion-action-sheet-controller`. The method `create()` takes an options object with the following possible properties.

- `header` - The title of the action sheet.

- `subHeader` - The subtitle of the action sheet.

- `cssClass` - The extra CSS classes to add to the action sheet.

- `backdropDismiss` - Whether the action sheet should be dismissed when the backdrop is tapped.

- `buttons` - The array of buttons to display in the action sheet.

Each button in the of array of `buttons` is a JavaScript object with the following possible properties.

- `text` - The text of the button.

- `icon` - The icon of the button.

- `handler` - The handler function to invoke when the button is pressed.

- `cssClass` - The extra CSS classes to add to the button.

- `role` - The role of the button. Possible values are `destructive`, `selected`, and `cancel`.

The return value of `create()` is a `Promise<HTMLIonActionSheet Element>` instance. After the promise is resolved, we can use methods `present()` or `dismiss()` of `HTMLIonActionSheetElement` to present or dismiss the action sheet, respectively. When the action sheet is dismissed by user tapping the backdrop, the handler of the button with role `cancel` is invoked automatically. When working with Angular, we can use the service `ActionSheetController` from Ionic Angular.

Action sheets also emit different life-cycle related events.

- `ionActionSheetDidLoad` - Emitted after the action sheet has loaded.

- `ionActionSheetDidUnload` - Emitted after the action sheet has unloaded.

- `ionActionSheetDidPresent` - Emitted after the action sheet has presented.

- `ionActionSheetWillPresent` - Emitted before the action sheet is presented.

- `ionActionSheetWillDismiss` - Emitted before the action sheet is dismissed.

- `ionActionSheetDidDismiss` - Emitted after the action sheet is dismissed.

Listing 12-1 shows an action sheet with three buttons.

Listing 12-1. Action sheet

```
export class ActionSheetComponent {
  actionSheet: HTMLIonActionSheetElement;

  constructor(private actionSheetCtrl: ActionSheetController) { }

  async chooseAction() {
    this.actionSheet = await this.actionSheetCtrl.create({
      header: 'Choose your action',
      backdropDismiss: true,
```

```
      buttons: [
        {
          text: 'Delete',
          role: 'destructive',
          icon: 'trash',
          handler: this.deleteFile.bind(this),
        },
        {
          text: 'Move',
          icon: 'move',
          handler: this.moveFile.bind(this),
        },
        {
          text: 'Cancel',
          role: 'cancel',
          icon: 'close',
          handler: this.close.bind(this),
        }
      ]
    });
    return this.actionSheet.present();
  }

  close() {
    this.actionSheet.dismiss();
  }

  deleteFile() {
  }

  moveFile() {
  }
}
```

Figure 12-1 shows the screenshot of the action sheet.

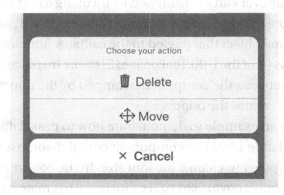

Figure 12-1. Action sheet

Popover

A popover floats on top of the current page. Popovers are created by wrapping existing components. We use the method create() of the component ion-popover-controller to create popovers. The method create() has only one parameter, which is a JavaScript object containing the following properties.

- component - The component that's wrapped in the popover.

- componentProps - The data object to pass to the popover component.

- showBackdrop - Whether to show the backdrop.

- backdropDismiss - Whether the backdrop should be dismissed when clicking outside of the popover.

- cssClass - Extra CSS classes to add.

- event - The click event object to determine the position of showing the popover.

361

The return value of `create()` is a `Promise<HTMLIonPopoverElement>` instance. The popover can be dismissed by invoking `dismiss()` of the resolved `HTMLIonPopoverElement` instance. The method `dismiss()` can accept an optional object that passed to the callback function configured by `onDidDismiss()` of the `HTMLIonPopoverElement` instance. This is how data is passed between the component wrapped by the popover and the component that creates the popover.

Now we use an example to demonstrate how to pass data when using popovers; see Listing 12-2. The component contains some text, and we want to use a popover to change the font size. In the `PopOverComponent`, we use the injected `PopoverController` instance to create a new `HTMLIonPopoverElement`. When invoking `create()`, the component to show is `FontSizeChooserComponent`, and we pass the current value of `fontSize` to the component in the `componentProps`. The event object of the click event is passed as the value of the property `event`, so the popover is positioned based on the position of the click event. If no event is passed, the popover will be positioned in the center of the current view. We use `present()` to show the popover. We then use `onDidDismiss()` to add a callback function to receive the updated value of `fontSize` from the popover.

Listing 12-2. PopOverComponent

```
import { Component, OnInit } from '@angular/core';
import { PopoverController } from '@ionic/angular';
import { FontSizeChooserComponent } from '../font-size-chooser/
font-size-chooser.component';

@Component({
  selector: 'app-pop-over',
  templateUrl: './pop-over.component.html',
  styleUrls: ['./pop-over.component.css']
})
```

```
export class PopOverComponent {
  fontSize = 16;
  constructor(private popoverCtrl: PopoverController) { }

  async changeFontSize(event) {
    const popover = await this.popoverCtrl.create({
      component: FontSizeChooserComponent,
      componentProps: {
        fontSize: this.fontSize,
      },
      event,
    });
    await popover.present();
    return popover.onDidDismiss().then(({data}) => {
      if (data) {
        this.fontSize = data.fontSize;
      }
    });
  }
}
```

The template of PopOverComponent is very simple. It has a button to create the popover. The font size of the <div> element is updated using the directive ngStyle. See Listing 12-3.

Listing 12-3. Tempate of PopOverComponent

```
<ion-app>
  <ion-header>
    <ion-toolbar>
      <ion-title>Popover</ion-title>
    </ion-toolbar>
  </ion-header>
```

```
<ion-content padding>
  <div [ngStyle]="{'font-size': fontSize + 'px'}">
    Hello world
  </div>
  <ion-button (click)="changeFontSize($event)">Font size
  </ion-button>
</ion-content>
</ion-app>
```

In the FontSizeChooserComponent, the injected NavParams can be used to retrieve the popover instance and data object passed to it. The popover instance is used to dismiss the popover and pass the current value of fontSize. See Listing 12-4.

Listing 12-4. FontSizeChooserComponent

```
import { Component } from '@angular/core';
import { NavParams } from '@ionic/angular';

@Component({
  selector: 'app-font-size-chooser',
  templateUrl: './font-size-chooser.component.html',
  styleUrls: ['./font-size-chooser.component.css']
})
export class FontSizeChooserComponent {
  fontSize: number;
  popover: HTMLIonPopoverElement;
  constructor(private navParams: NavParams) {
    this.fontSize = navParams.data.fontSize;
    this.popover = navParams.data.popover;
  }
```

```
save() {
  this.popover.dismiss({
    fontSize: this.fontSize,
  });
  }
}
```

In the template of FontSizeChooserComponent, we use an ion-range component to let the user select the font size. See Listing 12-5.

Listing 12-5. Template of FontSizeChooserComponent

```
<ion-list>
  <ion-list-header>Font size</ion-list-header>
  <ion-item>
    <ion-range [(ngModel)]="fontSize" pin="true" min="8"
    max="32">
      <ion-icon slot="start" name="remove"></ion-icon>
      <ion-icon slot="end" name="add"></ion-icon>
    </ion-range>
  </ion-item>
  <ion-item>
    <ion-button expand="full" (click)="save()">OK</ion-button>
  </ion-item>
</ion-list>
```

Figure 12-2 shows the screenshot of the font size chooser.

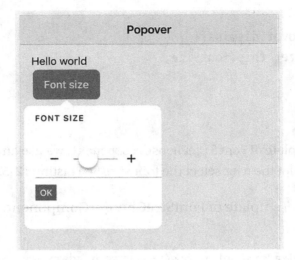

Figure 12-2. *Font size chooser*

Slides

The slides component is a container for multiple views. The user can swipe or drag between different views. Slides are commonly used for tutorials and galleries.

Slides are created using components ion-slides and ion-slide. ion-slides is the container component for ion-slide components inside of it. When creating the ion-slides, we can use the property options to configure it. Ionic slides uses Swiper as its implemention. The property options takes the same value as in the Swiper API (http://idangero.us/swiper/api/). The property pager controls whether to show the pagination bullets.

After the slides component is created, we can also programmatically control the slide transitions using the following methods.

- slideTo(index, speed, runCallbacks) - Transition to the slide with the specified index.

- slideNext(speed, runCallbacks) - Transition to the next slide.

- `slidePrev(speed, runCallbacks)` - Transition to the previous slide.

- `getActiveIndex()` - Get the index of the active slide.

- `getPreviousIndex()` - Get the index of the previous slide.

- `length()` - Get the total number of slides.

- `isBeginning()` - Get whether the current slide is the first slide.

- `isEnd()` - Get whether the current slide is the last slide.

- `startAutoplay()` - Start autoplay.

- `stopAutoplay()` - Stop autoplay.

In Listing 12-6, we create an `ion-slides` component with the reference variable set to `slides`. It contains three `ion-slide` components.

Listing 12-6. Slides

```
<ion-slides #slides>
  <ion-slide>
    Slide 1
  </ion-slide>
  <ion-slide>
    Slide 2
  </ion-slide>
  <ion-slide>
    Slide 3
  </ion-slide>
</ion-slides>
<div>
  <ion-button (click)="prev()">Prev</ion-button>
  <ion-button (click)="next()">Next</ion-button>
</div>
```

It has two buttons to go to the previous or next slide. The component SlidesComponent in Listing 12-7 has a @ViewChild property slides that binds to an ElementRef object. The property nativeElement returns the ion-slides element. The property loaded is used to check whether the slides component is loaded. The method componentOnReady returns a Promise that resolved when the component is ready. The method isValid() is required to check whether the Slides component is ready to use.

Listing 12-7. SlidesComponent

```
import { Component, ViewChild, ElementRef, OnInit } from
'@angular/core';

@Component({
  selector: 'app-slides',
  templateUrl: './slides.component.html',
  styleUrls: ['./slides.component.css']
})
export class SlidesComponent implements OnInit {
  @ViewChild('slides') slidesElem: ElementRef;
  loaded = false;
  slides: any;

  ngOnInit() {
    this.slides = this.slidesElem.nativeElement;
    this.slides.componentOnReady().then(() => {
      this.loaded = true;
    });
  }

  prev() {
    if (this.isValid()) {
      this.slides.slidePrev();
    }
  }
```

```
next() {
  if (this.isValid()) {
    this.slides.slideNext();
  }
}

isValid(): boolean {
  return this.loaded && this.slides != null;
}
}
```

Figure 12-3 shows the screenshot of the slides component.

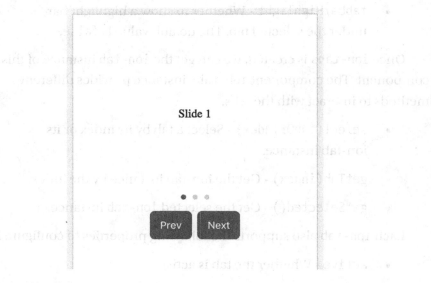

Slide 1

Prev   Next

Figure 12-3. *Slides*

Tabs

Tabs are commonly used components for layout and navigation. Different tabs can take the same screen estate, and only one tab can be active at the same time.

Tabs components are created using the component `ion-tabs`, while individual tabs are created using `ion-tab`. `ion-tabs` supports the standard properties `color` and `mode` and the following special properties.

- `tabbarHidden` - When this property is true, hide the tab bar.

- `tabbarLayout` - The layout of the tab bar. Possible values are `icon-top`, `icon-start`, `icon-end`, `icon-bottom`, `icon-hide`, `title-hide`.

- `tabbarPlacement` - The position of the tab bar. Possible values are `top` and `bottom`.

- `tabbarHighlight` - Whether to show a highlight bar under the selected tab. The default value is `false`.

Once `ion-tabs` is created, we can get the `ion-tab` instance of this component. The component `ion-tabs` instance provides different methods to interact with the tabs.

- `select(tabOrIndex)` - Select a tab by its index or its ion-tab instance.

- `getTab(index)` - Get the ion-tab instance by the index.

- `getSelected()` - Get the selected `ion-tab` instance.

Each `ion-tab` also supports the following properties to configure it.

- `active` - Whether the tab is active.

- `href` - The URL of the tab.

- `label` - The title of the tab.

- `icon` - The icon of the tab.

- `badge` - The badge to display on the tab button.

- badgeStyle - The color of the badge.

- disabled - Whether the tab button is disabled.

- show - Whether the tab button is visible.

- tabsHideOnSubPages - Whether the tab is hidden on subpages.

ion-tab also emits the event ionSelect when it's selected.

In the template file of Listing 12-8, we create an ion-tabs with the reference name set to tabs. Each ion-tab has its title and icon. The first tab has a button to go to the second tab.

Listing 12-8. Template of tabs

```
<ion-tabs tabbar-placement="top" #tabs>
  <ion-tab label="Tab 1" icon="alarm">
    Tab One
    <ion-button (click)="gotoTab2()">Select Tab 2</ion-button>
  </ion-tab>
  <ion-tab label="Tab 1" icon="albums">
    Tab Two
  </ion-tab>
  <ion-tab label="Tab 1" icon="settings">
    Tab Three
  </ion-tab>
</ion-tabs>
```

In the TabsComponent of Listing 12-9, we use the decorator @ViewChild to get the reference to the ion-tabs element and use its method select() to select the second tab.

Listing 12-9. Tabs

```
import { Component, OnInit, ViewChild, ElementRef } from
'@angular/core';

@Component({
  selector: 'app-tabs',
  templateUrl: './tabs.component.html',
  styleUrls: ['./tabs.component.css']
})
export class TabsComponent implements OnInit {
  @ViewChild('tabs') tabsElem: ElementRef;
  tabs: any;
  constructor() { }

  ngOnInit() {
    this.tabs = this.tabsElem.nativeElement;
  }

  gotoTab2() {
    this.tabs.select(1);
  }
}
```

Figure 12-4 shows the screenshot of tabs.

Figure 12-4. *Tabs*

Modal

Modals take up the whole screen space to present the UI to users. Modals are commonly used to gather information from users before they can continue. The `ion-modal` components are created using the method `create(opts)` of the component `ion-modal-controller`. The parameter `opts` is an options object to configure the modal. The following options are supported when creating modals.

- `component` - The component to show in the modal.

- `componentProps` - Parameters passed to the component.

- `showBackdrop` - Whether to show the backdrop or not. The default value is `true`.

- `backdropDismiss` - Whether the modal should be dismissed by tapping on the backdrop. The default value is `true`.

- enterAnimation - The animation to use when the
  modal is presented.

- leaveAnimation - The animation to use when the
  modal is dismissed.

The usage pattern of ion-modal-controller and ion-modal is similar
to ion-popover-controller and ion-popover. We can use ion-modal-
controller to show the same font-size chooser; see Listing 12-10.

Listing 12-10. Use modal to show font-size chooser

```
@Component({
  selector: 'app-modal',
  templateUrl: './modal.component.html',
  styleUrls: ['./modal.component.css']
})
export class ModalComponent implements OnInit {
  fontSize = 16;
  constructor(private modalCtrl: ModalController) { }

  ngOnInit() {
  }

  async changeFontSize(event) {
    const popover = await this.modalCtrl.create({
      component: FontSizeChooserComponent,
      componentProps: {
        fontSize: this.fontSize,
      },
    });
```

```
    await popover.present();
    return popover.onDidDismiss().then(({data}) => {
      if (data) {
        this.fontSize = data.fontSize;
      }
    });
  }
}
```

To close the modal, we can get the reference to the ion-modal using the property data.modal of NavParams.

Figure 12-5 shows the screenshot of FontSizeChooserComponent opened with a modal.

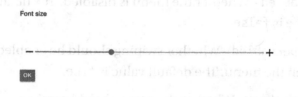

Figure 12-5. *FontSizeChooserComponent opened with a modal*

Menu

The component `ion-menu` creates menus that can be opened by clicking a button or swiping. `ion-menu` has the following properties.

- `contentId` - The id of the content component.

- `menuId` - The id of the menu.

- `side` - The side of the view to place the menu. Possible values are `start` and `end`. The default value is `start`.

- `type` - The display type of the menu. Possible values are `overlay`, `reveal`, and `push`. The default value depends on the platform.

- `disabled` - Whether the menu is disabled. The default value is `false`.

- `swipeEnabled` - Whether swiping should be enabled to open the menu. The default value is `true`.

- `persistent` - Whether the menu should persist on child pages. The default value is `false`.

Menu Toggle and Button

The component `ion-menu-toggle` can toggle the open or close status of a menu. The property `menu` of `ion-menu-toggle` specifies the id of the menu to toggle. We can also use `start` or `end` as the value of this property. The property `autoHide` specifies whether the toggle should be hidden when the corresponding menu is not active.

The component `ion-menu-button` is actually an `ion-menu-toggle` that wraps an `ion-button` with a menu icon.

Menu Controller

Using ion-menu-toggle is generally enough to control the visibility of the menu. However, when there are multiple menus at both sides, or the visibility of the menu depends on complex logic, it's better to use ion-menu-controller. It has the following methods.

- open(menuId) - Open the menu with specified id or side.

- close(menuId) - Close the menu with specified id or side. If no menuId is specified, then all open menus will be closed.

- toggle(menuId) - Toggle the menu with a specified id or side.

- enable(shouldEnable, menuId) - Enable or disable the menu with a specified id or side. For each side, when there are multiple menus, only one of them can be opened at the same time. Enabling one menu will also disable other menus on the same side.

- swipeEnable(shouldEnable, menuId) - Enable or disable the feature to swipe to open the menu.

- isOpen(menuId) - Check if a menu is opened.

- isEnabled(menuId) - Check if a menu is enabled.

- get(menuId) - Get the ion-menu instance with a specified id or side.

- getOpen() - Get the opened ion-menu instance.

- getMenus() - Get an array of all ion-menu instances.

- isAnimating() - Check if any menu is currently animating.

377

Listing 12-11 shows the template of using menus. We create two menus at the start and end side. The ion-menu-button toggles the menu at the start side. If the property contentId is not specified for the ion-menu, it looks for the element with the attribute main in its parent element as the content.

Listing 12-11. Template of using menus

```
<ion-app>
  <ion-menu side="start">
    <ion-header>
      <ion-toolbar>
        <ion-title>Start Menu</ion-title>
      </ion-toolbar>
    </ion-header>
    <ion-content>
      <ion-list>
        <ion-item>
          <ion-button (click)="openEnd()">Open end</ion-button>
        </ion-item>
      </ion-list>
    </ion-content>
  </ion-menu>
  <ion-menu side="end">
    <ion-header>
      <ion-toolbar>
        <ion-title>End Menu</ion-title>
      </ion-toolbar>
    </ion-header>
  </ion-menu>
```

```
  <div main>
    <ion-header>
      <ion-toolbar>
        <ion-buttons slot="start">
          <ion-menu-button menu="start">
            <ion-icon name="menu"></ion-icon>
          </ion-menu-button>
        </ion-buttons>
        <ion-title>App</ion-title>
      </ion-toolbar>
    </ion-header>
    <ion-content>
      Content
    </ion-content>
  </div>
</ion-app>
```

The MenuComponent in Listing 12-12 uses MenuController to open the menu at the end side.

Listing 12-12. MenuComponent

```
import { Component } from '@angular/core';
import { MenuController } from '@ionic/angular';

@Component({
  selector: 'app-menu',
  templateUrl: './menu.component.html',
  styleUrls: ['./menu.component.css']
})
```

```
export class MenuComponent {
  constructor(private menuCtrl: MenuController) { }

  openEnd() {
    this.menuCtrl.open('end');
  }
}
```

Figure 12-6 shows the screenshot when the start menu is opened.

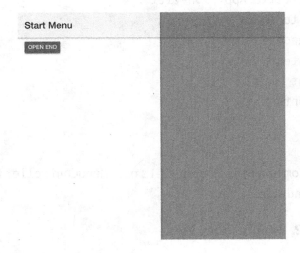

Figure 12-6. *Start menu opened*

Summary

In this chapter, we discussed how to use other common Ionic 4 components that are not used in the example app, including action sheet, popover, slides, and tabs. For each component, we provided a concrete example to demonstrate the usage. In the next chapter, we'll discuss some advanced topics in Ionic 4.

CHAPTER 13

Advanced Topics

In this chapter, we discuss some advanced topics, including platform, theming, colors, config, storage, push notifications, and React integration. These advanced topics are useful in many usage scenarios.

Platform

We have seen the class Platform in previous chapters. It can be used to interact with the underlying platform. We used the method ready() of Platform to wait for the Cordova platform to finish initialization. The class Platform also has other methods.

- platforms() – Depends on the running device, the return value can be an array of different platforms. Possible values of platforms are android, cordova, core, ios, ipad, iphone, mobile, mobileweb, phablet, tablet, windows, and electron. When running on the iPhone emulator, the return value of platforms() is ["ios","iphone"].

- is(platformName) – Checks if the running platform matches the given platform name. Because the method platforms() can return multiple values, the method is() can return true for multiple values.

© Fu Cheng 2018
F. Cheng, *Build Mobile Apps with Ionic 4 and Firebase*,
https://doi.org/10.1007/978-1-4842-3775-5_13

- `versions()` – Gets version information for all the platforms. When running on the iPhone emulator, the return value of `versions()` is `[{"name":"iphone"}, {"name":"ios", "settings":{"mode":"ios","tabsHigh light":false,"statusbarPadding":false,"keyboard Height":250,"isDevice":true,"deviceHacks":true}}]`.

- `isRTL()` – Checks if the language direction is right to left.

- `width()` and `height()` – Gets the width and height of the platform's viewport, respectively.

- `isPortrait()` and `isLandscape()` – Checks if the app is in portrait or landscape mode, respectively.

- `ready()` – This method returns a promise that is resolved when the platform is ready and we can use the native functionalities. The resolved value is the name of the platform that was ready.

- `url()` – Gets web page's URL.

- `getQueryParam(key)` – Gets query parameter.

There are three important `EventEmitters` in the `Platform` that are related to app states. The `EventEmitter` `pause` emits events when the app is put into the background. The `EventEmitter` `resume` emits events when the app is pulled out from the background. These two `EventEmitter`s are useful when dealing with app state changes. The `EventEmitter` `resize` emits events when the browser window has changed dimensions.

Theming

Ionic provides different look and feels based on the current platform. The styles are grouped as different modes. Each platform has a default mode that can also be overridden. It's possible to use iOS styles on Android devices.

There are two modes: md for Material Design styles, ios for iOS styles. The platform ios uses the mode ios by default, and other platforms use the mode md by default.

Once the mode is selected for the app, the html element will have the attribute mode set to the mode name, for example, <html mode="ios">. The element <ion-app> will have the mode name as a CSS class name, for example, <ion-app class="md"> for the mode md. This class name can be used to override styles for different modes. In the code below, we add extra styles only for the mode md.

```
.md {
  font-size: 16px;
}
```

Ionic components have the property mode to set the mode. This mode overrides the platform's default mode for this component only. In Listing 13-1, we declare two ion-range components with different modes.

Listing 13-1. Different modes for ion-range components

```
<ion-app>
  <ion-header>
    <ion-toolbar>
      <ion-title>Range</ion-title>
    </ion-toolbar>
  </ion-header>
  <ion-content padding>
    <ion-list>
      <ion-item>
        <ion-label slot="start">md</ion-label>
        <ion-range mode="md" value="50">
          <ion-icon mode="md" slot="start" name="sad"></ion-icon>
          <ion-icon mode="md" slot="end" name="happy"></ion-icon>
        </ion-range>
```

```
    </ion-item>
    <ion-item>
      <ion-label slot="start">ios</ion-label>
      <ion-range mode="ios" value="50">
        <ion-icon mode="ios" slot="start" name="sad">
        </ion-icon>
        <ion-icon mode="ios" slot="end" name="happy">
        </ion-icon>
      </ion-range>
    </ion-item>
  </ion-list>
</ion-content>
</ion-app>
```

Figure 13-1 shows the screenshot of these two ranges running on the iPhone emulator. We can see that the styles of these ranges and icons are different.

Figure 13-1. *Ranges and icons with different modes*

Ionic has different Sass variables to configure the styles. These variables can be overridden in the file `src/theme/variables.scss`. For example, the variable `$button-md-font-size` configures the button font size of mode md. The default value is 14px. We can add the code below to the file `variables.scss` to change the variable's value.

```
$button-md-font-size: 16px;
```

Colors

The file `variables.scss` defines several variables related to colors; see
Listing 13-2. The variable `$colors` is a map for named colors. These color
names can be used in the property `color` for components. We can update
values of these colors to change the theming.

Listing 13-2. Colors in `variables.scss`

```
:root {
  /** primary **/
  --ion-color-primary: #488aff;
  --ion-color-primary-rgb: 72,138,255;
  --ion-color-primary-contrast: #fff;
  --ion-color-primary-contrast-rgb: 255,255,255;
  --ion-color-primary-shade: #3f79e0;
  --ion-color-primary-tint: #5a96ff;

  /** secondary **/
  --ion-color-secondary: #32db64;
  --ion-color-secondary-rgb: 50,219,100;
  --ion-color-secondary-contrast: #fff;
  --ion-color-secondary-contrast-rgb: 255,255,255;
  --ion-color-secondary-shade: #2cc158;
  --ion-color-secondary-tint: #47df74;

  /** tertiary **/
  --ion-color-tertiary: #f4a942;
  --ion-color-tertiary-rgb: 244,169,66;
  --ion-color-tertiary-contrast: #fff;
  --ion-color-tertiary-contrast-rgb: 255,255,255;
  --ion-color-tertiary-shade: #d7953a;
  --ion-color-tertiary-tint: #f5b255;
```

```
/** success **/
--ion-color-success: #10dc60;
--ion-color-success-rgb: 16,220,96;
--ion-color-success-contrast: #fff;
--ion-color-success-contrast-rgb: 255,255,255;
--ion-color-success-shade: #0ec254;
--ion-color-success-tint: #28e070;

/** warning **/
--ion-color-warning: #ffce00;
--ion-color-warning-rgb: 255,206,0;
--ion-color-warning-contrast: #000;
--ion-color-warning-contrast-rgb: 0,0,0;
--ion-color-warning-shade: #e0b500;
--ion-color-warning-tint: #ffd31a;

/** danger **/
--ion-color-danger: #f53d3d;
--ion-color-danger-rgb: 245,61,61;
--ion-color-danger-contrast: #fff;
--ion-color-danger-contrast-rgb: 255,255,255;
--ion-color-danger-shade: #d83636;
--ion-color-danger-tint: #f65050;

/** light **/
--ion-color-light: #f4f4f4;
--ion-color-light-rgb: 244,244,244;
--ion-color-light-contrast: #000;
--ion-color-light-contrast-rgb: 0,0,0;
--ion-color-light-shade: #d7d7d7;
--ion-color-light-tint: #f5f5f5;
```

```
/** medium **/
--ion-color-medium: #989aa2;
--ion-color-medium-rgb: 152,154,162;
--ion-color-medium-contrast: #000;
--ion-color-medium-contrast-rgb: 0,0,0;
--ion-color-medium-shade: #86888f;
--ion-color-medium-tint: #a2a4ab;

/** dark **/
--ion-color-dark: #222;
--ion-color-dark-rgb: 34,34,34;
--ion-color-dark-contrast: #fff;
--ion-color-dark-contrast-rgb: 255,255,255;
--ion-color-dark-shade: #1e1e1e;
--ion-color-dark-tint: #383838;
}
```

Config

For each mode, Ionic has default configuration values for different properties. For example, the component ion-spinner checks the configuration property spinner for the loading spinner to use when no spinner name is specified. These configurations can be overridden in different ways.

In the class AppModule, we use the method IonicModule.forRoot() to create the module imports. This method can take a second parameter that configures the properties for different platforms. In Listing 13-3, we configure the spinner property to always use the value lines.

Listing 13-3. Override default configurations

```
@NgModule({
  imports: [
    IonicModule.forRoot(MyApp, {
      spinner: 'lines',
    })
  ]
})
```

When testing in the browser, we can also use the URL query string to configure the properties. The query string parameters are added like `ionic:<NAME>=<value>`. For example, the URL `http://localhost:8100/?ionic:spinner=lines` configures the property `spinner` to use the value `lines`.

Ionic has the global object `Ionic.global` to get and set configuration values. The configuration is essentially a map of key/value pairs. The configuration object provides the following methods.

- `set(key, value)` - Sets a configuration value.

- `get(key, fallback)` - Gets a configuration value.

- `getBoolean(key, fallback)` - Gets a Boolean configuration value.

- `getNumber(key, fallback)` - Gets a number configuration value.

In Angular we can inject the service `Config` to get the configuration object.

Storage

In the Hacker News app, we store all the user data in the Firebase database, so the user can access all the data across different devices. For some cases, it's not required that the data needs to be shared between different devices.

For this kind of data, we can store the data on the device. In this case, we can use the key/value pairs storage provided by Ionic. The package `@ionic/storage` is already installed as part of the starter template, so we can use it directly.

The storage stores key/value pairs. The value of each pair can be data of any type. If the value is a JavaScript object, it's serialized to a JSON string before saving. When the data is retrieved, the JSON string is deserialized back to a JavaScript object. The Ionic storage package wraps the localForage library (`https://github.com/localForage/localForage`). It provides a common API to access different storage engines, including SQLite, IndexedDB, WebSQL, and localstorage. The actual engine used in the runtime depends on the availability of the platform. The best storage engine to use is SQLite, because it's natively supported on iOS and Android platforms. We can install the plugin `cordova-sqlite-storage` to make SQLite available on different platforms.

```
$ cordova plugin add cordova-sqlite-storage --save
```

We use the class `Storage` from `@ionic/storage` to interact with the underlying storage engine. The module created by `IonicStorageModule.forRoot()` should be imported. The instance of class `Storage` can be injected into components. `Storage` has the following methods.

- `get(key)` – Gets the value by key.
- `set(key, value)` – Sets the value of the given key.
- `remove(key)` – Removes the given key and its value.
- `clear()` – Clears the whole store.
- `keys()` – Gets all the keys in the store.
- `length()` – Gets the number of keys.
- `forEach(callback)` – Invokes the callback function for each key/value pair in the store.

Most of the operations in Storage are asynchronous. The return values of methods get(), set(), remove(), and clear() are all Promise objects that resolved when the operations are completed. In Listing 13-4, we use set() to set the value first, then use get() to read the value and assign it to the property value.

Listing 13-4. Storage

```
import { Component, OnInit } from '@angular/core';
import { Storage } from '@ionic/storage';
@Component({
  selector: 'app-page-home',
  templateUrl: 'home.page.html',
  styleUrls: ['home.page.scss'],
})
export class HomePage implements OnInit {
  value: any;
  constructor(private storage: Storage) { }

  ngOnInit() {
    const obj = {
      name: 'Alex',
      email: 'alex@example.org'
    };
    this.storage.set('value', obj)
      .then(_ => this.storage.get('value')
        .then(v => this.value = v));
  }
}
```

The method `IonicStorageModule.forRoot()` accepts an optional object to configure the storage engine. This object has the following properties.

- `name` - Name of the storage.

- `storeName` - Name of the store.

- `driverOrder` - The array of driver names to test and use. The default value is `['sqlite', 'indexeddb', 'websql', 'localstorage']`.

Push Notifications

Push notifications play an important role in mobile apps and are used in many apps. Push notifications can be used to deliver messages to the user when the app is running in the background. They also can deliver data to the app to update the UI when the app is running in the foreground. Firebase offers the feature Cloud Messaging (`https://firebase.google.com/docs/cloud-messaging/`) to deliver messages to client apps.

We need to install the Cordova plugin `cordova-plugin-fcm` (`https://github.com/alexcheng1982/cordova-plugin-fcm`) to use Firebase Cloud Messaging (FCM). The Firebase configuration files for iOS and Android, that is, the `GoogleService-info.plist` and `google-services.json`, should be downloaded and copied into the project's root directory. FCM provides three key capabilities.

- It can send notification messages or data messages.

- It allows specifying different targets for messages distributions, so they can be single devices, groups of devices, or devices subscribed to topics.

- The client apps can also send messages to the server.

The following command is used to install the plugin `cordova-plugin-fcm`.

```
$ cordova plugin add https://github.com/alexcheng1982/cordova-
plugin-fcm.git --save
```

There are two types of messages in FCM: notification messages and data messages. Notification messages are displayed by FCM when the app is running in the background. When the notification is tapped, the app is brought to the foreground and the message is handled by the app. Notification messages have a predefined structure for FCM to consume. Data messages are handled by the app. They contain custom key/value pairs with meanings specific to different apps. Data messages are handled when the app is running in the foreground. Both types of messages have a maximum payload size of 4KB. If the app needs to keep updating the UI based on the server-side data, using data messages is a good choice.

We use JSON to describe FCM messages. In Listing 13-5, the property `notification` represents the notification object. The property `data` represents the custom key/value pairs. It's possible to contain both notification and data payloads in the same message. For these kind of messages, when the app is running in the background, the notification is displayed by FCM. When the notification is tapped, the data payload is handled by the app; When the app is running in the foreground, the whole message body is handled by the app.

Listing 13-5. FCM messages in JSON format

```
{
  "token" : "",
  "notification" : {
    "body" : "You got a new message.",
    "title" : "New message"
  },
```

```
  "data" : {
    "from" : "alex",
    "content" : "Hello!"
  }
}
```

Messages can be sent using the Firebase console or FCM REST API (https://firebase.google.com/docs/cloud-messaging/http-server-ref). We use Android as the example to show the usage of FCM. If the app only needs to receive notification messages, then after installing the plugin cordova-plugin-fcm, no code changes are required. The app can automatically support receiving notification messages. If the app needs to receive data messages, then we need to add the code to process the message payload.

The sample scenario is to display a name that pushed to the app using notifications. In Listing 13-6, the class NotificationPage is the page to show the name. FCM is the JavaScript object provided by @ionic-native/fcm. We use the method FCM.onNotification() to add a callback handler for notifications. Because using FCM requires the native plugin, the call to FCM.onNotification() is added in the resolve callback of Platform.ready(). The notification callback handler receives the data as the argument. We use the data to update the value of the property name. The data object contains the property wasTapped to check if this message is received after the user tapped the notification.

Listing 13-6. Display name using notifications

```
import { Component, OnInit, NgZone } from '@angular/core';
import { Platform } from '@ionic/angular';

@Component({
  selector: 'page-notification',
  templateUrl: 'notification.html'
})
```

```
export class NotificationPage implements OnInit {
  name: string;
  constructor(public platform: Platform,
                        private zone: NgZone) {}

  ngOnInit() {
    this.platform.ready().then(() => {
      (window as any).FCMPlugin.onNotification(data => {
        this.zone.run(() => {
          this.name = data.name;
        });
      });
    });
  }
}
```

The format of the data object passed to the notification callback handler is different than the format in Listing 13-5. There is no nested properties notification or data in the object; see Listing 13-7.

Listing 13-7. The format of data object

```
{
  "body":"You got a new name!",
  "title":"New name",
  "name":"Alex",
  "wasTapped":false
}
```

Now we can test the notifications using the Firebase console. Open **Cloud Messaging** in the sidebar and click **New Message** to create a new message. In the dialog of Figure 13-2, **Message text** is the text to display in the notification. In the **Target** section, we need to specify the targets to receive notifications. In the **Advanced options** section, we can specify the message title. It's required to add the custom data for the name to display.

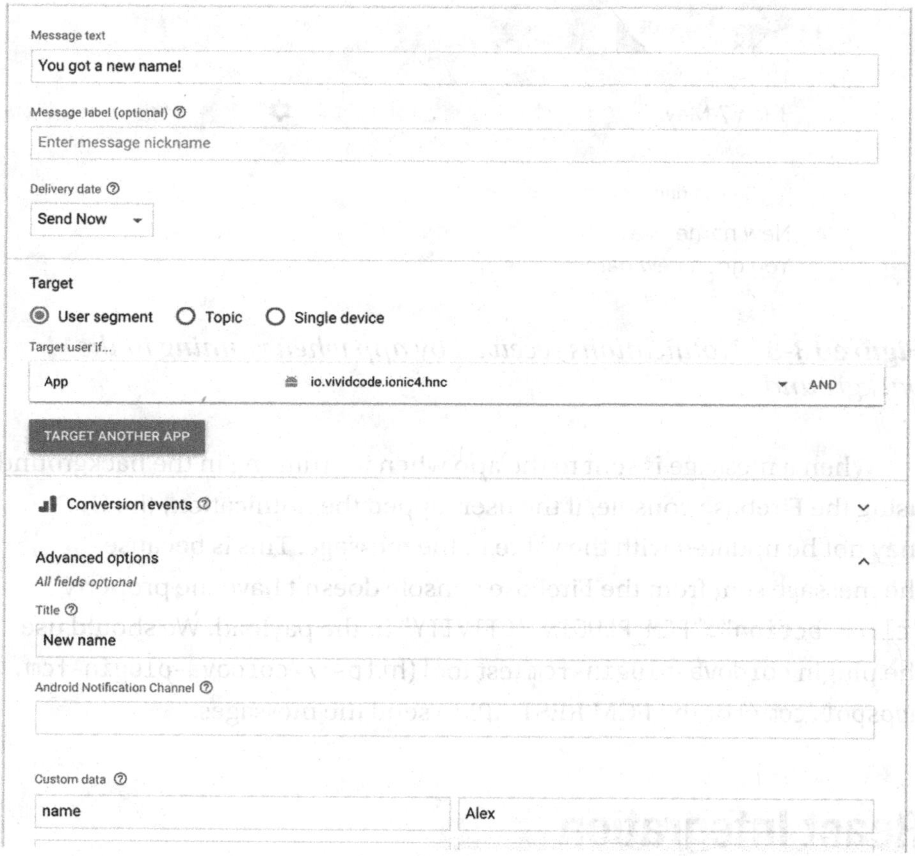

Message text

You got a new name!

Message label (optional) ⑦

Enter message nickname

Delivery date ⑦

Send Now   ▾

Target

◉ User segment   ○ Topic   ○ Single device

Target user if...

App   🗄 io.vividcode.ionic4.hnc   ▾   AND

TARGET ANOTHER APP

📊 Conversion events ⑦   ⌄

Advanced options   ⌃
All fields optional
Title ⑦

New name

Android Notification Channel ⑦

Custom data ⑦

name   Alex

Figure 13-2. *Create a new message*

When the app is running in the foreground and we send a message, the UI will be updated. When the app is running in the background, a notification message is displayed. When the notification is tapped by the user, the app is brought to the foreground and the value is updated. Figure 13-3 shows the screenshot of the displayed notification.

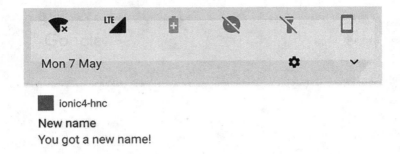

Figure 13-3. *Notifications received by app when running in the background*

When a message is sent to the app when it's running in the background using the Firebase console, if the user tapped the notification, the UI may not be updated with the value in the message. This is because the message sent from the Firebase console doesn't have the property `"click_action":"FCM_PLUGIN_ACTIVITY"` in the payload. We should use the plugin `cordova-plugin-fcm` test tool (`https://cordova-plugin-fcm.appspot.com/`) or the FCM REST API to send the messages.

React Integration

As we mentioned before, Ionic Core just consists of a set of custom elements built with Web Components standards. Being framework agnostic makes it very easy to integrate with other frameworks. Integration with React is very simple. We just need to load Ionic Core files in the React app and use the components directly. We can either use Ionic Core files served in a public CDN or copy these files to a local directory `/public`. We also need to update `index.html` to include the file using `<script>`. Listing 13-8 shows the sample code to use Ionic Core in React.

Listing 13-8. Sample React app with Ionic Core

```
import React, { Component } from 'react';

class App extends Component {
  render() {
    return (
      <ion-app>
        <ion-header>
          <ion-toolbar>
            <ion-title>App</ion-title>
          </ion-toolbar>
        </ion-header>
        <ion-content>
          <ion-button>Test</ion-button>
        </ion-content>
      </ion-app>
    );
  }
}

export default App;
```

Summary

In this chapter, we discussed some advanced topics in Ionic 4, including Platform, theming, Config, Storage, and push notifications. These topics may not be used in every app, but they can be very useful when you need to customize your app. Using push notifications is a good way to engage better with you users. In the next chapter, we'll discuss how to add end-to-end tests and continuous integration for Ionic 4 apps.

CHAPTER 14

End-to-End Test and Build

In the previous chapters, we focused on the implementation of different user stories and the Ionic framework itself. In this chapter, we'll focus on some nonfunctional requirements, including end-to-end test with Protractor and build with Headless Chrome and GitLab CI. These steps are essential for real-world app development. After reading this chapter, you should know how to apply these practices.

End-to-End Test with Protractor

Protractor (`http://www.protractortest.org/`) is an end-to-end test framework for Angular applications. The name "Protractor" comes from the instrument that is used to measure angles, indicating its close relationship with Anguar. Most of the end-to-end testing tools are using Selenium WebDriver (`http://www.seleniumhq.org/projects/webdriver/`) to drive a browser as a user would. You can use the WebDriver API directly, or use tools like Nightwatch.js (`http://nightwatchjs.org/`) or WebdriverIO (`http://webdriver.io/`), which wrap the WebDriver API to provide an easier-to-use API. Protractor also uses WebDriver API, but it has a close integration with Angular to make find elements much easier.

We use npm to install Protractor and the dependent package `webdriver-manager` that manages the Selenium server for testing.

© Fu Cheng 2018
F. Cheng, *Build Mobile Apps with Ionic 4 and Firebase*,
https://doi.org/10.1007/978-1-4842-3775-5_14

```
$ npm i -D protractor webdriver-manager
```

Then we need to update `webdriver-manager` to install drivers for different browsers. This is done by running the command `update` of `webdriver-manager`. Because we didn't install the package `webdriver-manager` globally, we must use the full-qualified path to access the binary of `webdriver-manager`.

```
$ node_modules/webdriver-manager/bin/webdriver-manager update
```

After the command `update` is finished, we can start the Selenium server using the command below.

```
$ node_modules/webdriver-manager/bin/webdriver-manager start
```

To make sure that `webdriver-manager` is updated, we can add a `postinstall` script to `package.json` to run `webdriver-manager update` after the packages installation.

Protractor Configuration

Protractor is configured using the file `protractor.conf.js` in the directory e2e; see Listing 14-1. This file contains different settings. Refer to this page (`http://www.protractortest.org/#/api-overview`) for more information about the configuration.

- `seleniumAddress` - Set the Selenium server address. `http://localhost:4444/wd/hub` is the default Selenium address, so the property `seleniumAddress` can be omitted.

- `allScriptsTimeout` - Set the timeout settings to 15 seconds.

- `specs` - Set the pattern to find all specs files. Here we use all the files with the suffix `.e2e_spec.ts` in the directory `src`.

- capabilities - Set the capabilities requirements for Selenium server. Here we require using Chrome.

- directConnect - Connect directly to the browser without using a Selenium server. This option can be enabled for Chrome and Firefox to speed up the execution of test scripts. When this property is set to true, Selenium-related settings are ignored.

- baseUrl - Set the base URL for testing.

- framework - Set the testing framework. Jasmine is the recommended framework.

- jasmineNodeOpts - Set the options for Jasmine.

- beforeLaunch - Set the action to run before any environment setup. Here we register the directory e2e to ts-node, so ts-node compiles TypeScript code on-the-fly during the execution of the script.

- onPrepare - Set the action to run before the specs are executed. Here we configure Jasmine to add one reporter. SpecReporter is used to output the testing result to the console.

Listing 14-1. protractor.conf.js

```
const { SpecReporter } = require('jasmine-spec-reporter');

exports.config = {
  allScriptsTimeout: 15000,
  specs: [
    './src/**/*.e2e-spec.ts'
  ],
```

```
capabilities: {
  browserName: 'chrome',
},
directConnect: true,
baseUrl: 'http://localhost:4200/',
framework: 'jasmine',
jasmineNodeOpts: {
  showColors: true,
  defaultTimeoutInterval: 30000,
  print: function() {}
},
beforeLaunch() {
  require('ts-node').register({
    project: 'e2e/tsconfig.e2e.json'
  });
},
onPrepare() {
  jasmine.getEnv().addReporter(new SpecReporter({ spec: {
  displayStacktrace: true } }));
  browser.waitForAngularEnabled(false);

  // The css_sr selector is copied from https://github.com/
  angular/protractor/issues/4367.
  // The related PR (https://github.com/angular/protractor/
  pull/4786/) is not merged yet.
  by.addLocator('css_sr', (cssSelector, opt_parentElement,
  opt_rootSelector) => {
    let selectors = cssSelector.split('::sr');
    if (selectors.length === 0) {
      return [];
    }
```

```
    let shadowDomInUse = (document.head.createShadowRoot ||
    document.head.attachShadow);
    let getShadowRoot = (el) => ((el && shadowDomInUse) ?
    el.shadowRoot : el);
    let findAllMatches = (selector, targets, firstTry) => {
      let using, i, matches = [];
      for (i = 0; i < targets.length; ++i) {
        using = (firstTry) ? targets[i] :
        getShadowRoot(targets[i]);
        if (using) {
          if (selector === ") {
            matches.push(using);
          } else {
            Array.prototype.push.apply(matches, using.
            querySelectorAll(selector));
          }
        }
      }
      return matches;
    };

    let matches = findAllMatches(selectors.shift().trim(),
    [opt_parentElement || document], true);
    while (selectors.length > 0 && matches.length > 0) {
      matches = findAllMatches(selectors.shift().trim(),
      matches, false);
    }
    return matches;
  });
  }
};
```

The `baseUrl` we use for testing is `http://localhost:4200`, which is the URL of the Angular dev server. In the function `onPrepare`, we also call `browser.waitForAngularEnabled(false)` to disable the waiting for pending asynchronous tasks to finish in Angular (`https://github.com/angular/protractor/blob/master/docs/timeouts.md#waiting-for-angular`). Otherwise, all the tests will fail with timeout errors: `Timed out waiting for asynchronous Angular tasks to finish after 15 seconds while waiting for element with locator`. This is because Firebase uses WebSocket to connect to the server and the connection is treated as in-progress asynchronous task.

In the function `onPrepare`, we also add a custom Protractor locator `css_sr`. This selector enables selection of elements inside of shadow trees. Ionic Core components uses Shadow DOM by default. The DOM elements inside of their shadow roots cannot be selected using existing CSS selectors in Protractor. There is already a pending GitHub pull request (`https://github.com/angular/protractor/pull/4786/`) to add this selector to Protractor. Once this pull request is merged, we no longer need to add it in the function `onPrepare`.

The file `package.json` already has the script `e2e` to run Protractor. We can run `npm run e2e` or `ng e2e` to start the Protractor tests.

Top Stories Page Test

After Protractor is configured, we add the first end-to-end test suite for the top stories page. The spec file is written with Jasmine, so we can leverage what we already know in writing unit tests; see Listing 14-2. The first test spec verifies that there should be 20 stories. The method `browser.get(")` loads the page in the browser. Because we already configure the `baseUrl` in `protractor.conf.js`, the empty string means loading the base URL. The functional call `browser.wait(EC.presenceOf(element(by.css('app-top-stories'))), 5000)` uses the `ExpectedConditions` (`https://www.protractortest.org/#/api?view=ProtractorExpectedConditions`)

provided by Protractor to wait for certain conditions to be met. The condition presenceOf means the element matching the given CSS selector must exist in the DOM. Here we wait for the element app-top-stories to be created. The method element.all(by.css('app-item')) finds all <app-item> elements, then we verify the number to be 20.

In the second spec, we use the method browser.executeScript() to execute some JavaScript code in the browser. The script document.getElementsByTagName("ion-infinite-scroll")[0]. scrollIntoView(); makes the content to scroll to show the component ion-infinite-scroll, which triggers the loading of more items. We then verify the number of items should be 40. The method browser. sleep(5000) makes the tests to sleep 5 seconds to allow the loading to finish.

Listing 14-2. Test spec for the top stories page

```
import { browser, element, by, ExpectedConditions as EC } from
'protractor';

describe('top stories page', () => {
  it('should show 20 stories', () => {
    browser.get(");

    browser.wait(EC.presenceOf(element(by.css('app-top-
    stories'))), 5000);
    const stories = element.all(by.css('app-item'));
    expect(stories.count()).toEqual(20);
  });

  it('should show more stories when scrolling down', () => {
    browser.get(");

    browser.wait(EC.presenceOf($('app-top-stories')), 5000);
    let stories = element.all(by.css('app-item'));
    expect(stories.count()).toEqual(20);
```

```
browser.executeScript('document.getElementsByTagName("ion-
infinite-scroll")[0].scrollIntoView();');
browser.sleep(5000);
stories = element.all(by.css('app-item'));
expect(stories.count()).toEqual(40);
  });
});
```

Note   The way we use `browser.sleep` to wait for actions to be finished in Protractor tests is not ideal. Most of Protractor APIs actually return Promise objects that can be easily chained together to write faster and more reliable tests. Protractor also has a good integration with Angular. Unfortunately, we have to use `browser.waitForAngularEnabled(false)` to get test specs executed. This is a special case for using Firebase. If your app doesn't have the same issue, you should always use Protractor's Angular support.

Page Objects and Suites

In the test specs of Listing 14-2, we can see a lot of code duplication. We can refactor the test code using the Page Objects pattern (`https://martinfowler.com/bliki/PageObject.html`). A page object describes a page and encapsulates all logic related to this page. These page objects can be reused in different tests.

In Listing 14-3, `TopStoriesPage` is the class for the top stories page. The method `get()` loads the page, `scrollDown()` scrolls down to trigger the loading of more items, `getStoriesCount()` gets the number of stories in the page. TypeScript files of page objects usually have suffix `.po.ts`.

Here we use two convenient shortcuts, $ and $$, to replace the usage of element and by in Listing 14-2. $ is the shortcut of element(by.css()), while $$ is the shortcut of element.all(by.css()).

Listing 14-3. Page object of the top stories page

```
import { $, $$, browser, ExpectedConditions as EC } from
'protractor';
export class TopStoriesPage {
  get() {
    browser.get(");
    browser.wait(EC.presenceOf($('app-top-stories')), 5000);
  }

  scrollDown() {
    browser.executeScript('document.getElementsByTagName("ion-
    infinite-scroll")[0].scrollIntoView();');
    browser.sleep(5000);
  }

  getStoriesCount() {
    browser.wait(EC.presenceOf($('app-item')), 5000);
    return $$('app-top-stories app-item').count();
  }
}
```

Listing 14-4 is the actual test spec for the top stories page. In the method beforeEach(), an object of TopStoriesPage is created for each test spec and used to interact with the page.

Listing 14-4. Test spec of top stories page

```
import { browser, element, by } from 'protractor';
import { TopStoriesPage } from './top-stories.po';

describe('top stories page', () => {
  beforeEach(() => {
    this.topStoriesPage = new TopStoriesPage();
    this.topStoriesPage.get();
  });

  it('should show 20 stories', () => {
    expect(this.topStoriesPage.getStoriesCount()).toEqual(20);
  });

  it('should show more stories when scrolling down', () => {
    expect(this.topStoriesPage.getStoriesCount()).toEqual(20);

    this.topStoriesPage.scrollDown();
    expect(this.topStoriesPage.getStoriesCount()).toEqual(40);
  });
});
```

We can also group test specs into different suites. In the protractor.
conf.js, we can use the property suites to configure suites and their
included spec files; see Listing 14-5.

Listing 14-5. Protractor test suites

```
exports.config = {
  suites: {
    top_stories: './src/top_stories.e2e_spec.ts',
  },
};
```

Then we can use `--suite` to specify the suites to run.

```
$ protractor --suite top_stories
```

User Management Test

We continue to add test specs for user management-related features. The class LogInPage in Listing 14-6 is the page object for the login page. In the method get(), we go to the index page and call the method gotoLogin() to navigate to the login page. In the method logIn(), we use sendKeys() to input the test user's email and password, then click the button to log in. Here we use the selector css_sr added in Listing 14-1 to select the input elements inside of ion-input components. ::sr in the css_rs is used to separate the selector used in the main DOM tree and selector used in the shadow root. In the method canLogIn(), we check the existence of the login button. In the method isLoggedIn(), we check the existence of the logout button. In the method logOut(), we click the logout button to log out the current user.

Listing 14-6. Page object of login page

```
import { browser, element, by, $ } from 'protractor';

export class LogInPage {
  get() {
    browser.get(");
    browser.sleep(5000);

    this.gotoLogin();
  }

  gotoLogin() {
    $('#btnShowLogin').click();
    browser.sleep(2000);
  }
```

```
logIn(email: string = 'a@b.com', password: string =
'password') {
  element(by.css_sr('ion-input::sr input[name=email]')).
  sendKeys(email);
  element(by.css_sr('ion-input::sr input[name=password]')).
  sendKeys(password);
  $('#btnLogin').click();
  browser.sleep(5000);
}

canLogIn() {
  return $('#btnShowLogin').isPresent();
}

isLoggedIn() {
  return $('#btnLogout').isPresent();
}

logOut() {
  $('#btnLogout').click();
  browser.sleep(1000);
}
}
```

With the class LogInPage, the test suite for user management is very simple; see Listing 14-7. When the page is loaded, we check the user can do the login. After we call the method logIn(), we check the user is logged in. The we call the method logOut() and check the user can do the login again.

Listing 14-7. Test spec of login page

```
import { LogInPage } from './login.po';

describe('user', () => {
  it('should be able to log in and log out', () => {
    const loginPage = new LogInPage();
    loginPage.get();
    expect(loginPage.canLogIn()).toBe(true);
    loginPage.logIn();
    expect(loginPage.isLoggedIn()).toBe(true);
    loginPage.logOut();
    expect(loginPage.canLogIn()).toBe(true);
  });
});
```

Favorites Page Test

The page object of the favorites page in Listing 14-8 uses the class LogInPage to handle the login. In the method addToFavorite(), we find the first item element with a Like button, which is the item to add to the favorites. We click the Like button to add it and return the item's title. In the method isInFavorites(), we go to the favorites page and check that the title of the newly liked item is in the array of the titles of all items.

Listing 14-8. Page object of the favorites page

```
import { browser, by, $, $$ } from 'protractor';
import { LogInPage } from './login.po';

export class FavoritesPage {
  logInPage: LogInPage = new LogInPage();
```

411

```
get() {
  this.logInPage.get();
  this.logInPage.logIn();
}

viewFavorites() {
  $('#btnShowFavorites').click();
  browser.sleep(5000);
}

addToFavorite() {
  const itemElem = $$('app-top-stories app-item').filter
  (elem => {
    return elem.$('.btnLike').isPresent();
  }).first();
  if (itemElem) {
    const title = itemElem.$('h2').getText();
    itemElem.$('.btnLike').click();
    browser.sleep(2000);
    return title;
  }
  return null;
}

isInFavorites(title: string) {
  this.viewFavorites();
  expect($$('app-favorites-list h2').map(elem => elem.
  getText())).toContain(title);
}
}
```

Listing 14-9 is the test spec of the favorites page. The test spec checks that items can be added to the favorites.

Listing 14-9. Favorites page test

```
import { FavoritesPage } from './favorites.po';

describe('favorites page', () => {
  beforeEach(() => {
    this.favoritesPage = new FavoritesPage();
    this.favoritesPage.get();
  });

  it('should add stories to the favorites', () => {
    const title = this.favoritesPage.addToFavorite();
    if (!title) {
      fail('No stories can be added.');
    }
    this.favoritesPage.isInFavorites(title);
  });
});
```

Build

After we add unit tests and end-to-end tests, we need to introduce the concept of continuous integration that makes sure every commit is tested.

Headless Chrome for Tests

Currently we use Chrome to run unit tests, which is good for local development and debugging, but it makes the continuous integration harder as it requires managing external browser processes. It's not recommended to use PhantomJS for tests any more. A better choice is to use the headless browser Headless Chrome (https://developers. google.com/web/updates/2017/04/headless-chrome).

413

Switching from Chrome to Headless Chrome is an easy task; we just need to update the settings browsers in karma.conf.js to be ['ChromeHeadless']. When running for continuous integration, we should use the option --single-run to close the browser after the test.

We can configure Headless Chrome to use different options. In Listing 14-10, the browser CustomHeadlessChrome extends from ChromeHeadless with different flags. The flag --no-sandbox is required if Chrome is running as the root user. It's better to create a new Karma configuration file karma.ci.conf.js to be used when running on continuous servers. In this case, we can add a new script ci:test to run the command ng test --karma-config src/karma.ci.conf.js.

Listing 14-10. Configure Headless Chrome

```
module.exports = function (config) {
  config.set({
    browsers: ['CustomHeadlessChrome'],
    customLaunchers: {
      CustomHeadlessChrome: {
        base: 'ChromeHeadless',
        flags: ['--disable-translate', '--disable-extensions',
        '--no-sandbox']
      }
    },
  });
};
```

For end-to-end tests, we also need to update Protractor to use Headless Chrome. Listing 14-11 shows the Protractor configuration file protractor.ci.conf.js for continuous integration. This file extends from standard protractor.conf.js and overrides the configuration for Chrome. The option --headless makes Chrome running in headless mode.

Listing 14-11. protractor.conf.js for CI

```
const parentConfig = require('./protractor.conf').config;

exports.config = Object.assign(parentConfig, {
  capabilities: {
    browserName: 'chrome',
    chromeOptions: {
      args: ['--headless', '--disable-gpu', '--window-
      size=800x600', '--no-sandbox'],
    }
  }
});
```

To use this Protractor configuration file, we need to create a new script ci:e2e to run the following command.

```
ng e2e --protractor-config e2e/protractor.ci.conf.js
```

Gitlab CI

We can integrate the app build process with different continuous integration servers. Here Gitlab CI is used as an example. If you have a local Gitlab installation, you need to install Gitlab Runner (https://docs. gitlab.com/runner/) to run CI jobs.

Gitlab uses Docker to run continuous integrations. We add the file .gitlab-ci.yml in the root directory to enable CI on Gitlab; see Listing 14-12. We use the alexcheng/ionic as the Docker image to run. In the before_script, we use npm to install the dependencies. The first job unit-test runs the unit tests using npm run ci:test; the second job e2e-test runs the end-to-end tests using npm run ci:e2e.

Listing 14-12. .gitlab-ci.yml

```
image: alexcheng/ionic:latest

cache:
  key: ${CI_COMMIT_REF_SLUG}
  paths:
    - node_modules/

before_script:
  - npm i

unit-test:
  script:
    - npm run ci:test

e2e-test:
  script:
    - npm run ci:e2e
```

Summary

In this chapter, we discussed how to use Protractor to test Ionic 4 apps and use Gitlab CI to run continuous integration. Apart from the unit tests we added in the previous chapters, end-to-end tests are also very important in testing Ionic 4 apps to make sure that different components are integrated correctly. Continuous integration is also important for the whole development life cycle that guarantees every code commit is tested. In the next chapter, we'll discuss some topics about publishing the app.

CHAPTER 15

Publish

After the app has been developed and tested, it's time to publish it to app stores. In this chapter, we'll discuss tasks related to app publish. An app needs to have proper icons and splash screens. Ionic provides a way to generate these icons and splash screens. Ionic Deploy is the tool to deploy new versions with live updates. Ionic Monitor can capture error logs generated in apps for error diagnostics.

Icons and Splash Screens

Before the app can be published, we need to replace the default icons and splash screens. Ionic can generate icons and splash screens from source images to create images of various sizes for each platform. We only need to provide an image for the icon and another image for the splash screen, then Ionic can generate all necessary images. Source images can be .png file, .psd file from PhotoShop or .ai file from Adobe Illustrator.

For icons, the source image should be file `icon.png`, `icon.psd` or `icon.ai` in the directory `resources` of the Ionic project. The icon image should have a size of at least 192 x 192 px without the round corners. For splash screens, the source image should be file `splash.png`, `splash.psd` or `splash.ai` in the directory resources. The splash screen should have a size of at least 2732 x 2732 px with the image centered in the middle.

We use the command `ionic resources` to generate those resource files for icons and splash screens; see Listing 15-1.

© Fu Cheng 2018
F. Cheng, *Build Mobile Apps with Ionic 4 and Firebase*,
https://doi.org/10.1007/978-1-4842-3775-5_15

Listing 15-1. Generate resources

```
// Icons only
$ ionic resources --icon

// Splash screens only
$ ionic resources --splash

// Both icons and splash screens
$ ionic resources
```

Generated icons and splash screens are saved to the subdirectory ios and android of the directory resources.

Deploy to Devices

We can deploy the app to a device for testing. For iOS, open the generated project in the directory platforms/ios with Xcode and use Xcode to deploy to the device. For Android, open the generated project in the directory platforms/android with Android Studio to deploy to the device.

Ionic CLI commands ionic run ios and ionic run android can also be used to deploy apps to the device.

Ionic Deploy

After we publish the app's first version to app stores, we need to continuously release new versions to the users. Usually, these new versions need to go through the same review process as the first version, which may take a long time to finish. This can delay the delivery of new features and bug fixes. For Cordova apps, since the majority code is written in HTML, JavaScript, and CSS, it's possible to perform live updates without installing new versions. These static files can be replaced by the wrapper to update to the new versions. Ionic Pro provides the deploy service to perform live deployments.

You'll need an Ionic Pro account to use this feature. After being logged in to Ionic Pro, we need to create a new app in the dashboard and link the app to Ionic Pro. Because we already created the Ionic app, the following command is used to link it. You can find the `app_id` in the dashboard.

```
$ ionic link --pro-id <app_id>
```

Ionic Pro uses a Git-based workflow to manage app updates. The command `ionic link` will prompt to set up the Git repository. Just follow the instructions displayed when running `ionic link` to finish the setup. Here we use Ionic Pro as the Git repository. A new Git remote called `ionic` is added to the repository, and we can push the current code to this remote. After the link, the file `ionic.config.json` is updated to include the property `pro_id`.

In the Ionic Pro dashboard for the app, go to the tab **Code** and select **Channels**. Two channels Master and Production have already been created. Master channel is for binaries for development, while Production channel is for binaries for app stores. Clicking the button **Set up deploy** next to a channel shows a dialog with instructions on how to set up the deploy. There are three options of how updates are installed.

- "background" mode checks for updates when the app is opened from a completely closed state. It will download the update in the background when the user is using the app. The update is applied when the app is closed and opened the next time.

- "auto" mode checks for updates when the app is opened from a completely closed state. It will wait on the splash screen until the update is downloaded and applied. This mode forces users to always use the latest version.

- "none" mode doesn't download or apply updates automatically. The entire update process is managed by you using the plugin API. This is not recommended as it may break the app with broken updates. Using background and auto mode won't have this issue as the updates in these two modes are done in the native layer.

We are going to use the background mode for the app. The dialog already shows the command to run to install the plugin `cordova-plugin-ionic`.

```
$ cordova plugin add cordova-plugin-ionic --save \
--variable APP_ID="<app_id>" \
--variable CHANNEL_NAME="Master" \
--variable UPDATE_METHOD="background"
```

After a commit is pushed to the Git repository, a new build will run. You can check the builds in the tab **Builds**. For each build, it can be manually deployed to a channel. A channel can also be configured to auto-deploy builds in a Git branch.

View and Share with Ionic View

We can easily view and share the app with Ionic View (`https://ionicframework.com/pro/view`). Ionic View is an app created by Ionic that allows users to view Ionic apps without installing them. It's very easy to share the app with others. The viewer needs to have Ionic View app installed. In the Ionic Pro dashboard, clicking the button **Share app** shows the dialog to share the app.

Monitoring

Error monitoring is another feature provided by Ionic Pro to automatically track runtime errors in Ionic apps. The errors can map to original, non-transpiled source code to quickly identify the cause of issues. To use this feature, we need to have the package @ionic/pro installed.

```
$ npm i @ionic/pro
```

Source maps are required to provide stracktraces that map back to the original TypeScript code. Source maps can be uploaded using the command ionic monitoring syncmaps or manually on the app's dashboard. Source maps files can be found in the directory www. Source map files for all modules need to be uploaded.

Errors can also be captured manually using the Ionic Pro API. Listing 15-2 shows the CustomErrorHandler that uses Ionic Pro to capture errors.

Listing 15-2. CustomErrorHandler

```
import { Pro } from '@ionic/pro';
import { ErrorHandler, Injectable } from '@angular/core';

Pro.init('<APP_ID>', {
  appVersion: '<APP_VERSION>'
});

@Injectable()
export class CustomErrorHandler implements ErrorHandler {
  handleError(err: any): void {
    console.error(err);
    Pro.monitoring.handleNewError(err);
  }
}
```

CustomErrorHandler is added to the root module; see below.

```
{ provide: ErrorHandler, useClass: CustomErrorHandler }
```

When any error occurred in the app, we can see the error in the tab **Monitoring** of the app's dashboard; see Figure 15-1. Clicking an error shows its stacktrace.

Figure 15-1. *Errors in Ionic Pro dashboard*

Summary

In the last chapter of this book, we discussed some important topics about publishing the app to app stores, including adding icons and splash screens and using Ionic Pro to perform live updates to published apps.

In this book, we used the Hacker News app as the example to demonstrate the whole life cycle of building mobile apps with Ionic 4 and Firebase. We started with the introduction of hybrid mobile apps and programming languages, frameworks, libraries, and tools used in the development; then we implemented different user stories.

During the implementation, we discussed details about Ionic 4 components and Firebase. We also covered some advanced topics of Ionic 4. Toward the end, we discussed some nonfunctional topics, including end-to-end tests, continuous integration, and app publish. After reading this book, you should be able to build your own mobile apps with Ionic 4 and Firebase.

Index

A

Action sheet, 357
<a> elements, 243
Android
    Chrome DevTools, 22–23
    emulator, 26–28
    Genymotion, 15
    Java for, 2
    PATH environment
        variable, 14
    SDK, 13–14
angular.json file, 107
Angular Router, 259
    loadChildren property, 260
    to NgRx store, 262–264
    root routing module, 261
    RouterStateUrl, 261
    routing module for
        comments, 259
    stateKey property, 263
    useHash property, 260
Apache Cordova, 4
app.component.html
        template file, 114
app.component.ts file, 113–114
App files
    app, 110
    assets, 108

    components, 110
    environments, 109–110
    index.html, 108
    pages, 110
    theme, 109
app.module.ts file, 111–112
app-routing.module.ts file, 112–113
Autonomous custom
        elements, 72–75
Avatars, 124

B

Basic app structure
    app files
        app, 110
        assets, 108
        components, 110
        environments, 109–110
        index.html, 108
        pages, 110
        theme, 109
    config files
        angular.json, 107
        config.xml, 105
        ionic.config.json, 107
        package.json, 105
        tsconfig.json, 106
        tslint.json, 107

© Fu Cheng 2018
F. Cheng, *Build Mobile Apps with Ionic 4 and Firebase*,
https://doi.org/10.1007/978-1-4842-3775-5

U, V

W, X

Y, Z

Printed in the United States
By Bookmasters